Global Business

Cashman Dudley
An imprint of Gulf Publishing Company
Houston, Texas

Global Business

LAWRENCE E. KOSLOW AND ROBERT H. SCARLETT

308 TIPS TO TAKE YOUR COMPANY WORLDWIDE

Global
Business

Cashman Dudley
An imprint of Gulf Publishing Company
P.O. Box 2608 □ Houston, Texas 77252-2608

10 9 8 7 6 5 4 3 2 1

Library of Congress Cataloging-in-Publication Data

Koslow, Lawrence E.
    Global business : 308 tips to take your company worldwide / Lawrence E. Koslow and Robert H. Scarlett.
        p.   cm.
    Includes bibliographical references and index.
    ISBN 0-88415-753-9 (alk. paper)
    1. International business enterprises—Management.   I. Scarlett, Robert H.   II. Title.
    HD62.4.K677   1999
    658′.049—DC21   99-17561
                                                                CIP

Printed in the United States of America.
Printed on acid-free paper (∞).

DEDICATIONS

To my grandson, Michael James Hublou;
his parents, Larisa Koslow and Chad Hublou;
and his aunt, Melinda Koslow
for their love and inspiration.

LEK

To my father, Robert D. Scarlett,
an international business pioneer;
and to my mother Jane Scarlett Hennings,
who persevered to raise four children
while moving from continent to continent
and from country to country.

RHS

CONTENTS

OVERVIEW, 1

DEVELOPING AN INTERNATIONAL PLAN, 22

CROSS-CULTURAL AWARENESS, 29

ECONOMIC INTEGRATION, 43

IMPORTING, 59

EXPORTING, 68

TRANSPORTING GOODS
INTERNATIONALLY, 83

PLANNING
INTERNATIONAL OPERATIONS, 91

INTERNATIONAL
FINANCIAL MANAGEMENT, 98

INTERNATIONAL TAX PLANNING, 128

MARKETING AND SALES, 135

INTERNATIONAL
HUMAN RESOURCES, 148

RISK MANAGEMENT AND CORPORATE SECURITY, 169

INTERNATIONAL LEGAL MANAGEMENT, 173

MARKET ENTRY STRATEGIES—GLOBAL BUSINESS WITHOUT LEAVING HOME, 186

MARKET ENTRY STRATEGIES—DIRECT MARKETING FROM THE HOME COUNTRY, 196

MARKET ENTRY STRATEGIES—SELLING THROUGH INTERNATIONAL AGENTS AND DISTRIBUTORS, 199

INTERNATIONAL FRANCHISING, 223

TECHNOLOGY LICENSING, 230

DETERMINING WHAT TO LICENSE, 240

MANAGING LICENSEES, 247

PROTECTING INTELLECTUAL PROPERTY, 251

INTERNATIONAL ALLIANCES: NON-EQUITY, 254

INTERNATIONAL ALLIANCES: EQUITY, 257

MAJOR ISSUES IN FORMING AN IEJV, 264

ESTABLISHING DIRECT OPERATIONS ABROAD, 270

ACQUIRING A LOCAL COMPANY, 286

RELATIONSHIPS WITH SUBSIDIARIES, 291

FAMILY BUSINESS CONSIDERATIONS, 298

CAPITALIZING ON
INTERNATIONAL TRENDS, 303

INTERNATIONAL NEGOTIATIONS, 319

INTERNATIONAL ETHICS, 328

REFERENCES, 332

INDEX, 333

Acknowledgements

The authors are indebted to the many colleagues, friends, and loved ones that contributed to the completion of this work. Some contributed ideas; others contributed their experiences. Some served as sources of inspiration, while others gave encouragement. Many contributed their time and effort.

Interviewees

A good many working executives and other observers of the international business scene kindly agreed to be interviewed by the authors. They offered bits of uncommon wisdom that found their way into this book. A complete listing of all such people would be very long indeed; but we would like to at least mention the following: Tom Anderson, Barry Becket, Steve Burnham, John Jones, Rushworth Kidder, Dale Lapakko, Scott Meriwether, Stan Obino, Ricardo Robles, David Roland, Lewis Russell, Lee Sundet, and Hroar Toppenberg.

Sources of Inspiration

Given the special effort that the authors made to incorporate the experience of international business professionals in all parts of the world, and with companies of all sizes, we would like to thank those who offered their example and their insights as inspiration for this work. In particular, **Lawrence E. Koslow** would like to thank Averell Elliott, Homa Firouztash, Dale Furnish, Gregg Gliechert, Russell Johnson, Gottfried and Mieke Kellermann, Kathryn Leary, Herbert Leshinsky, Emilio Lopez, Mauro Pando, Pamela Pappas Stanoch, David Ruhala, Jose Carlos Tobon, Fred Welz, Laurie Wolfe and a special thanks to Gerald R. Giombetti whose memory will always inspire him. **Robert Scarlett** would like to thank Johnny Escribano, Jeff Hanson, Claudia Jiménez de Torres, Herr Walter Küper, Herr Roland Küper, Ing. J. Alberto Leal Osório, Ing. Gustavo Menéndez Salazar, Ing. Joél Ramirez Pérez, Victor Salgado, Carlos A. Torres Hurtado, Alcy A. Vidal, Alcy Vidal Filho, and Minoru Yasuda. Finally, both authors would like to acknowledge the assistance of our able partners in **The Global Business Connection, LLC.** These are Corrine Seltz, Ricardo Vallejos, and Thomas Gryskiewicz.

Manuscript Production

Preparing the manuscript for this work took a lot of extra time and effort on the part of quite a few people. We would like to recognize Marian Heinemann for overseeing and coordinating this production effort; and we join her in thanking Jodie Becker, Rose Greven, Carol Haight, Marilynn Hallen, Kristin Johnson, Tracy Johnston, Laureen Jost, Renee Kleinjan, Krispin Lam, Teresa Lyon, Linda McCormick, Mary Moe, Marty Nagan, Amy Peterson, Laura Reinhardt, Jan Stahura and Julie Witt-Ramos for all the detail work.

Most of all, we would like to thank our wives and partners, Teresa and Sibylle, for the many specific insights they contributed to the work and for their patience with us as we attempted to juggle our writing activities, the demands of our professions, and our family lives, all at the same time.

Lawrence E. Koslow
Robert H. Scarlett

PREFACE

The move of the marketplace toward globalization is like a giant jigsaw puzzle and, for today's most successful businesses, the pieces are coming together. As more and more companies attempt to understand how the global puzzle works, they may not be able to keep up with the world markets unless their leaders and employees understand how to create a truly global business.

This book's purpose is to organize the multitude of information available into 308 tips that every business professional can understand. Some of these tips will provide answers that can be immediately applied to the issue at hand. Most, however, will be useful in providing the framework for further analysis—or, stated another way, they will assist the businessperson in knowing how to ask the right questions.

Two examples of the tips found in the book illustrate the question-answer dichotomy. In discussing how a business determines its readiness for global expansion, for instance, we can only raise the most salient points that a company should consider, such as the assessment of the global readiness of the company's products and services. In discussing the preparation for international travel, however, we can be more specific in providing information, such as checklists to follow for international travel.

While this book covers a multitude of subjects, we have divided the subject matter into a number of logical sections. Each section of this book is designed to stand alone by containing the necessary material to understand the theme (for example, international financial management), or to provide the elements necessary to complete a particular type of international business transaction (as in franchising). Additionally, each section is cross-referenced.

We are particularly proud of three sections of this book that we believe break new ground in the literature of international business. The first is the section called Family Business Considerations. In this section, we point out some of the key trends that are particularly favorable to the globalization of family businesses. Also discussed are how to develop global family networks and how international expansion may be used to address certain issues that are specific to a family business, such as succession planning and providing opportunities for non-family members.

A second groundbreaking area is the section on international ethics. Here we examine the difficult issues presented by the ethical differences between cultures. Also explored are some of the attempts by the business community to create global codes of conduct, along with some of the ways in which companies are globalizing their corporate philanthropy.

Finally, this book explores some of the evolving international trends and their potential meaning to the international business community. The availability of this information will allow companies to make middle- and long-term planning decisions as they move into the new millennium.

Lawrence E. Koslow
Robert H. Scarlett

OVERVIEW

In this first section we will examine some of the preliminary questions that need to be answered before a company can decide if, when, and how to enter or expand in international markets. Also included will be discussions on how to prepare for the initial overseas trips, how to determine when you should go, and how to provide for your safety and comfort.

Additional tips will discuss how to set up country files and how to organize for effective international expansion. After reviewing this section, you should be in a position to determine whether you are ready to address the more specific issues of international expansion.

1. Understanding International Business

What is international business? What does it mean to go international? A company begins the international process by first becoming aware of the influences of international activities on its present and future business. This includes an analysis of the makeup of its products and services, an understanding of its capabilities, an analysis of its existing marketplace, a view of where its industry is going, and finally, an understanding of what the competitors are doing, or are likely to do, in the near future. This takes place both internally and externally.

Internal Internationalization

From a practical point of view, a company can become involved in international business without ever exporting from its home market. Just think of the mass retailers and grocery chains who import from all over the globe. Examples of internal internationalization are:

☐ Importing
☐ Sourcing or obtaining foreign components or labor
☐ Representing a foreign business in your home market
☐ Licensing foreign technology
☐ Providing services to foreign companies

External Internationalization

Once you begin to market your products and services abroad, you now have to consider a wholly different set of variables. There are many ways in which to address the international marketplace. These include the following:

☐ Selling products abroad from the domestic base
☐ Selling to or through trading companies
☐ Using agents or co-marketers
☐ Using foreign distributors as your marketing channels
☐ Licensing and franchising intellectual property and/or know-how
☐ Using strategic alliances, consortia, or equity joint ventures

2. Determining Your Readiness for Global Expansion

Deciding to enter the global marketplace or to expand operations abroad is never easy. Some companies are pulled into the international marketplace by promises of larger revenues and profits; others are pushed into it by the need to keep up with their competitors. One of the biggest reasons why companies fail in expanding abroad is that they enter these markets piecemeal, with no overall assessment of global possibilities. A preliminary global assessment might include the following six steps:

Assess your domestic market. Is there still growth potential? Is your customer base diversified enough? Are profits more than adequate? If there is still growth potential at home, you may prefer to conquer St. Paul, for instance, before you take on São Paulo. Consider that you can also "go international" by adding foreign products to your existing lines of business.

Look for clues in your industry. What is being discussed at industry meetings? Are your competitors entering world markets? Most importantly, are your customers going international? If your company is a supplier to a multinational corporation in your domestic market and the multinational expands into other territories, you may need to expand or take the risk that a competitor will become the supplier for the multinational.

Assess whether there is a market for your products or services. It is difficult to name a single product or service that cannot be sold across borders in one way or another. Some products and services just do not transfer well because they are over-engineered or geared strictly to local tastes (for example, ant eggs in Mexico). If you have such a product, you are generally better off trying to increase your market share in your home market.

Assess whether your products and/or services are ready for global markets. Does the product need to be modified to function abroad? Other countries, for example, use different systems of measurement. Do you need to translate instructions and warranties? If you make the needed modifications, will your product still be competitive?

Assess whether you are willing to commit the resources to go global. What internal constraints must be considered? Are you willing to commit financial resources to learn how to do the business? Are human resources available? Are you concerned about a possible dispersion of your corporate focus?

Assess opportunities that may be unique to your company. If your products are seasonal, could you find markets abroad for them during your off-season? During winters, for example, could you sell your lawn mowers or ice cream to countries in the Southern Hemisphere? Would the global markets allow you to harvest your products—expanding their life cycles by selling in markets that are not state-of-the-art? Can you try a new product abroad before bringing it to the home market (for instance, products requiring Federal Drug Administration [USA] approval)?

3. Motivations for Foreign Expansion— Proactive

Some companies are *pulled* into the international marketplace by the possibility of expansion and larger profits, while other companies are *pushed* into international business by the limitations of their home markets or the demands of their existing customers.

Some of the proactive reasons why companies would choose international expansion are as follows:

☐ **To respond to requests from abroad.** This is the most common manner in which companies make their first international sale. Foreign visitors to your domestic market may learn of, or use, your products. Domestic catalogs and other marketing devices often find their way into places you would never expect, and trade shows often result in foreign inquiries.

☐ **To beat competitors to new markets.** Being first has some great advantages, especially if you do it right. Ask Coca Cola how hard it was to get into the Russian market after Pepsi Cola had already established itself.

☐ **To diversify their customer base.** A company may wish to diversify its customer base by creating and increasing its foreign market outlets. If the domestic customer base is composed of a few large customers, the successful expansion into the international marketplace should lead to a larger customer base with less dependency on individual customers.

☐ **To create incremental revenues and profits through international expansion.** Assuming excess capacity and large fixed costs, the economies of scale created may exceed the additional costs of marketing the product abroad. This would result in incremental revenue and profits for the company.

4. Motivations for Foreign Expansion— Reactive

Many companies enter global markets in a reactive manner. Initially, they would prefer to avoid expansion, but some or all of the following factors listed force them to enter international markets.

The domestic market has low or no-growth potential. Especially for mature industries, they may face a no-growth or downsizing situation, or they may attempt to continue their expansion by opening up foreign markets.

Current customers have gone overseas. Many companies are pushed into international markets by their customers. If they don't follow their customers overseas, they risk the possibility of losing them to their foreign competitors (or even to internationally-based domestic competitors).

Domestic workforces need to be preserved. Exports create local jobs. These jobs are often the highest-paying and offer the most interesting work.

Lower manufacturing and labor costs can be taken advantage of. To remain competitive—even in your home market—it may be necessary to enter foreign markets to source labor, components, or finished product.

5. Compelling Reasons for Going International

☐ The domestic market is either saturated or has low growth potential.
☐ The opportunity is there to beat competitors to new markets.
☐ Customers located overseas provide a vast new market that will diversify your customer base.
☐ Greater profits can be achieved through incremental production.
☐ The need for product diversification at home is minimized.
☐ Product life cycles are extended.
☐ New products can be tested before launching them in your home market.
☐ Jobs for your domestic workforce can be preserved.
☐ Lower manufacturing and labor costs can be realized.
☐ Foreign technologies and management know-how can be utilized.
☐ Seasonal cycles for your products can be lengthened.
☐ Products can be distributed and serviced more efficiently.
☐ Indirect channels can be replaced with direct channels.
☐ Requests from abroad can be responded to.
☐ Government programs and incentives abroad can be taken advantage of.
☐ New products can be acquired for the home market.
☐ Business cycles can be more effectively utilized.
☐ Hostile corporate acquisitions can be avoided.
☐ Companies are more attractive to potential buyers.
☐ The business's value can be increased.
☐ Better employees can be attracted and retained.

6. Developing Global Market Awareness

If you are reading this book, you are probably already aware of the extent to which your company is a "player" in the global market place. Here is a way to gauge the extent to which your industry and company are materially affected by global market forces:

Ownership: Is your company owned exclusively by investors native to your country?

Processes and technology: Historically, did the processes and the technology used by your company originate in your home country?

Raw materials: Do the raw materials used in your company all originate within your home country? If so, are these materials available in other areas of the world? Does your home country government limit or tax their importation into your country? Are the costs of your raw materials affected by world commodity prices?

Customers: Are any of your customers foreign-owned?

Competitors: Are any of your competitors foreign-owned or affiliated?

Distribution: Do any of your products end up in foreign destinations, as components of another product or piece of equipment?

Your answers to these questions will provide a basis upon which you can determine to what extent your company and its industry are global and if your global involvement represents a threat or a profitable growth opportunity for your company. However, to complete this analysis, it is crucial that you also have a comprehensive view of your present market. For example:

☐ Who are your customers? Who are your most desirable/profitable customers? What makes them desirable/profitable?

☐ What is your product/service and how is it delivered? Does your sales force—and/or other distribution channels—add value for the customer?

☐ Roughly, how big is your present market?

☐ What drives growth in demand for your product or service in your present market?

☐ Who are your competitors and from where do they originate? Are they all local or regional? Do you have any international competitors? What is your share of the present market?

☐ Who are your suppliers? Where are their sources?

☐ Historically, where has the best technology in your industry come from?

☐ What are the factors most critical for the success of your product or service in your present market? These factors include product quality, unique features, technical support, distribution, financing, inventory, and delivery.

7. Entering a New Foreign Market: Take this Reality Test

"Everybody else is doing it!" This was not a good enough excuse for your parents, nor is it a good reason to enter a new foreign market with an existing product line. Here is a little test you should take when you first feel the impulse to enter the new foreign market:

☐ How will entry into this new foreign market help your company or business unit achieve its strategic business goals?

☐ How will entry affect your position vis-à-vis your key competitors?

☐ How will entry affect your ability to serve your present customers?

☐ Does this market appear to have good long-term potential—and is the potential enough to justify the investment required?

☐ Does your company have sufficient capacity to meet the estimated demand for your product or service? Will there be a high opportunity cost, if capacity is limited?

☐ Does your company possess the talent and skills to support a position in this market?

☐ How do you envision sustaining a position in the market, once you have entered it?

If you know enough about the targeted foreign market to consider entering it, then these questions should be easy to answer. Making yourself answer them will also help you prepare to make the case to others whose approval and support may be required.

8. Developing Expertise on Foreign Markets

To find attractive opportunities for growth in foreign markets and to prepare to compete effectively once you enter them, it is important to develop a system for quickly gaining the market knowledge and expertise you will need to increase your chances for success. Your system should help you monitor key factors like the following:

Emerging political developments
Investment trends (flight capital risk)
"Competitor currency" developments and trends
Foreign exchange market developments
External events/trends, including actions of yours
   and other governments
Liquidity—developments affecting repatriation
   of revenues, earnings, assets
Competition—and your company's intelligence on competitors
Regulatory events, trends

9. Cross-Cultural Considerations

Cross-cultural considerations are present in every business transaction. But the further afield you take your business, the larger the impact these considerations can have on the success of your business. Here are some tips for recognizing and responding to these cross-cultural issues:

☐ Be aware of your own "culture" and how you acquired it.
☐ Study the history/geography/climate and the political/economy of your counterpart's country.
☐ When in contact, observe and listen carefully; avoid early conclusions about another person's "culture."
☐ Exercise humility—accept the fact that you will never completely understand another person's culture.
☐ Show respect for the culture by learning the language and showing interest in the country.
☐ Learn, observe, and practice local etiquette.

☐ Explain your own culture, but only when asked.
☐ Look for common interests and build the business relationship
on them.

10. Preparing for Entry into a Specific Target Market

Acquire knowledge of your own market, then size up the foreign target market. This is not a job for "bean counters." Someone with entrepreneurial instincts and broad market and industry knowledge would be best suited for this kind of analysis. Today, you can use the Internet, consultants, or other secondary sources to obtain much of the information you will need.

First, identify your potential customers. Compare them with your most desirable/profitable customers in your present market. Make note of any similarities and differences. Then, identify your likely competitors and determine from where they originated. Are they local, regional, national, or international in their reach? Do you already compete with any of them in your present market? Identify your competitors' primary suppliers and their sources of raw material, if possible. Compare these suppliers with those that you depend on. Note any comparative advantages or disadvantages.

List the factors that would appear to be most critical to the success of your product or service in the target market. Compare them with the success factors in your present market. If a product or service comparable to your own currently exists in the target market, describe its features and compare them with those of your product or service. If no such product or service exists, take additional time to understand why.

Estimate market size for your product or service. A good guess based on clearly-stated assumptions is enough. You can always revise the assumptions and the estimates, as more information becomes available. Also, describe what factors or trends drive growth in demand for your type of product or service in the target market. Compare these factors and trends with those in your present market. Note any differences.

For some companies, this can all be done in a few minutes; for others, it may require weeks of research. Either way, much of it can and should be done before the first plane ticket is purchased.

In addition to the sources available via the Internet, here are other "intelligence" sources you should consider:

Your country's department of commerce, international trade
    administration, or foreign commercial service
Your provincial, state, or local trade promotion office
Your local libraries
Industry associations
Freight forwarders with experience
Banks with correspondent relations
Business people with international experience
Students and other visitors from the target county

11. Alternative Ways to Penetrate a Foreign Market

Once you have done enough research to identify a truly attractive foreign market for your product or service, there are a number of alternative entry strategies you may want to consider:

Use trading companies
Rely on Original Equipment Manufacturers (OEMs), who purchase
    your components or products and integrate them into their own
    products
"Piggy-back" on channels of companies already in the market
Appoint agents, and/or distributors
Establish a branch office for direct sales support, and another for
    indirect sales support
Establish a sales subsidiary
Form an alliance with another manufacturer
Establish a manufacturing and sales subsidiary
License a local manufacturer-distributor
Develop a franchise

12. The International versus the Global Company

Almost all companies entering the international marketplace begin as international companies. Some, however, develop into truly global companies. In this section, we will clarify the differences between the terms and discuss what the tradeoffs are in attempting to become a global company.

An *international company* is one in which its foreign operations are often thought of as appendages for producing and/or selling products that were designed and engineered in the home market. Central direction comes from corporate headquarters and the top echelons of the company are dominated by the nationals of the home country. Often, the company pursues a strategy designed to bring the bulk of the profits to the corporate headquarters.

A *global company* is one in which top management makes decisions with little regard to national borders. These decisions are made to maximize global revenues, income, and profits. Global companies are not adverse to moving people from country to country and to promoting foreign nationals to top positions. They seek Research and Development (R & D) from anywhere it is available. The idea is to create a stateless corporation, one that is more or less independent of state regulations.

As cross-border trade and investment grows, the case for creating the global company is compelling. Japanese high-technology companies are able to enter the U.S. market by doing final assembly in Mexico. Medical devices and products are tested first in Europe to avoid the difficulties posed by the FDA in the U.S. Significant raw material and labor savings may be accomplished by moving some production to developing nations. Having a multinational group of corporate executives creates a significant symbiosis of talent.

However, the costs of creating and maintaining a global company may or may not be worth the effort. The costs of moving people abroad are high. Manufacturing and sourcing decisions cannot be made quickly unless significant productive capabilities are created and maintained. Products may not be so easily made globally. Finally, trying to go stateless will ultimately be dependent upon whether most governments will choose to go along with stateless corporations or try to strengthen their regulatory and tax authorities.

The companies who have become closest to becoming stateless are the ones that are willing to do it in a first-class manner. These companies tend to treat their stakeholders well and exhibit high ethical standards. Therein lies the tradeoff; recent experience has shown that if a company wants to achieve the greatest amount of independence, the best manner of doing so is to self-govern by being the best corporate citizen it can be.

13. American, Western European, and Japanese Company Operational Styles

Companies worldwide have developed different styles of going global based on their histories and typical manners of doing business. While the following analysis deals in stereotypes and each company must be looked at individually, the information does give some general ideas of their different operational styles:

U.S.A.

☐ A large internal market, resulting in less dependency on foreign sales, has slowed the globalization of American companies.
☐ Most large companies are publicly traded, so American companies tend to think in shorter timeframes and are less relational (people-to-people oriented) than European companies.
☐ Because of the dominant, economic position of the U.S.A. during the 1950s and 1960s, American companies expanded by taking their products abroad rather than by developing global products.
☐ Because of a management tradition that stressed formal planning and controls, American companies developed a worldwide network of subsidiaries tied very tightly to their corporate parent in the U.S.A.

Western Europe

☐ Smaller internal markets fueled international expansion as a necessity.
☐ Given the colonial traditions and the fact that more European companies were family-owned, these companies were likely to be more relational (dependent on personal relationships) and

Europeans tended to create companies that are highly sensitive to local needs and opportunities.
☐ European subsidiaries were more like a portfolio of local companies than a tightly organized group reporting to the corporate headquarters. As long as the local company performed adequately, it was left pretty much alone.

Japan

☐ Restricted by severe government-imposed regulations which required an export-based strategy, the Japanese developed global products and marketed them worldwide.
☐ Global marketing allowed the Japanese to first develop excellent economies of scale and then to stylize products for large markets, such as the U.S. auto market.
☐ While the Japanese were the most successful at global products, they are the least relational of the three groups and have the biggest problems with their foreign customers and suppliers.

14. Preparing for a Trip Abroad

Traveling abroad can be very expensive and is often hard on the body as well as the mind. Before you decide to go, consider the following:

☐ Define, in writing, the principal purpose(s) of your trip, including a preliminary itinerary.
☐ Check with at least two other persons in your office (or in those to be visited) to determine if the purpose of the trip and the itinerary make sense at this time.
☐ Determine if the principal purpose and goals can be accomplished without the necessity of travel.
☐ Check to see if all actions necessary to make the trip possible are arranged *before* the trip is scheduled. Considerations may include:
  • All necessary background information
  • Marketing and sales materials
  • Time available to obtain visas and to meet medical requirements
  • Availability of travel and hotel reservations
☐ Check to see if the trip conflicts with national or company holidays; monthly, quarterly or year-end closings; vacations; or other events which could make the trip untimely.

15. Making Travel Arrangements

Overseas travel can't simply be turned over to your secretary or travel agent. Careful planning is a necessity. In making international travel arrangements, consider the following:

☐ Determine suitable flight and hotel reservations.
☐ Carry a flight schedule book to determine alternative flights.
☐ Schedule flights on weekends or evenings whenever possible to take advantage of either more meeting time and/or fewer days away from the office.
☐ Consider business or first class travel, if the flights are extremely long or if work is scheduled to begin upon arrival. The traveler may have upgrades as part of a frequent flyer program. If your company does considerable international travel, it might be possible to work out a special arrangement with the appropriate airline(s).
☐ Determine details about the hotel as it relates to the place of business and travel safety.
☐ Check to see if any meals are included in the price of the room.
☐ Does the traveler have credit cards that allow for upgrades, late check-outs, and other extra amenities?
☐ Check to see if the quoted price includes all amenities.
☐ Consider the hotel as a place to hold the meetings as it may be a neutral destination that could lessen the home advantage.
☐ Make sure the traveler has credit cards with high limits, and that the cards are accepted in the countries to be visited.
☐ Have the traveler check his or her medical records to assure that all shots and prescriptions are maintained throughout the end of the trip.
☐ Make sure that the traveler has the appropriate powers of attorney to execute necessary documents.
☐ Check passport for expiration dates and current visas. Don't expect that a visa can be obtained in a third country since many countries require that the visa must be obtained in the traveler's country of residence.
☐ Consider special safety rules for traveling in developing countries.
  • Avoid fancy watches and jewelry. Dress modestly, and don't attempt to dress like a local.
  • Do not hail taxicabs on the street. Have your local business contacts call taxicabs for you or use cab stands to assure you obtain a licensed cab.

- Avoid public transportation unless locals say it is safe to use it.
- Consider carrying small denomination U.S. currency notes in addition to or instead of traveler's checks. U.S. dollars are accepted everywhere and are easy to cash. The best strategy is credit cards and U.S. currency in small denominations.

16. Travel Necessities

In addition to the right clothes and toilet items, consider bringing the following with you when you travel:

☐ Tickets and any frequent-user cards.
☐ Passport and all appropriate visas. Determine what types of visas are necessary. Some countries will require business visas for any business reasons; for others, a tourist visa may be sufficient.
☐ Copies of the itinerary, as well as information on alternative flights.
☐ Extra passport photos (to use if passport is lost or additional visas are required).
☐ Photocopies of initial passport pages, in case your passport is lost, to establish information needed for a replacement. Consider having multiple passports if you travel frequently to countries that require visas.
☐ Power(s) of attorney, if needed.
☐ Business cards. Consider having them made in different languages. Consider also that placement of names in relation to the company name may differ in different cultures.
☐ For laptops, be sure to carry extra batteries, have a lock that can be attached to a heavy object, carry an adapter for electrical current, and have your MIS department design an icon(s) that can work with various phone systems.
☐ Medical kit with sufficient supply of prescriptions.
☐ Customs declaration of foreign-made objects taken on the trip (watch, camera, etc.) to facilitate reentry.

17. The Pre-Trip Checklist

Just like the pre-flight checks performed by an airline crew, it is wise to develop and maintain a good "pre-trip" checklist for each

country you do business in. Here are some additional items which
should be included on such a list:

☐ Immigration and immunization requirements
☐ Maps and guidebooks
☐ Currency and exchange rates
☐ Communications systems
☐ Guides that denote time zone differences, language, customs, and
  etiquette
☐ Appropriate gifts
☐ Appropriate clothing for occasions, climate
☐ Personal contacts list

18. Security Precautions for Travel

Travel to major cities or remote areas can be risky, whether you are
in your own country or abroad. Here are a few tips for managing the
risks that come with traveling abroad for business:

☐ Choose a travel agent that is personally familiar with travel
  conditions to and from, as well as in and around your destination.
☐ Avoid burdening yourself with highly visible and valuable
  equipment or accessories that may attract thieves and be difficult
  or cumbersome to keep secure during your trip.
☐ Remove all tags from previous flights and make sure your luggage
  is easily identifiable, without calling attention to it.
☐ Understand the language. The confusion that comes with not
  having a clue to the local language can increase your vulnerability.
☐ Know your territory. The more you know about the history,
  current events, language and customs of your destination, the less
  vulnerable you will be.
☐ Keep your hands free. The more over-burdened you are with
  luggage and other belongings, the more vulnerable you will be.
  Use local skycap services or carts, to increase your control over
  these circumstances.
☐ Look like you know where you are going. Wandering around and
  looking lost will increase your vulnerability. Prepare in advance,
  then quietly observe what others do and follow suit, or arrange to
  be met and escorted.

☐ Avoid "standing out." Dress comfortably for travel and for the destination climate. Do not flaunt wealth or privilege in the way you dress.

☐ Avoid "rip-off" havens. Consider choosing more modest hotels that cater to the local business community, rather than to tourists.

☐ Know the local transportation system and know where you are going. Know how much it should cost and how much time it should take to reach your destination.

19. Personal Comfort When Traveling

Considering the magnitude of the investment in time and expense, for you as well as for your counterparts, it is important to plan and take precautions that will ensure your personal comfort and enhance your productivity while traveling internationally. Here are a few tips:

☐ *"Know thyself"* well enough to know your personal "travel risk factors," such as:
  • Do you tire easily?
  • How much sleep do you need at night?
  • Are you able to take short sleeping breaks?
  • Are you affected by altitude- or motion-sickness?
  • Does it usually take you a while to adjust to time-zone and/or climactic changes?
  • Are you a hearty eater, or a careful eater?

☐ For lengthy trips to far-off destinations, plan a "humane" schedule according to your personal needs, considering these factors:
  • Allow time for pre-trip rest, if possible.
  • Prepare for maximum feasible rest during travel.
  • Allow time for rest and adjustment to time-zone and climactic differences, upon arrival at your destination.

☐ Take precautions to manage your personal health risk factors related to the travel itself:
  • Motion-sickness preventatives
  • Nasal sprays or other measures, medicated or non-medicated, to keep your sinuses, nasal passages, and ear canals clear and your mucous membranes moist

- Equipment to aid in sleeping or napping—cover for the eyes, ear-plugs, neck-support pillow—and a travel alarm clock, so you won't worry about missing a meal or a change of planes
- Bottled water, to counteract high-altitude dryness and the dehydrating effects of coffee, tea, and alcohol

☐ Take precautions to manage risk factors associated with eating and drinking. For example, homeopathic physicians sometimes recommend that a traveler take acidophilus bacteria supplements several days before departing and regularly during the trip. This helps the traveler's digestive system retain its normal functions while being exposed to alien bacteria that might otherwise disrupt digestion.

20. The Constraints of Going International

In making your assessment of international opportunities, be sure to give some consideration to reasons why a company may choose *not* to go international, or may delay that decision until conditions change.

☐ *Internal resource constraints*—The company lacks the financial, human, productive, or developmental resources to enter into international markets. The level of internal resources needed will be largely dependent upon the approach or strategy taken to enter the international marketplace. A distribution network would take less resources than wholly-owned subsidiaries but the margins may not exist to develop a viable distribution network.

☐ *Experience constraints*—A company at the threshold of international expansion needs to determine if it has the basic experience level to enter into any type of international activities. A certain level of experience is needed in the following areas:
- Payments and collections
- Shipping and documentation
- Maintaining legal protection—contracts and intellectual property registration
- International negotiation

☐ *Limited international opportunities.* Is there a market for the products? Is the product cost-competitive? Can it be made cost-competitive? Does your product meet the quality or perceived quality standards on the international marketplace?

☐ *Dispersion of corporate focus.* Will international operations take away resources that can be better used in R&D or in the domestic market?

☐ *Trade Restrictions.* Are the products subject to large tariffs, import licenses, boycotts, and embargoes? Are they subject to complicated administrative procedures, quality standards, or onerous local rules and regulations?

21. Attributes of a Good International Executive

Do you have what it takes to be a good international executive? Here's a list of attributes that have been associated with success in international dealings:

Flexibility and adaptability: Rigid personalities need not apply. People chosen to work on international assignments must be able to adapt to different working styles, different working schedules, different time zones, and different concepts of time.

Interpersonal skills: Grumpy Old Men need not apply. Friendly, outgoing people, with a broad knowledge of the world around them and an ability to converse on several levels, are better suited for international assignments.

Entrepreneurial skills: Bureaucrats need not apply. International assignments often require an ability to quickly recognize problems and opportunities, and a disposition to decide quickly how best to respond to them—all without assistance from the home office. For this reason, it is best to assign people who are self-assured and who have a thorough understanding of their industry, their company, and who have proven "business" judgement.

Technical competence: Beginners need not apply. International counterparts expect to deal with people who really know their business. Do not send a boy to do a man's work. If the assignment requires a combination of entrepreneurial decision-making skills and specific technical competence that cannot be found in one person, then send two.

Commitment, drive, and physical/mental stamina: Nine-to-fivers need not apply. International assignments often require long hours, early mornings, late nights, and week-end business travel.

Cultural awareness: Cultural "chauvinists" need not apply. People who have open minds and are curious to learn about other cultures seem to perform better on international assignments. The greater the cultural awareness, the greater the influence that can be exercised.

Language proficiency: Monolinguists need not apply. The greater the language proficiency, including proficiency in your own language, the greater the effectiveness on international assignments.

Ability to juggle multiple priorities: Uni-dimensional people need not apply. International assignments often involve a number of tasks that must be performed—all at the same time. People who can handle stress with equanimity and manage conflicting priorities are best suited for this kind of work.

22. Considering a Product's International Potential

In today's increasingly competitive global market, product news travels faster than ever, even across national boundaries. If you are planning to launch a new product in your primary domestic market, you should immediately begin to determine its international potential. Here are some steps you might want to consider:

☐ Update your knowledge of governing patent and trademark laws and rules in the foreign markets you might enter. This will help you establish timelines and sequences for introducing the product in various markets. In some markets, it is very easy to lose patent and trademark protection, unless you follow procedures that may be quite different from those that apply in the U.S. or Western Europe.

☐ In the development stage, get input on needs, requirements, and features from customers, distributors, or agents in selected foreign markets. By soliciting a broader range of end-user input, you may be able to launch a product that has wider appeal and greater profit potential.

☐ In the design stage, incorporate features that will make the product easier to adapt to special requirements in the overseas markets you intend to serve. It is important to consider responding to those requirements in this early stage, especially in those markets where special standards sometimes serve as arbitrary, non-tariff, barriers.

☐ Before launching the product, determine which customs classifications will likely apply, anticipate customs duties, and plan the export and foreign distribution. It is sometimes possible to avoid excessive duties by carefully selecting the product classification. This is also a good time to consider such things as a total or partial "break-down and reassemble," in order to lessen the impact of duties.

By considering these four steps, you will be able to increase the probability that your new product introduction will be "export ready," as well as a domestic success.

Developing an International Plan

Once you have decided to go international, it is now time to develop and establish your international plan. This section is designed to provide the reader with a step-by-step analysis for creating such a plan. Six areas are explored that must be considered in developing the plan. This includes everything from goal definition, to how to fit your plan into the overall company plans.

23. Determining Your Specific International Goals

Questions regarding international goals can be as different as "Where do we source products?" to "Should we establish manufacturing in France to accompany our marketing subsidiary?" The answers to these questions can be concrete (e.g., a goal of U.S.$100 million in sales by the year 2005), or qualitative (e.g., estimating Indonesian market for your products), but they should be as clear as possible.

Clarity, to start, is important because it also should be recognized that goals in the international marketplace will take longer to develop and are more likely to be subjected to reassessment and change. Therefore, while short-term goals should be established, longer-term goals (three years or more) should be as specifically stated as possible. Examples of such goals might be:

☐ International sales as a percentage of total sales
☐ Unit and revenue sales by territory
☐ Market share of territory
☐ Customer base by territory
☐ Product mix by territory
☐ Distribution channels by territory
☐ Maintenance/service channels by territory
☐ International training budget
☐ International advertising budget
☐ Literature requirements

☐ Legal concerns, such as development of agreements, protection of intellectual property, and effective termination provisions
☐ Financial concerns, such as aging accounts receivable, alternative collection formats, and the limitation, or elimination, of currency exposure

24. Territory Evaluation and Selection

Territory evaluation and selection is concerned with where to buy and sell, along with where and what to produce. *Where to buy* deals with the purchase of components and/or finished products and may have nothing to do with *where you sell*, especially if your product is sourced in low-income countries and sold in the "developed" world. *Where to produce* may be tied to where you sell. For example, you may choose to produce in Ireland or Portugal to be able to sell "European products" in the European Economic Community (EEC). European and Japanese companies are now "producing" in Mexico to meet the North American Free Trade Agreement (NAFTA) rules of origin guidelines, that will allow for duty-free sale to the U.S.A. and Canada.

In regard to marketing and sales, you need to consider whether you will develop your international plan on the basis of regional groups or individual countries. The regional approach might have you develop a plan for Europe, Asia, or Latin America, while a country plan would have you target key national markets like France, Japan, and Mexico. Smaller companies should probably begin with targeting key countries before trying to develop elaborate regional plans.

Another consideration is which countries to target. Companies in the U.S. almost always start with Canada because of language, cultural, and market similarities, and then move to Great Britain, Mexico, and Australia. However, companies may begin with countries where their products are in demand (such as Saudi Arabia or Venezuela, for petroleum production equipment), or where there is a strong ethnic tie. One client insisted on beginning its international business in the Czech Republic because it was the country of his ancestors.

Finally, a company developing its international plan should try to seek a balance between the risk of overlooking opportunities versus the possibility of exhausting valuable resources in examining too many opportunities. This, to a certain extent, depends on the type of international business selected. Using agents and/or distributors would probably allow the company to concentrate on more markets than would establishing marketing subsidiaries with their own direct sales force.

Overall, the following variables should be considered in territory evaluation and selection:

Market Size. While it is the key variable, it is important also to view market size in relation to the company's products. It should also be considered, especially in the area of consumer products, that Brazil, China, India, Indonesia, and Mexico may have more consumers in the middle and upper classes than do the medium-sized countries of Europe.

Competitive Risk. Large market size may look less impressive if your competitors already have a good head start in the territory. This may require using more assets to reach the market share, which may be accessed far more readily in a territory where the competitors have a weaker position. Ease of market access and the ability to retain and grow market position must be considered.

Territorial Fit in Relation to the Company's Capabilities and Policies. This covers the following subcategories:

Geography: Ability to get products to the geography and to distribute within the geography

Language: Ease of translation, importance of the native language(s) to the citizens

Market similarities: Open or closed economies, methods of advertising and promotion, degree of development of marketing and distribution channels

Internal costs and red tape: The cost of services and materials needed to sell the product, complexity of license and other government regulations

Availability of people: Either an educated workforce for the subsidiary, or the availability of business partners as agents, distributors, licensees, or joint venture partners

Monetary Risk. This basically can take two forms: risk exposure from a currency that is fluctuating greatly in relation to the home currency and government restrictions on repatriation of sales proceeds, profits, royalties, and/or investment.

Political Risk. Government stability and the ability to rely on government promises from one regime to another; the possibility of terrorism, riots, or strikes that could stop business and perhaps even destroy assets.

25. Obtaining Support for an International Plan

In almost every case, upper management is always willing to give at least lip service to taking their company "international." The problem is that many in upper management do not understand what is necessary to build an international business. In many countries, the United States being perhaps the best example, top management is still oriented toward quarterly results and are not willing to give international projects and sales the time and resources necessary to develop them. It cannot be stressed enough that upper management understand the objectives, costs, problems, and rewards of international business. Without that understanding and support, even the best international plans are doomed to failure.

26. Legal and Financial Homework

The questions most frequently asked when companies are first entering the international marketplace are usually these:

How do we get paid?
How do we protect our intellectual property?
What happens if disputes arise?

While these questions are not the only legal and financial issues a company must be aware of, these are, by far, the most important.

Obtaining Payment

Each company should determine the level of risk it is willing to take, and what forms of international payment systems it is willing to accept. In determining what type of international payment system the company should adopt, the following general principles should be considered:

☐ Availability of risk capital of the seller
☐ Credit worthiness of the buyer
☐ Degree of profit margin in the goods
☐ Industry standards

☐ Use of goods—for manufacturing, a different and longer payment
   scheme may be needed than for finished products for direct sale
☐ Government policies regarding foreign exchange, which may make
   it difficult to collect in hard currencies, even if the buyer is willing
   to pay its accounts

Companies beginning a relationship with a buyer who is relatively
unknown will normally begin with cash before delivery, or letters of
credit. They then may move to allow a small amount on open
account with restricted credit until that amount is paid, and after the
relationship is fully established, move to a revolving line of credit or
complete open account.

Protecting Intellectual Property

Despite the existence of several international treaties and conventions (International Convention for the Protection of Industrial Property, or the Paris Convention; the Patent Cooperation Treaty; and the
Universal Copyright Convention), holders of intellectual property
rights still must rely on national laws and regulations to protect their
intellectual property. This requires country-by-country registration,
which is both time-consuming and expensive.

On the practical level, this is one area in which smaller companies
are at a considerable disadvantage over their larger counterparts.
Consider, for example, a relatively common and simple situation of a
small company with three trademarks and the desire to appoint
agents and/or distributors in 20 countries. Sixty trademark registrations (three registrations times 20 countries) would likely cost
between U.S.$60,000 and U.S.$75,000, forcing the company to make
a considerable up-front investment before it can even offer products
for sale. This situation becomes even more complex and expensive
when litigation is involved. However, there are some ways to protect
intellectual property within reasonable expense and effort:

☐ Only register those trademarks that you know you are going to
   use, because such registration is subject to *use requirements*.
☐ Limit your international focus to include only those countries
   where you have a likelihood of doing a reasonable amount of
   business. Do not respond positively to the unsolicited letter from
   Bolivia, for example, if you do not see possibilities in that country.

☐ In the areas of technology transfer and licensing, consider nonlegal ways of protecting your intellectual property (e.g., hold something back such as licensing a key component, or put safeguards in your software).

☐ Rely as much on partnership selection as you do on establishing legal protection. The best protection for intellectual property is to be dealing with honest and trustworthy people.

☐ Consider sharing legal costs. Require, or request, your foreign partner to pay some of the costs of local registration in their country. However, make sure that all registrations are in the name of your company.

Dispute Resolution

Disputes arising from companies of different nationalities are always more complicated than domestic disputes. Bringing legal disputes before local courts is fraught with all kinds of dangers, including likely bias by the court toward the local party. Additionally, the costs of service of process, depositions, and translations can make it too expensive to litigate, except when very large amounts are involved. Even winning does not assure you will be able to collect; even if you do collect, it does not assure that you will be able to convert your recovery to the currency of your choice.

Therefore, it is essential that each legal agreement contain a provision for conciliation short of arbitration and, if that fails, contain a provision for an internationally-recognized form of arbitration. The form and type of these provisions should be determined by your attorney, but there are several international conventions that offer a broad variety of dispute resolution mechanisms.

27. Internal Preparedness

International business cannot be conducted in a vacuum. At some point, nearly every part of the company will be involved in the transaction. Using a relatively simple sales transaction—exporting a product—the following table illustrates that the transaction cannot be made solely by your marketing or sales department, but requires the coordination of many departments of the company.

Company Functions Involved in Export Sales

Scope	Department(s)
Is the product available for export?	Marketing/Manufacturing
Does the product meet foreign requirements?	Engineering/Quality control
Needed modifications	Engineering
Can the product be supported technically?	Marketing services/Engineering
Can the product be exported?	Legal
Cost of exporting product	Materials/Customer services
Order invoicing	Customer services/MIS
Sales support literature	Marketing services
Foreign currency issues	Finance/Treasury
Warranty terms and conditions	Quality control/Accounting/Legal
Customer credit-worthiness?	Finance
Export sales terms and conditions	Finance/Accounting/Legal
Agreements	Legal/Marketing

28. Fitting the International Plan into the Company

As the above table illustrates, the decision to take a company across borders should be one in which all major elements of the company are informed and, if possible, involved. Additionally, this involvement is essential to determine how the international plan will fit into the overall plan. A company cannot simply look to international sales as another revenue generator, unless it has assessed whether they may set off other forces that could negatively impact the company, or send it down roads it does not want, or is unprepared, to travel. There are many ways to enter the global marketplace and, as you will see, some involve limited risk. Whichever way is chosen, however, it should not be undertaken until the impact on the entire company is understood and accounted for.

CROSS-CULTURAL AWARENESS

Whether you are doing business in your home market or overseas, much of your success depends on how well you understand and can work with critical "human" factors. No matter how technically competent you may be, your ability to communicate and build business and personal relationships across national and cultural boundaries will determine your individual effectiveness and the ultimate success of your enterprise.

The following sections will give you some foundations for creating your own unique approach to cross-cultural awareness and communications. You will find a useful mixture of general principles and practical advice, organized so you can easily find the human factors that interest you the most.

29. *Becoming WorldWise*™

In an increasingly competitive global marketplace, to be world-wise is to be market-wise. In business, the most market-wise generate the most attractive profits in any segment of any industry. Window on the World, Inc., a U.S. firm based in Minneapolis, Minnesota, has been providing training and consultation services for multinational companies since 1985. According to their *Becoming WorldWise*™ training program, here's what you should do to start becoming market-wise on a global scale:

Know your global market

☐ Who are your customers in your current markets?
☐ What are the characteristics of your most desirable customers?
☐ Where else in the world are there concentrations of similar customers?
☐ What are the trends or special circumstances that affect the attractiveness of your product or service to your customers in your current markets?

☐ Do these same trends or special circumstances affect the attractiveness of your product or service in other markets around the world?

Know your global industry

☐ How is your industry structured in your current markets?
☐ Do you have relatively new technology or old? Where did the original technology come from?
☐ Do the participants have narrow, specialized product lines or highly diverse product lines?
☐ Is the ownership family/private, publicly-traded, or state-owned?
☐ Is the market dominated by a few large participants or are there many, smaller participants?
☐ Is distribution mainly direct or indirect? Does it vary greatly within your current markets?
☐ Is it highly regulated?
☐ Are there strong industry associations?
☐ In other markets, is the industry structure the same as it is in your current markets, or is the structure substantially different?

Know your direct competitors

☐ Who are your competitors in your current markets?
☐ Do they compete with you in all of your current markets?
☐ Do any of them serve markets you presently do not serve?
☐ In which market did your competitors originate?
☐ Which markets appear to have the largest and which markets appear to have the smallest number of competitors?
☐ How do each of your competitors differentiate themselves in your current markets and do they differentiate themselves the same way in other markets?

Know your suppliers

☐ Do all of your suppliers originate within your current markets?
☐ Do all of your competitors in your current markets rely on the same suppliers?
☐ What trends or special circumstances affect your suppliers in your current markets?

☐ What trends or special circumstances affect your potential suppliers in other markets?

By answering questions like these, you will be able to determine where your company fits into your market and your industry in truly global terms. This "world-wise" perspective will help you plot a profitable course for your business.

30. Greetings and Introductions

First impressions really do count, and much of your credibility as a transnational businessperson may rest on your ability to properly "meet and greet" people of different nationalities and cultures. Here are some tips to help you prepare for any eventuality:

☐ Before traveling overseas, or before welcoming your overseas visitor to your own country, do a little "homework" on the other country in question. Learn about customary greetings and arrival "protocol," either from written materials, local expatriates, or associates who have traveled to the country in question.

☐ Determine to what extent your visitor or overseas host has traveled to your country or had contact with persons of your nationality. This may influence your visitor's or your host's expectations for the first contact. If your visitor or host has little experience in your country or with any other person of your nationality, it is wise to expect and for you to apply, as well, a higher degree of formality to the initial contact or greeting.

☐ Be aware of "formalities," such as codes of dress, manners, conduct, and gift exchanges that may be customary in the home country of your visitor or counterpart. Chances are, your first contact will be more formal than you may be accustomed to in your home market. Your guest or host will very likely attempt to show respect in ways that they are most accustomed.

☐ Follow the "Golden Rule"—with a twist. Always do unto others as you would have them do unto you, but be aware of the differences in expectations and customs that may exist. Although you may be accustomed to getting "right down to business," your guest or host may expect to have some time first to unwind and get acquainted with you socially on neutral ground.

31. Dressing for Success

Around the world, the way people dress often communicates credibility (or the lack of same) in very subtle ways. Here are some tips to keep in mind:

☐ Become familiar with "dress code" traditions and the variations on these traditions in your destination country. The way you dress, especially in your initial encounters, can be taken as a sign of respect or as a slight.

☐ Keep in mind that significant differences in the "dress code" may exist between appropriate dress for daytime work and evening entertainment, between urban and rural, between suburban and "financial centers," and between capital cities and regional centers.

☐ When in doubt, dress "up"—dress conservatively. Deference to dress codes will convey that you are an educated and cultivated person. Remember, you can always take a coat, jacket, or tie off if invited to do so.

☐ Always keep climactic conditions in mind (hot and humid vs. dry and cool); consider umbrellas and appropriate footwear, among other items.

☐ Adopt "native" dress only when appropriate (e.g., the "guayabera" in some Caribbean Island nations, coastal regions, and some Central American countries).

☐ Assume that quality will be noticed.

☐ In some social circumstances, foreigners are perceived to be well-to-do; and if they don't "put on their best," it may be perceived as an insult. So, don't dress "down" in these situations. You may be perceived as "condescending" or "patronizing."

☐ Shorts and tennis shoes are not acceptable business or social attire in many parts of the world.

☐ Pay special attention to the social mores in countries known to enforce strict religiously-derived codes—particularly with respect to dress and social behavior of women.

☐ After relationships and trust have been established, sometimes it is appropriate to take your cues from your host or counterpart and dress on a par with him or her.

☐ Keep in mind that it is up to you to do your homework—not up to your host. Even an attentive host will not risk *your* embarrassment by correcting you or pointing out the error in what you are doing. On the contrary, a good host will always want you to feel comfortable and accepted.

32. Entertaining and Being Entertained

In many parts of the world, entertaining is not just an extracurricular activity. It is a key method for establishing the business relationship—or determining whether or not there will be a business relationship. Wherever you may find yourself, you must prepare for entertaining, and prepare to be entertained. Allow time for entertainment when you plan your schedule. This is likely to occur well before you discuss the first point on your business agenda.

Entertaining and being entertained are fundamental prerequisites in building business relationships in most parts of the world. Do your homework on the social expectations for guests and for hosts in the destination country. For example, is entertainment likely to be done in hotels and restaurants or at private homes? Are gifts (flowers, wine, etc.) appropriate to the host or hostess if you are meeting with them in a private home? It is also important to know the appropriate topics of conversation, as well as cultural taboos to avoid.

Is punctuality expected—or entirely unexpected? When is it acceptable to leave? The international traveler must also know the appropriate table manners, according to the host's culture. The importance of toasting should not be overlooked—as well as that of reciprocity.

33. Knowing What Gifts to Give

In most countries in the world, gift exchanges between prospective business associates are common. It is part of the process of establishing trust and mutual respect. The thoughtful choice of a gift can profoundly influence the credibility of the giver. Remember that "knowledge is power." In this case, it is the knowledge of the culture and gift-giving traditions of your host country that will give you the power to succeed in establishing successful business relationships.

Long before your departure, it would be wise to read as much as you can about your destination country, its history, and its customs—

particularly the role that gift giving plays in building relationships. Also, consult with colleagues who have lived and worked in your destination country, along with expatriates living in your home community. Seek the advice of others, as well, who specialize in intercultural communications.

Be mindful that the increasing globalization of business practices has eroded adherence to many traditions, including gift-giving traditions. Expectations and practices may vary within your destination country as well and may depend on such things as education, relative social standing, and private or public sector affiliation.

When selecting and presenting gifts, it is better to be too formal than too casual. A sincere attempt to honor local gift-giving traditions will establish you as a well-educated and serious person—attributes that are important for success in most parts of the world.

"When in doubt, ask." If you find yourself already in the country and unprepared, don't hesitate to ask for advice on gift selection from your company's local representative or from a trusted associate. If you have no such contacts to rely upon, consult with your hotel's concierge or even the hotel manager. Although it might take a little longer, your country's local diplomatic or commercial representatives should be able to offer guidance on the selection of gifts and other protocol.

34. Making Contacts and Appointments

The protocol for making contacts and appointments varies from one country to another, and may vary from region to region within a country, as well. To get off on the right foot, do your homework. Read up on the business and social customs of your counterpart's country of origin. Seek advice from colleagues who have already done business there or from expatriates in whom you can place your trust.

Make sure you are approaching the right person, given the relative importance of the roles that each of you play in your respective organizations. If you are the chief executive of your company, you should be prepared to initiate contact with the person of equivalent authority in the counterpart organization, even though you may wish, ultimately, to interview someone at a lower echelon within the organization. You will often be expected to have the "blessing" of the superior before making contact with the subordinate.

"Cold calling" is normally not effective. It is usually advisable to send a letter or fax to introduce yourself, your company or product line, and the purpose of your correspondence before making telephone contact. In some business cultures, people are not accustomed to accommodating people they do not yet know, or to whom they have not been introduced or referred by a mutual acquaintance.

In your correspondence, be sure to spell the names of your counterparts correctly and *include all appropriate titles*. Format the address correctly and accurately, and use the appropriate language, whenever possible, maintaining a degree of "formal cordiality" in the initial correspondence.

Follow up your letter or fax with a phone call to determine a suitable meeting time and place. Depending on the nature of your business with your counterpart, this may or may not be an "in office" meeting. Be prepared to have that first encounter in a restaurant, hotel lobby, or other place that is conducive to getting acquainted. Adjust your expectations to fit local perceptions of time and the relative importance of punctuality. In some parts of the world, be prepared for occasional "no-shows" or substantial waits in the reception room. It is important not to take such events personally. Adjust your appointment planning to the local logistical realities, so you don't arrive frustrated and "off-balance." Allow adequate time between appointments.

Depending on your relative stature, don't enter a private office unless you have been acknowledged and invited in. Remain standing until your host invites you to take a seat. Be prepared to accept offers of hospitality, such as coffee or tea, and for the exchanging of gifts, during pre-arranged initial encounters.

Also, depending on your relative stature, it may be up to you to make the first move to courteously indicate the end of the meeting and to thank the host as you leave. In some business cultures, you may have to be the first to arise from your chair.

35. Adapting to Different Cultures

"Another day, another culture." Every day, even in our hometowns, we face the need to make at least minor adaptations to different cultures, although we probably characterize this as simply "getting along with people." Sometimes, the cultural differences are so subtle that we may not be aware of them or the slight adjustments we automatically make to adapt to them.

As human beings, we are endowed with all the tools we need in order to adapt to different cultures: the abilities to observe, to reason, and to communicate. It is attitude and commitment, however, that distinguish successful adapters from unsuccessful ones.

Attitude and Commitment Check—"Know thyself"

Do you really enjoy meeting people you have never met before? If you do, this will affect your attitude and create a positive perception in the minds of your counterparts. If you don't, maybe you should adopt a role which does not require you to lead the way in establishing relationships across cultures.

Are you naturally curious about people and life in other parts of the world? If you are, this will help you sustain the "small talk" that often accompanies the process of getting acquainted across cultures.

Do you believe strongly that your culture is superior to all others, and that you have nothing to learn from other cultures? Then—just as it's said in the game of Monopoly—stop, go directly to jail, do not pass "go," and do not collect the $200!

Do you consider people as individuals, or do you rely on common stereotypes to guide your expectations regarding people from cultures different than your own? If you rely on stereotypes, you will miss many important clues regarding the true nature and potential of the relationship you are trying to establish with your counterpart. (Note: stereotypes are not all bad, if they are based on broad and deep experience within a particular culture. It is extremely important to set the stereotype aside, however, when getting acquainted with any particular individual; otherwise, it will prevent you from observing, reasoning, and communicating in a manner that is appropriate for that particular individual.)

Listen to and Observe your Counterpart— "Stop, Look and Listen"

Review what you know (or think you know) about your counterpart, including that person's position in the company, industry background, current title, authority, age, education, and family background. As you observe, make mental notes of your counterpart's appearance, including height, weight, and manner of dress. Compare this with others in the same local context.

Also, note your counterpart's manner of speaking, including his or her grasp of foreign languages, grammar, and vocabulary. Compare this, too, with others in the same context. Study your counterpart's interactions with others—the respect or deference shown, use of authority, and apparent influence—including his or her interactions with you.

Reason

Analyze your observations and compare your counterpart with the stereotype you "brought with you." Try to explain any differences between what you expected (stereotype) and what you found (observation) to be true about your counterpart. Then develop a working "hypothesis" about your counterpart, to help guide your communications and further observation as you get better acquainted.

Communicate

If possible, demonstrate respect for your counterpart and his or her culture by communicating in the language of your counterpart. In most parts of the world, people who can speak more than one language are automatically assumed to be well-educated. This perception will help you gain the confidence and trust of your counterparts.

Let your observations be your guide in choosing the appropriate manner of dressing, behaving, and speaking ("communication" includes all three) in the early stages of your relationship with your counterpart. Be sure to reciprocate any respect or deference shown to you by your counterpart, especially while in public or in groups.

36. The Pitfalls of Polite Conversation

For those conducting business internationally, there are many opportunities to carry on polite conversation as you become acquainted with your host, guest, negotiating counterparts, or other associates and officials that you may meet along the way. Such conversations, casual as they may seem, can be an important prelude to doing business, or a complementary means for confirming who you are in the eyes of your counterparts.

To reinforce your credibility, while also enjoying polite conversation, speak your counterpart's language whenever possible, especially if you are a guest in your counterpart's country. Just showing an interest in your counterpart's language can increase your standing. Also, don't complain about "inconveniences" you have suffered during your trip or during your introduction to the host country. Such complaints can be taken as criticism of the host country's customs and traditions.

Although you may occupy "center stage" as a special guest, it is wise to maintain a polite reserve and draw others into the conversation. Remember not to dominate the conversation. Don't offer opinions on narrow political issues or religious topics, and try to avoid contradicting opinions offered by your counterpart; instead, try to maintain a sympathetic, yet humble, demeanor.

Do show curiosity about your counterpart and those things that seem important to him or her, such as art, music, sports, travel, current events, hobbies, and collections, as well as children and family. Don't introduce business topics into the conversation, especially if you are the guest. To do so may cause you to appear "pushy" and uninterested in getting acquainted with your counterpart.

37. The Importance of Business Cards

How can a simple business card be all that important? After all, in some parts of the world, they are filed away immediately. Although the practice may be evolving in different ways in different parts of the globe, it is important to remember the status of business cards and the ceremony that may accompany their exchange in some parts of the world.

Business cards serve as "letters of introduction"—a representation of "who you are" and "what you can do." The address on the cards should include the name of your "home" country; otherwise, by assuming that your counterparts will know where Topeka, Kansas is, you may appear arrogant. Abbreviations should be avoided, unless they are universally recognized. "USA," for example, is acceptable, as are the abbreviations for many other countries. When in doubt, however, spell it out! Consider using your full given name, rather than your "nickname," and incorporate titles or academic degrees into your name. Use a business title that is descriptive and communicates your relative position within the organization.

Consider how to carry, present and receive business cards. Be aware that, in some parts of the world, business cards are handled with great care and exchanged with some degree of reciprocal ceremony. For this reason, be sure to carry a supply of your business cards in an attractive card case; this card case can be kept in your briefcase or in your suit pocket. In most parts of the world, business cards should definitely not be carried in a back pocket. This is particularly offensive in many Asian countries. Be sure any cards presented are in "mint" condition—not smudged, dog-eared, or written upon.

Observe the local card-exchanging customs and follow them as closely as you can. When in doubt, receive your counterpart's business card with both hands; and read it carefully—to demonstrate respect for the person presenting you with the card. As a guest, you should be prepared to offer and present your card first, so it is important to do your "homework" before your first encounter.

38. Language and Culture

If you want to establish long-term business relationships, it is important to recognize the relationship between language and culture. Language provides an indispensable window through which the international business person can observe and better understand the culture of his or her business counterpart. Also, language often defines the nationality or "affinity group" within a nation; therefore, it is important for you to understand that language and culture are so intertwined that it is not possible to truly understand a culture without also understanding the language of that culture.

In international business, or in business across cultures within one's own country, knowledge of the counterpart's or the customer's language is essential at all phases of the business venture. This includes determining:

☐ If there is a market for your product or service
☐ How to successfully adapt the product or service
☐ How to respond to orders and distribute the product
☐ How to sustain the product or service in the market

In successful, long-term, cross-cultural business relationships, the parties have to find a way to understand each other and to build trust. To the extent that a shared language is a prerequisite for building understanding and trust between people, then a shared language is also a prerequisite for building a successful, long-term business relationship.

In business, the choice of a "shared language" is most often governed by the practical language skills of each of the two parties. It is important to keep in mind, however, that the party with the greater language skills will often have a greater business advantage. If you rely exclusively, though, on your own language as the "shared language," then you are ceding an important negotiating advantage to the other party and cutting off your access to information that may be essential for a long-term, "win-win" type of business relationship. To the extent that mutual respect is essential for a successful, long-term business relationship, an effort to understand the other party's language and culture is also essential.

39. Learning Foreign Languages

In today's world, there are more than 1,000 spoken languages. Of these, at least 250 are spoken by at least one million people. If you include the African trading languages of Swahili and Hausa, about 14 of these languages are regularly used in transnational commerce. To determine which language or languages you should strive to learn, first consider that the international language of business is the language of the customer.

For the reader of the English edition of this book, it is important to note that Mandarin Chinese, Hindi and Spanish are more widely spoken than English. Thanks to the worldwide reach of the one-time British Empire, however, British English has become a "default" language for commerce across language boundaries in many parts of the world. It is still important to remember, however, that only about 13 percent of the world's multilingual people speak English.

The importance of language may depend on whether you intend to do business "between" countries or "within" countries—keeping in mind that, in some countries, several languages may be in common use. The importance of language also may depend on the role you personally intend to play in the international undertaking. If your role requires you to take charge of an overseas assignment, clearly you will need to be able to communicate in the language or languages used in your host country.

40. English—The Language of Convenience

Even though British English has evolved to become the language of convenience in the conduct of international commerce throughout many parts of the world, it is important not to take the use of English for granted. It is quite possible that your counterpart's native language, culture, and national identity are all intertwined, and it may be wise to show respect for your counterpart and his language by showing interest in it and learning some of its fundamentals.

In most parts of the world, "English" means "British English," which is different in spelling and in common usage than American English. American common usage does not translate well (or at all) into British English.

American Spelling		British Spelling
Center	vs.	Centre
Theater	vs.	Theatre
Analyze	vs.	Analyse
Program	vs.	Programme
Neighbor	vs.	Neighbour
Humor	vs.	Humour

Figure 1. Examples of British vs. American English Spelling and usage

American Usage		British Usage
Gas	vs.	Petrol
Hood	vs.	Bonnet
Trunk	vs.	Boot
Rubber	vs.	Condom
Eraser	vs.	Rubber
Make a decision	vs.	Take a decision

Figure 2. Examples of differences in common usage

41. Building Language Capabilities

Those involved in international business have demonstrated an ability to acquire new knowledge and skills. The following self-directed learning methods may help you build your own language capabilities:

☐ Review and become aware of your own language and its grammatical structure.

☐ Assess your attitude toward learning languages. Is it fun, an interesting challenge, or a necessary "evil"? Your attitude will have much to do with how easily you build your language capability.

☐ Determine whether you learn best on your own, one-on-one, or in a group. For practice, what combination of seeing, hearing, and speaking activities will likely work best for you? Also, don't rule out other senses as learning aids—such as smell, touch, and taste.

☐ If you prefer to work on your own, or if you have no time to devote to classes, consider using some combination of books, recording tapes, videos, CD-ROMs, or information available via the Internet, to build your own learning program.

☐ If you are able to devote time to classes, try to pick one that offers you an opportunity to acquire vocabulary that might be used in your industry.

☐ Take every opportunity to immerse yourself in the language—to train your ear to distinguish the sound of words the way they are actually spoken.

42. Language Solutions

If, while conducting international business, you find that you must communicate with counterparts who do not speak your language, or who have limited proficiency in your language, here are some suggestions:

☐ Find someone in your own company who is a native speaker and enlist him or her to assist you with translations and protocol.

☐ Find a qualified interpreter, preferably someone with substantial experience in the languages in question and who is willing to learn something about your business, as well as the context of the communications.

☐ Rely on interpreters provided by your counterparts—although this is not the most desirable alternative, as they will often interpret in favor of their clients.

☐ In any case, it is always advisable to learn enough of the local language to at least identify yourself properly and attend to the formalities of an introduction.

ECONOMIC INTEGRATION

Although nations have always entered into trade agreements, in recent decades the growth in the number and comprehensiveness of such agreements and the resulting economic integration around the world has increased dramatically. In this post-WWII era, countries have increasingly entered into trade alliances and created trading blocks based on common regional interests.

This section gives you an overview of the major trading blocks around the world and the extent of the economic integration that is occurring within and between these blocks.

43. Levels of Economic Integration

The degree of economic integration is best measured by the relative ease of cross-border trade between the member nations. However, the large number of these efforts to ease trade or create preferences makes this measurement a bit difficult.

Thousands of minor bilateral trade agreements exist all around the world. There are traditional trade preferences that former colonial powers extend to their former colonies, such as the British Commonwealth. There are also significant and comprehensive regional trade agreements like the European Union; the North American Free Trade Agreement (NAFTA); the Mercado Común del Sur (MERCOSUR), also known as the South American Common Market in the southern part of South America; and the Association of South East Asian Nations (ASEAN); as well as the major global trade regulatory agreements like the General Agreement on Tariffs and Trade (GATT) that have evolved into formal institutions like the World Trade Organization (WTO).

To comprehend the nature and the degree of regional economic integration, and to determine how it might affect your business strategy, you may use the following criteria to guide your analysis:

All economic sectors: Are there some economic activities, like banking or insurance, or some natural resources, that are excluded from such arrangements?

All trade financial activity: Are all areas of importation and
exportation handled in like manner, or does the arrangement call
for special handling of trade finance in certain sectors?

All investment activity: Are investments governed in the same manner
throughout the integrated territories?

Taxation: Have tax laws been brought into conformity throughout
the integrated territory?

Standards: Are technical quality, safety, and consumer-protection
standards the same throughout the integrated territories?

Currency: Is the same monetary system and currency used throughout
the territories?

Labor law: Have the labor laws been brought into conformity?

Social policy: Have education and social welfare policies been
brought into conformity?

Immigration policy: Are citizens able to move freely from one
country to another within the integrated territories?

44. Major Regional Trade Agreements

Here are the major regional trade agreements, along with a brief
description of their origins:

European Union (EU)

This process of trade integration began with the signing of the Treaty
of Rome in 1957 by six member states—Germany, France, Italy, the
Netherlands, Belgium, and Luxembourg—and it continued to evolve
over the ensuing decades. By 1998, the EU incorporated a core group of
15 sovereign nations, 11 of which have joined together to form a monetary union. These countries are Austria, Belgium, Denmark, Finland,
France, Germany, Greece, Ireland, Italy, Luxembourg, the Netherlands,
Portugal, Spain, Sweden, and the United Kingdom. These 15 EU countries have a combined Gross Domestic Product (GDP) approaching
U.S.$7.5 trillion and a combined population approaching 380 million.

North American Free Trade Agreement (NAFTA)

The NAFTA integration process began with the Free Trade Agreement (FTA) entered into by the U.S. and Canada in 1989. These two

countries already had long-standing preferential trade agreements covering a large number of industry sectors before they took this final step toward free trade. With the incorporation of Mexico in 1994, NAFTA now has a combined GDP of more than U.S.$9 trillion and a combined population of almost 400 million.

Asian Free Trade Area—Association of South East Asian Nations (AFTA—ASEAN)

In Asia, the economic integration process is relatively new. In 1995, the seven ASEAN members saw the need to create greater trade negotiation leverage, in view of the pace at which economic integration was occurring in Europe and in North and South America. They expect to complete tariff and trade negotiations by the year 2003. Seven countries are currently members of AFTA, including Brunei, Indonesia, Malaysia, the Philippines, Singapore, Thailand, and Vietnam—creating a combined GDP of about U.S.$1.8 trillion and a combined population greater than 450 million.

Mercado Común Del Sur or South American Common Market (MERCOSUR)

Although there is a long history of regional trade negotiation in Latin America, the most ambitious in recent years is the MERCOSUR that incorporates the "Southern Cone" countries of Argentina, Brazil, Paraguay, and Uruguay. The initial steps toward integration were completed in 1994. With the addition of Chile, as sort of an affiliate member, the combined GDP of MERCOSUR is now almost U.S.$1.4 trillion and the combined population exceeds 220 million.

Gulf Cooperation Council (GCC)

The six member states of the GCC make up one of the most economically powerful trade groups in this region. It was formed in 1980, largely in response to concerns about the effects of the Iran-Iraq war. Current members are Bahrain, Kuwait, Oman, Qatar, Saudi Arabia, and the United Arab Emirates. These states have a combined GDP of U.S.$351 billion and a combined population of 29 million.

Economic Community of West African States (ECOWAS)

In 1975, 16 African states created ECOWAS in the hopes that it would develop into an integrated common market. Some progress has been made toward a customs union but many elements of economic integration are still missing. Member states include Benin, Burkina Faso, Cape Verde, Gambia, Ghana, Guinea, Guinea-Bissau, Ivory Coast, Liberia, Mali, Mauritania, Niger, Nigeria, Senegal, Sierra Leone, and Togo. With a combined GDP of U.S.$262 billion and a combined population of 217 million, these 16 nations make up the largest trading community in Sub-Saharan Africa.

Other Trade Agreements and Affiliations

In all of the regions mentioned, there are many other types of trade agreements that are not as comprehensive or as inclusive as those mentioned above. It is important to research all trade agreements that may affect the movement of product, personnel, and financial assets in and out of the areas of interest to you.

45. European Economic Integration

The key elements of European economic integration are expressed in terms of tariffs, immigration, currency, design standards, quality standards, social policy, economic policy, finance and investment, and public infrastructure.

Tariffs—To be reduced or eliminated between participating countries; external tariffs to be agreed upon

Immigration policy—To be liberalized to the extent that evidence of citizenship will not be required upon crossing borders between member countries

Currency—To be replaced by one common currency, the euro

Design standards—To be revised to create common standards that will be applied universally within the member countries

Quality standards—To be uniform throughout the trading area; the *ISO* standards will continue to be promulgated

Social policy—To be integrated and made uniform over time

Economic policy—To be centralized and managed jointly through new regional mechanisms

Finance and investment—To be regulated by a centralized regional mechanism

Public infrastructure—To continue to be integrated and interconnected and marked in universally recognizable ways

46. The Integrated European Market

Depending on the degree of integration ultimately achieved, the implications of the European market may be enormous—not only for Europeans, but also for the rest of the world, as it will involve:

☐ One of the world's largest markets
☐ A currency that can compete with the U.S. dollar and the Japanese yen
☐ A strong, competitive corporate finance market
☐ A stronger and more competitive sovereign debt market
☐ Greater "transaction" efficiencies within the market
☐ Greater economies of scale for manufacturing
☐ More cost-efficient sourcing from within the market
☐ Spawning grounds for stronger competitors

47. The "Euro" as a Common Currency

On January 1, 1999, 11 of the 15 members of the European *Economic and Monetary Union* (EMU) implemented the first phase in their plan to adopt the "euro" as a common currency (see tip #122). The participating countries are Austria, Belgium, Finland, France, Germany, Ireland, Italy, Luxembourg, the Netherlands, Portugal, and Spain. Denmark, Sweden, and the United Kingdom chose not to participate, at least initially; and Greece was not able to meet the stringent economic convergence criteria adopted by the Union.

The participating countries have adopted irrevocable conversion rates that became effective on January 1, 1999, and the euro became the official currency for all 11 countries. No euros are scheduled to be put in circulation, however, until January 1, 2002. Also, as of January 1, 1999, the euro took over all the functions performed by the European Currency Unit (ECU), that had been in use since 1979.

48. Selecting a Base in the EEC

Even after the unified currency is fully implemented, there will continue to be significant differences in labor costs, manufacturing overhead, and distribution expense, as you go from one country or
province to another within the *European Economic Community*.
Here are some factors to consider when you are looking for the best
place to "set up shop" to serve the EEC:

- *Customers:* Depending on the nature of your industry, proximity to
  customers may or may not be important. In any case, it is advisable
  to know where your customers are located within the EEC.
- *Competitors:* In EEC countries where a particular competitor
  industry is dominant, you should continue to expect to find non-
  tariff barriers to entry. You may want to consider an EEC country
  that is not dominated by direct competitors.
- *Manufacturing costs:* Depending on the labor content of your
  product, manufacturing costs may vary widely, from one country
  to another within the EEC.
- *Raw materials and components:* To the extent that the proximity of
  these inputs is important to your success, it is advisable to examine
  how to optimize your sourcing within the EEC. Some countries may
  offer greater advantages than others, in this respect.
- *Distribution costs:* The cost of order fulfillment may vary widely
  within the EEC.
- *Regulatory costs:* Keep in mind that, in addition to the imposed
  costs of regulations that affect your operations, there may be
  regulations or restrictions designed to discourage
  commercial/industrial growth in some areas and encourage it in
  other areas within the EEC.
- *Taxes:* Even though there is a great deal of convergence in the fiscal
  policies of the participating countries within the EEC, you should
  be aware that there may still be significant differences in the
  taxation of business activities and profits within the EEC.
- *Cost of capital:* With the advent of the euro, it is fair to expect that
  the relative cost of capital will decline, due to greater market
  efficiencies and the effect of scale. However, there still may be
  significant differences in these costs from country to country.

49. Creating an EEC Company

Will it be necessary to create a new corporation, under EEC incorporation rules, to pursue market opportunities within the European market? Here are some factors to consider:

☐ *Know your critical success factors:* Before making a decision regarding your company's position within the European Economic Community, first consider what factors are likely to be most critical to your company's success within the EEC—keeping in mind that the "mission" of the EEC is to create favorable economic conditions for businesses based within the EEC borders.

☐ *Tax laws and laws of incorporation:* Are there features of EEC corporate law that make incorporation relatively attractive? Would incorporation within the EEC create any tax advantages?

☐ *Manufacturing logistics:* Would incorporation within the EEC offer attractive opportunities for sourcing management, labor, raw materials, components, or manufacturing technology (capital equipment)?

☐ *Distribution logistics:* Would EEC incorporation create potential for improving channels of distribution within the EEC—for reducing the cost of order fulfillment?

☐ *Financial logistics:* Would EEC incorporation create access to competitive corporate financing? Would it ease currency transaction costs? Would it create favorable accounting and translation conditions, from a parent company's point of view?

☐ *Regulatory issues:* Would EEC incorporation create a more attractive and consistent regulatory environment?

☐ *External barriers:* Would EEC incorporation enable your company to overcome tariff and non-tariff barriers to importation?

50. Key Elements in North American Integration

There are substantial differences in the level of integration, when you compare the European Common Market with NAFTA.

Movement of people: A business traveler will notice the obvious difference in the ease of travel, when comparing NAFTA with the

European Community. A European business traveler may travel freely from one country to another, without showing a passport or other documentation at the border. By contrast, a NAFTA business traveler must be able to show a passport or other official documentation and adhere to certain immigration procedures, going from country to country within NAFTA.

Movement of Goods: Within the European Community, merchandise and the merchandise carriers are relatively free to cross national borders, without customs inspection or application of duties. By contrast, within NAFTA, there are still substantial restrictions on the free movement of merchandise and merchandise carriers—and, in most instances, customs duties continue to be assessed.

Movement of funds: Notably, within the participating European Community countries, there will soon be just one currency and just one monetary system. Whereas, within NAFTA, there are three currencies and three distinct monetary systems.

Regulatory environment: Within the European Community, the participating countries have established a community-wide, law-making and regulatory process that is intended to cover such areas as environmental protection, labor standards, investment, intellectual property, etc. With NAFTA, each country has retained its individual sovereignty in these areas, although there are "side agreements" that have created the foundations for bilateral or multilateral cooperation in many of these same areas.

51. Understanding NAFTA

NAFTA, which went into effect on January 1, 1994, is a rather modest form of regional integration when compared with the European Economic Union but is, nonetheless, a huge departure from the past. Following suit on the FTA with Canada, NAFTA encompasses all three countries, Canada, the U.S.A. and Mexico, 400 million people and about U.S.$9 trillion in combined Gross Domestic Product.

NAFTA's broad purpose is to eliminate barriers to trade in, and facilitate the cross-border movement of, goods and services between the territories of the Parties.

The text of NAFTA covers:

☐ Trade in goods
☐ Trade in services

☐ Investment
☐ Intellectual property protection
☐ Competition policy
☐ Dispute resolution

Trade in goods:

☐ Eliminates import duties on many goods (about 50 percent of industrial goods tariffs) and mandates "national treatment" to goods of the other parties
☐ Eliminates most border restrictions (barriers) such as quotas, import licenses, and performance requirements
☐ Duties not immediately eliminated will be phased out over 15 years, in a four-part schedule ending in the year 2008
☐ Preserves the duty reductions already achieved under the U.S.-Canada FTA
☐ Harmonizes the three countries' customs procedures such as the "rules of origin," customs forms, and record-keeping requirements
☐ Eliminates customs user fees between Mexico and the U.S.A. by mid-1999. Such fees between the U.S.A. and Canada were eliminated in 1994.

Trade in services:

☐ Eliminates barriers to cross-border services, financial services, and professional services
☐ Licensing requirements still retained by each country but the expectation is that they will be transparent and no more burdensome than necessary
☐ Citizenship and residency requirements for service providers were to be eliminated by January 1, 1996
☐ Freedom of movement for workers is still restricted; however, temporary entry restrictions have been eased for business purposes, after-sale service providers, sales representatives and agents, and professionals, executives and management personnel
☐ NAFTA hopes to reduce the incentive for illegal border crossings by Mexican workers by raising Mexican wages and the standard of living within Mexico.

Investment:

- ☐ Open investment policy established—requiring national and Most Favored Nation (MFN) treatment for foreign investment from NAFTA countries
- ☐ Eliminates performance requirements, domestic content, and nationality requirements
- ☐ Some reservations still apply in Mexico, in that investment in Mexican industries such as petroleum, electricity, railroads, maritime transportation, and satellite communications, is still somewhat restricted.

Intellectual property:

- ☐ Strong protection for patents, copyrights, trademarks, know-how, trade secrets, and semiconductor technology
- ☐ Copyright laws include computer programs, as well as a long list of literary and artistic works.
- ☐ Trademark protection includes service marks and so-called famous marks that are well known in a territory, even if not registered there.
- ☐ Patent protection is to be available for a minimum of 20 years from the date of filing or 17 years from the date of grant.
- ☐ Layout and design of semiconductor integrated circuits is fully protected.
- ☐ NAFTA also harmonizes procedures and requires effective enforcement.
- ☐ Canada persisted in retaining a "cultural exemption" that allows it to exclude non-Canadian cultural materials, such as magazines, books, motion pictures, and sound recordings.

Competition policy:

- ☐ Requires coordination of laws and policies on competition and monopolies and pledges to prohibit anticompetitive business conduct, to give mutual legal assistance, notification and consultation to each other, and to exchange information on antitrust issues
- ☐ Recognizes Mexico's tradition of state-owned enterprises and monopolies, but prohibits state-owned enterprises from impinging on the right to open investment and requires that goods or services be made available on a non-discriminatory basis

☐ Designated monopolies must act in accordance with commercial considerations in selling or purchasing, and must not engage in anticompetitive acts in non-monopoly markets.

Dispute resolution:

☐ NAFTA contains a general dispute resolution mechanism, as well as specialized mechanisms relating to investment, anti-dumping appeals, and countervailing duty cases.
☐ Side agreements on labor and the environment have separate dispute resolution mechanisms.
☐ NAFTA parties retain the right to bring a dispute under GATT, as well as to a NAFTA panel.

52. Creating a NAFTA Product

Not all products found within the geographic area covered by NAFTA are NAFTA products. The goal of NAFTA is to limit the benefits of expanded trade to products originating in the U.S.A., Canada or Mexico. Here's how to go about making sure your product qualifies as a NAFTA product:

☐ Is it produced exclusively at facilities located within NAFTA countries?
☐ Is it composed of materials or components originating in a NAFTA country?
☐ Is it produced from non-NAFTA materials or components with a different tariff classification than the final product?

If you can answer "yes" to these questions, then your product likely qualifies as a NAFTA product, for these purposes.

The third question is often referred to as the *tariff shift*. In other words, there is no minimum local (inside NAFTA) content requirement. However, when non-NAFTA components and/or materials are used to make a product, the manufacturer must demonstrate that enough "value" is being added to cause a change in the tariff classification of the final product.

Evidence of this tariff shift is sufficient evidence to qualify a product as a NAFTA product, even though most or all of its materials and/or components are sourced outside of NAFTA.

Accordingly, a product brought into a NAFTA country for eventual re-export to another NAFTA country (the "spring-board" maneuver) would not be considered a NAFTA product, unless it was put through a process that caused it to be re-classified into a different tariff category.

53. The NAFTA Agreement on Environmental Cooperation

In August 1993, the U.S.A., Canada, and Mexico entered into a "side agreement" on environmental cooperation, largely in response to concerns that U.S. environmental interest groups had expressed about lax enforcement of environmental protection laws and rules within Mexico. This is what it is intended to do:

☐ Ensure that no country gains a competitive trade advantage by failing to enforce environmental laws.
☐ Create a *Commission on Environmental Cooperation* to address virtually any concern, including:
  • Transnational environmental issues
  • Environmental implications of process and production methods
  • Conservation of flora and fauna and natural areas
  • Approaches to governmental enforcement and compliance
☐ Establish a dispute resolution process, for use when there is a "persistent pattern of failure" by any of the three countries to effectively enforce its own environmental law.

54. The NAFTA Agreement on Labor Cooperation

On August 13, 1993, the U.S.A., Canada, and Mexico entered into a "side agreement" called the *Supplemental Agreement on Labor Cooperation,* largely in response to concerns expressed by organized labor interests in the U.S. This is what this agreement was intended to do:

☐ Create a trilateral *Commission for Labor Cooperation*
☐ Establish an enforcement mechanism to respond to a country's disregard of labor standards

☐ Require that each country provide for high labor standards and for due process for resolving complaints and disputes
☐ Requires each of the countries to address the following issues:
  • Freedom of association and protection of the right to organize
  • The right to bargain collectively
  • The right to strike
  • Prohibition of forced labor
  • Labor protection for children and young people
  • Minimum employment standards
  • Elimination of employment discrimination
  • Equal pay for women and men
  • Prevention of occupational injuries and illnesses
  • Compensation in cases of occupational injury and illness
  • Protection of migrant workers

55. The Enterprise for the Americas Initiative

At the *Summit of the Americas* in December, 1994, representatives from the U.S.A. and 33 other countries in the Americas initiated planning for hemispheric trade cooperation. The *Enterprise for the Americas Initiative (EAI)* was a response to the fear that growing trade regionalism within Latin America might impede future efforts to integrate trade within and among the North and South American continents. At the 1994 *Summit,* 34 nations agreed to remove barriers to trade among themselves by the year 2005. This consensus has begun to create the foundations for a *Free Trade Agreement of the Americas (FTAA).* Here are some FTAA "factoids" to consider:

☐ The FTAA would cover 34 nations, becoming the world's largest trading bloc.
☐ The combined GDP of the member nations would exceed U.S.$8 trillion.
☐ The market would comprise more than 750 million people.

Although planning for the FTAA continues, its actual implementation depends heavily on the leadership provided by the Executive Branch of government in the U.S.A. In turn, the Executive Branch requires negotiating authority that can only be granted by the American Congress.

56. Working with MERCOSUR

With so much attention focused on the European Common Market, NAFTA, and the prospects for economic integration in Asia, many business people overlook the significance of MERCOSUR—a customs union linking Argentina, Brazil, Paraguay and Uruguay, with a population of more than 200 million and a U.S.$1 trillion combined GDP. Chile has recently joined MERCOSUR and other membership prospects include Bolivia, Ecuador, Colombia, Peru, and Venezuela.

Although MERCOSUR is not as fully integrated as the European Union or NAFTA, it does have a similar potential for creating commercial advantages for those already inside or those who are willing to invest within these South American "Southern Cone" countries. Here are some of its salient features:

☐ Agreement on common *external* tariffs, to shelter internal commercial activity from external competition
☐ Agreement on gradually reduced *internal* tariffs and other barriers to trade between and among the four countries involved
☐ Openness to the inclusion within the external tariff wall of other neighboring countries

57. Global Trade Regulations Since 1945

In the beginning, there was Bretton Woods. In 1944, during the latter months of World War II, 44 nations attended the United Nations Monetary and Financial Conference in Bretton Woods, New Hampshire, to take measures designed to promote worldwide economic growth and development through the creation of institutions like the *World Bank*, the *International Monetary Fund (IMF)*, and the *International Bank for Reconstruction and Development*.

Later, in 1947, 27 members of the United Nations entered into a preliminary agreement to regulate international trade and commercial policy. The agreement became known as the *General Agreement on Tariffs and Trade (GATT)*.

This preliminary GATT round led to 45,000 tariff concessions among its participants, but it had no enforcement mechanism and it did not cover services, agriculture, foreign investment, intellectual property rights, and environmental issues.

Later, when the *International Trade Organization (ITO)* (whose charter was adopted in Havana in 1948 but failed to secure the approval of the U.S. Congress) did not come into existence, the GATT remained the only multilateral instrument governing trade from 1948 until the *World Trade Organization (WTO)* was established in 1995.

58. Replacing GATT with the World Trade Organization

The *Uruguay Round* of the General Agreement on Tariffs and Trade (GATT) created the World Trade Organization (WTO) in 1993. It was further defined in the *Marrakech Agreement* and went into force on January 1, 1995. The WTO is intended to facilitate the implementation of all the agreements and legal institutions negotiated in the Uruguay Round, including:

☐ Overseeing all future negotiations on the governance of world trade and payments
☐ Settling disputes between members
☐ Monitoring agreements
☐ Authorizing retaliation in cases of non-compliance with agreements and decisions

The WTO is considered the "third leg" of the Triad of institutions set up to coordinate global economic policy-making, as envisioned in the *Havana Charter* of 1947.

The other two "legs" are the *International Monetary Fund (IMF)* and the *World Bank*.

59. Bilateral and Multilateral Trade Agreements

In order to benefit from existing trade agreements, whether they are bilateral or multilateral, it is important to understand a little bit about the process that led to them and to be aware of the agreement provisions that have a bearing on the way you do business internationally. Here are some points to remember when you are reviewing your international business plans:

☐ Are there existing trade agreements between my home country and the countries I consider attractive markets for my company's products or services?

☐ How do these trade agreements affect the flow of goods and services between the two countries?

☐ How do they affect the cost of doing business?

☐ Do the agreements contain provisions that will change over time?

☐ What is the history of the trading relationship between the countries in question and what direction do these agreements appear to be going as you look to the future?

☐ Are there non-tariff barriers that are not addressed by these agreements?

☐ Do the countries that interest your company have bilateral or multilateral trade agreements with other countries, as well?

☐ Are the pertinent provisions more or less favorable than the provisions agreed to in your country's trade agreements?

☐ How do all of these agreements affect manufacturing costs specifically, or the cost of doing business in general, in your home country and in the country or countries you are most interested in?

☐ How do these trade agreements affect your customers, your distribution channels, your competitors, and your suppliers?

By giving some thought to these questions, you will be in a much better position to prepare realistic plans for serving the markets your company has targeted.

IMPORTING

While most people think of globalization as exporting, it is possible to become a global corporation by importing. Importing, however, is fraught with a number of complex issues, particularly when your home country is attempting to control imports to encourage use of local products and/or to save employment. Examples are tariff and non-tariff barriers, marking or labeling requirements, and issues of product nationality.

60. Importing as an International Strategy

Importing is the acquisition of goods, services, and intellectual property by a business located in one country from sellers or licensors in another country. Businesses choose to use importing as an international strategy when there are limited or no local goods available, and when foreign goods are of higher quality or are less expensive than local goods.

While businesses who seek to export have considerable public and private resources available to assist them, importers find very little assistance available. As a general rule, countries do not want to encourage imports. (Japan, however, is a major exception.) On the other hand, most governments are very interested in what is imported into their countries. Besides being a major source of tax revenues, governments are concerned about the selling of local products, ensuring the quality and safety of imported goods, and regulating how improted products are labeled or marked.

Importers need to be concerned about a variety of logistic, financial, commercial, legal and government issues in obtaining their goods, services and intellectual property. If these concerns can be met, importing as an international strategy allows businesses to become more global while dealing primarily with their own domestic market.

61. Foreign Trade Zones

Foreign Trade Zones (FTZs) are cost saving options available to importers in nearly every country in the world. Located in enclosed, policed areas within or near customs offices, FTZs are considered to be outside the customs territory of the country in which they are located.

Because FTZs are considered outside the customs territory, foreign goods may be brought into the FTZ without going through normal customs procedures and duties. While in the FTZ, products may undergo certain activities such as being repackaged, repaired, mixed, cleaned, salvaged, destroyed, assembled, manufactured, or relabeled.

Using an FTZ defers customs duties which allows your company to benefit. If a product is subject to import quotas, quantities in excess of those quotas can be stored in the FTZ until import is authorized. Products in the FTZ are also exempt from state or territorial taxes and charges.

Merchandise can be re-exported without duties or drawback (refunds of duties previously paid). An FTZ can then be used as a regional warehouse (e.g., Rotterdam for Europe; Panama City for Central America). The FTZ can also be used as a location to modify "generic" products for local markets.

Locating your business activities in an FTZ benefits the territory in which the FTZ is established and creates good will in that market for your business.

62. Mexican Turnkey and Shelter Programs

One viable-import related strategy is to develop production sharing in neighboring countries to assemble or manufacture products from your components but with the use of more cost-effective labor.

Mexican production sharing (originally called *maquiladoras)* allows companies of all nationalities to combine their technology and materials with low-cost Mexican labor, and to market the resulting product in the U.S.A. market. Today in Mexico there are more than 2,000 *maquiladora* plants, employing over 500,000 workers. *Maquiladora*-type operations can work in any of three ways:

Turnkey. The *maquiladora* owner (a Mexican national) takes all the risk in acquiring space, capital goods, employees, and raw materials, and manufactures the product to the customer's specifications. The customer agrees to pay (per fixed amount or individual unit) for a specific period of time.

Shelter. The same as a turnkey operation except that the customer provides the raw materials or semi-finished goods and manages the production process. The Mexican owners take all other risks.

Contract. The customer provides the capital and equipment, as well as raw materials and/or semi-finished goods. The Mexican owners provide the space, labor, and production management.

The customer is invoiced by the piece or on an hourly basis.

63. Setting Up an Import Department

Importers need to be concerned with a multitude of commercial, government, and legal matters. Therefore, companies importing large amounts of goods usually set up an import department (often part of a traffic department) with professional staff to meet the following needs:

☐ Monitoring the movement of goods from international to domestic carriers

☐ Selecting the appropriate carriers to ship components and receive completed product

☐ Assuring quality control of imported goods

☐ Working with exporters and contract manufacturers to assure logistics

☐ Working with the local customs office on:
  • Entry documents
  • Product content
  • Marking and labeling products
  • Duties and duty free items
  • Antidumping issues

☐ Establishment and maintenance of bonded and other warehouses

64. Non-Tariff Barriers

Tariffs have a public purpose of raising government revenues, protecting local industry, and improving the balance of trade through the creation of local production or the reduction of imports. With the strengthening of the World Trade Organization (WTO) and other regional organizations, the imposition of high tariff barriers has become more difficult. In recent years, a number of ingenious non-tariff barriers have been developed. Some of these are:

Quotas—Limitations, sometimes voluntary, on the amount of products or services that can be imported. For a long time, the U.S. placed quotas on the importation of sugar, usually allowing larger quotas to countries which are more favorable to American foreign policy interests.

Embargoes—Policies that set a limit of zero imports. Witness the American embargoes on Cuba, Libya, Iraq and Iran.

Voluntary export restraints (VERs)—Quotas imposed by the exporting country. Japan has had VERs on automobiles and semiconductors sold in the U.S.A.

Required counter-trade or co-production—Exchanged or imported goods must be enhanced with a certain percentage of local content.

Customs and administrative procedures—These include limiting points of entry, constantly reclassifying products, local language requirements, requiring import licenses, and limiting import to certain times of the year (for seasonal products).

Quality requirements—While sometimes justified, some so-called quality requirements are merely other examples of non-tariff barriers. Denmark, for instance, will only allow imported soft drinks if they are in reusable bottles, and Germany will not allow the importation of beer if it contains corn or rice. Japan also restricts the importation of rice based on its texture and stickiness.

Local requirements—In Japan, for example, you may find store size requirements that limit supermarkets and discount stores. Many countries refuse to allow certain franchise trade names and store configurations to be used in historic areas.

65. Importing Under Customs Laws

Every country has its own system of controlling imports. However, all have common elements that should be understood by all importers.

Understand customs services. Since one major function of customs is the collection of tariffs, it is often part of a country's treasury department or interior ministry. It is important to understand how customs is structured and at which levels different problems or issues are likely to be resolved.

Determine which goods are subject to duty. Determine whether goods may enter duty free if certified as part of a free trade zone or other economic union. Determine the tariff schedules and how your products may be classified under those schedules.

Understand how duties are assessed. The three most common methods of assessing duties are:

Duty assessed per unit

Ad valorem duties—assessed as a flat percentage of the total imputed value of the goods

Compound duties—which combine specific duties with ad valorem duties

Learn what you can do to protest assessments. In most countries, protests are made if the importer believes that the tariffs are too high or there are other problems. In the U.S.A., normally the duties are paid and the goods are "liquidated" (released from customs). Then the importer has 90 days to commence the protest.

Learn the local policies on bonded warehouses and foreign trade zones. These issues will be discussed in later tips.

Understand how products must be marked with regard to their place of origin or whether they need to be marked.

Understand and observe any record-keeping requirements. The U.S. system of importation is largely based on voluntary cooperation which means that customs will most likely accept what is on the documents. It is therefore necessary to keep very complete records in case your business is audited.

66. Imports—Marking and Labeling Requirements

Many countries require that all imported products be marked with the country of origin. The purpose of such laws is to inform the ultimate purchaser of where the product originated so the consumer can make an informed purchasing decision. In the U.S.A., these policies are under the jurisdiction of the Federal Trade Commission.

The hardest cases are where there is a combination of imported and domestic material. Here the general rule is whether the product manufactured in the foreign country has *lost its identity* when combined with the domestic material. Other words used to determine nationality are "significant transformation." Recently, American courts have ruled that watch bands manufactured in Hong Kong, but polished in the U.S.A., had to be labeled "made in Hong Kong," and the same was true for a Japanese-manufactured sunglasses lens when placed in a U.S. frame. Customs argued that the lenses did not lose their identity. However, the courts have also ruled that airlines are the ultimate consumers of frozen airline meals so that they did not have to be identified as to origin for those who actually consumed them.

Product markings must be large and clear enough to be read by a person with normal vision. They must also be in a conspicuous place (for instance, not in the battery compartment). It is preferred that the markings become part of the good itself but, if not, they should be attached in a manner which will allow the markings to remain during normal handling. In some cases, such as with produce, the goods themselves cannot be marked so it is necessary to mark their containers. Examples of items that do not have to be marked are works of art, unstrung beads, eggs, feathers, and flowers.

67. Antidumping, Foreign Subsidies, and Countervailing Duty Issues

Some countries, the U.S.A. included, try to protect their local industries against certain unfair trade practices such as dumping and unfair foreign subsidies. Dumping is the importation of product for sale below the product's "fair value." Unfair foreign subsidies include government subsidies in the country of production or with the manufacturer to make the products more competitive abroad.

Antidumping

Under American laws, "dumping" is the practice of selling goods in that market at a value less than what the same product would be sold for in the producer's home market. In the U.S.A., the industry or an "interested party" which claims to be adversely affected files a petition with the Commerce Department and the International Trade

Commission (ITC). Before antidumping duties can be imposed, the ITC must decide the likelihood of sales of foreign merchandise at less than fair value, *and* if the U.S.A. industry has been materially injured or threatened by reason of the dumped imports.

Foreign Subsidies and Countervailing Duties

The best example of a foreign subsidy would be a government rebate for exported products, but other examples could include grants, loans, exemption from taxes or reduced cost transportation on government-owned or subsidized carriers. In the U.S.A., the same two-part test is applied before countervailing duties are instituted. Such duties can remain in force until the situation changes.

68. Just-in-Time Goals

Achieving just-in-time (JIT) delivery has been a goal of many companies. JIT is a system in which there is little or no delay in time for shipment of components and/or parts and there is little need for inventory. To achieve your JIT goals, however, the following points should be kept in mind:

☐ JIT is a *total* system which cannot be adopted in part.
☐ JIT is a *balanced* system which must be used for mass production techniques. It does not work well in specialty production unless the specialty value-added is primarily in labor.
☐ JIT based on imports does not work well in countries with significant tariff and non-tariff barriers. That is why many Japanese companies have established bases in North America that are served by North American suppliers.
☐ JIT, because of the need for reduced inventory, requires that the components and parts delivered have few or no defects.
☐ A JIT system cannot be put in effect overnight, so the system must be developed over a period of time.
☐ JIT makes more sense the larger the volume of items produced in the manufacturing process.

69. Product Nationality Issues

This section on imports is the proper place to include a discussion on the nationality of products because the decision to import over use of indigenous products may turn on whether the nationality of the product is important to its distribution and sale.

In this section we will review the key considerations associated with nationality:

Government purchases. Although not as common as in the past, some government procurement agencies continue to provide preferences to local suppliers and/or local products.

Tariff reductions. In the forty-plus years since the founding of the General Agreement on Tariffs and Trade, or GATT, and now the World Trade Organization, or WTO, a series of bilateral and multilateral treaties has reduced the tariff on certain products between certain countries. Another approach is the granting of Most Favored Nations (MFN) status to some countries and not others. In the case of the U.S.A., for instance, this MFN status has resulted in massive imports from China but only sporadic imports from Vietnam, which does not have MFN status.

Marking and labeling. In many countries, imported products must be marked or labeled as foreign. This may put them at a consumer-oriented disadvantage against local products that do not have to be marked or labeled.

Subject to embargoes. Products from certain countries cannot enter the domestic markets. In certain countries, domestic products cannot be exported to the embargoed country (for example, U.S.A. products to Cuba and Iraq).

Export finance assistance. The nationality of products is sometimes critical to whether a government agency will assist with export financing. The Export-Import Bank of the United States, for example, will guarantee up to 85 percent of U.S. content of exports but only if the entire U.S. content of the products is more than 50 percent.

70. Product Nationality

It is sometimes difficult to determine nationality especially if the product is the result of parts and components from various nations. Some of the rules used to determine nationality are:

Value of the components. If the value of any of the parts and components of a country exceed 50 percent, the product is normally deemed to be national to that country.

Regional value content. In regional organizations such as the EEC, NAFTA, and MERCOSUR, the combined content value will be added together to determine the nationality within the region, such as a NAFTA product that is duty free in the entire NAFTA region.

Significant transformation. The non-origin materials used in production of the goods undergo a change in tariff classification. In this case, the goods will be deemed to have the nationality of the country in which the transformation took place.

De minimis. This is a term that means that even if a product does not undergo significant transformation, it will be deemed a product of the country of transformation if the foreign content is very limited (in NAFTA, less than 7 percent).

Finally, keep in mind that the rules of nationality may differ by product. For example, the NAFTA agreement has distinct rules for automotive products and computers.

EXPORTING

Exporting products and services goes to the very heart of global business and for most companies it might be all they choose to do. Not all exporting is the direct sale to a purchaser in another country. Some businesses sell to customers in their domestic markets who in turn export the product. In this case, the seller should still be interested in how its products are sold, used, and warranted as poor initial presentation might increase the difficulties for future sales.

Exporting, whether direct or indirect, raises a whole host of issues, such as product modification, packaging, pricing, and inventory. These and other issues will be discussed in this section.

71. Exporting—Pros and Cons

Making the decision to export requires that you examine the advantages and disadvantages of entering the international marketplace.

Advantages

☐ Sales and income through new markets are increased.
☐ Customer base is diversified and dependence on your home market is reduced.
☐ Increased income is available to become more competitive in the home market.
☐ Research and development expenditures are more affordable.
☐ Existing jobs are saved and more are created.
☐ Seasonal sales and other fluctuations are stabilized.

Disadvantages

☐ Existing products and/or packaging may need to be altered.
☐ New promotional materials need to be developed.
☐ Initial start-up costs must be budgeted.
☐ Additional administrative staff is required.
☐ Difficulty in currency conversions and/or collections may occur.

□ Additional capacity may be required.
□ Higher travel costs will be incurred.

72. Avoiding Surprises When Exporting

Once you have determined that your product definitely has a place in a particular overseas market, it's important to *"stop, look and listen,"* before stepping onto the export track. Much of the burden for taking these precautions rightfully falls on the shoulders of the importer or the importer's customs broker; but even experienced importers sometimes fail to anticipate obstacles to the profitable import of your particular kind of product. If you get the following questions answered before you take that overseas order, you will avoid some costly surprises:

□ Are there government-imposed restrictions or procedures that will add cost to the product you intend to export?
  • Does the host-country apply high import duties and other taxes to your product?
  • Do customs officials arbitrarily change product classifications or the invoice total of your shipment in order to increase tariffs on your product?
  • Does your product require an import license? If so, can licenses be easily obtained?
  • Do host-country patent laws create additional competitive or proprietary risks?
  • Is your product subject to import quotas?
  • Can your customers get access to foreign exchange—and at reasonable exchange rates?
  • Might host-country currency devaluations price your product out of the market, or make it difficult for you to offer finance terms?
  • Are there pre-import deposits or restrictions on commercial terms that will add cost to your product?
  • Are there port of entry inefficiencies, hidden duties, or excessive bureaucratic delays that will add cost or impede the timely delivery of your product?
  • Are competitors able to influence the application of laws or rules that might impede entry or add cost to your product?

☐ Are there non-tariff restrictions or barriers that will impede entry and/or add cost to your product?
  • Do host-country import or government purchasing policies discriminate against import of your product?
  • Does your product face unfair competition from state-owned enterprises or subsidies to competitors or other countries of origin?
  • Do your customers prefer to buy locally manufactured products of your type?
  • Are there any political or economic embargoes in effect that will affect the import of your product?
☐ Does your own country have any restrictions on what you can export?
  • Are your products scarce or of limited supply in the home market?
  • Are they of unique value to the home country's culture or history?
  • Do your products or their components require an export license (for example, computer products containing certain encryption devices from the U.S.A)?
  • Does your home country have an embargo on the country(ies) you wish to ship to?
☐ Are there other arbitrary restrictions or involved procedures that impede, delay or add cost to your product?
  • Are there unusually cumbersome customs formalities, such as, certificate-of-origin requirements or pre-export inspection requirements?
  • Are there arbitrary rulings on patent/trademark rights or special labeling requirements that will impede or add cost to your product?
  • Are local public health and safety laws likely to be twisted in order to impede or add cost to your product?
  • Are there any arbitrary technical standards that will impede or impose additional costs on your product?
  • Is there potential for arbitrary application of "anti-dumping" laws or countervailing duties to offset alleged subsidies enjoyed by your product?

As a starting point, be sure to request country and market access information from your own government. In the U.S.A., you should contact the U.S. Department of Commerce, International Trade Administration, or your state and local international trade organizations.

73. Markets that Seek to Promote Imports

While most countries do little to encourage imports, a few Asian countries have now begun to encourage imports as a vehicle to address the political problems which result in trade imbalances with the rest of the world. In the case of Japan, the services provided are substantial and should be used by businesses seeking entry into that market.

The Japanese External Trade Organization (JETRO) is a non-profit semi-governmental agency affiliated with Japan's Ministry of International Trade and Industry (MITI). Founded in 1958 to primarily promote Japanese exports, JETRO now devotes considerable expertise and resources to businesses seeking to enter Japanese markets. JETRO has at least one trade advisor in every key city normally located in the local trade office or World Trade Center.

Besides the trade advisors, JETRO provides trade and investment information, seminars, trade shows and missions and has established Business Support Centers in five key Japanese cities which provide fully equipped office facilities on a temporary basis, as well as spaces to exhibit literature and products.

In addition to the services provided by Japan, other countries such as Taiwan and South Korea sponsor buying missions to countries where they have substantial trade surpluses. While these are designed to foster goodwill, the sizes of purchases in recent years tend to make these more than token gestures.

74. Indirect Exporting from the Home Country

Indirect exporters come in an almost infinite variety that includes the manufacturer's export agents, export management companies (EMCs), export trading companies (ETCs), cooperative exporters (piggybackers), resident export buyers, and export commission agents. All have one thing in common—they allow you to export your products abroad *without* making a direct effort from your home country, or having to appoint foreign intermediaries. In effect, you sell your products to the indirect exporter which then exports them on its own behalf.

Companies will appoint indirect exporters for the following reasons:

☐ They lack international expertise.
☐ They are in the very early stages of exporting.
☐ They wish to avoid committing funds and/or personnel to all international markets or to unexplored markets.
☐ They wish to test-market their products, and allow for their trade names and trademarks to be known, before making a more serious commitment to the international marketplace.
☐ They wish to increase cash flows, economies of scale, and capacity through incremental sales.
☐ They desire to leverage the distribution networks and contacts of others.
☐ They hope to find a means of warehousing their products abroad without additional costs and commitments.

75. Problems with Indirect Exporting

Indirect exporting is not without its costs and its problems. The following list describes some of the key ones:

☐ Indirect exports will siphon off some of the gross profit margins through commissions and/or lower selling prices to the indirect exporters.
☐ Because indirect exporters are putting your products in the hands of others, they will limit your direct contact with the customers. Additionally, customer feedback, if any, will come filtered through the indirect exporters.
☐ Companies using indirect exporters will lose virtually all control over pricing. If the products are priced too high by the indirect exporter, your company may also lose significant sales.
☐ It will be difficult to provide product support, and the future market can be damaged.

☐ The indirect exporters may relabel the products, which will prevent product identification necessary for continued sales.

☐ If exclusivity is granted to the indirect exporter, they may tie up the market for some time with little effort being made on behalf of those products.

☐ They may prevent you from building up the knowledge base you will need to sell directly at a later time.

☐ While they may increase sales overall, there is no guarantee that these sales will be stable.

☐ The company may find it difficult to take over the markets of the indirect exporter when the relationship has ended.

76. Export Management Companies

Export management companies (EMCs) approach companies with the idea of becoming, in effect, their export departments. Most work on a retainer and/or a commission based on the sales they generate. They are paid by the exporter. A few will actually purchase products directly from the exporter for resale to customers abroad. Depending on the financial arrangements, EMCs will perform some or all of the following functions:

Consulting services. EMCs will often work with the exporter to determine the best foreign market for their products. This may include market analysis and identification, visits abroad to determine the most appropriate methods of distribution, and providing the exporter with assistance in export administration, product quality documentation, and selection and use of freight forwarders, insurance, banking, and translation services.

Advertising and promotion. EMCs will work with the exporters to prepare sales literature and, at times, advertisements for use in international markets. They may also represent the exporter at international trade shows and exhibits, and may assist the exporter in locating and appointing international agents and distributors.

Agent services. EMCs will often locate customers and assist the exporter in arranging the sale.

Financial and legal services. EMCs may assist the exporter in determining its international pricing, credit, and financial policies. They will assist in locating banks and in working with those banks to establish letters of credit, site drafts, and other financial instruments. Occasionally, EMCs have a legal capability that could be used to assist in the drafting of terms of sale, agreements, advising, and overseas patent and trademark protection, and, in some cases, negotiating on behalf of the exporter.

Purchase for resale. Occasionally, the EMC will actually purchase product from the exporter for resale to its own customers.

In choosing an EMC, the exporter should consider the characteristics cited in the EMC profile in the following table.

Export Management Company Profile

1. The EMC has sufficient size and resources to meet the exporter's needs.
2. The EMC is willing to share its expertise and to train the exporter in international business as part of its compensation.
3. It prices its services competitively.
4. The EMC will take the time to learn the exporter's business, including a full understanding of the after-sale requirements of the products.
5. It is well established in the community and can provide appropriate references.
6. The EMC/Exporter Agreement should clearly explain what the EMC will provide, including a reasonable estimation on the effort to be spent in promoting the products.
7. The EMC is willing to begin on a nonexclusive basis and to earn exclusivity upon demonstrated success.
8. It will not alter or relabel the exporter's products without the exporter's written permission.
9. The EMC has experience in advertising and sales promotion.
10. Its employees have the needed language capabilities.

77. Export Trading Companies

Export trading companies (ETCs) are, in many ways, similar to EMCs, except that they tend to be larger, and provide a wider range of services. The major difference, however, is that the ETC normally takes title to the goods and services, while the EMC normally services as a commissioned agent. The U.S.A., primarily as the result of the Export Trading Company Act of 1982, allowed ETCs to operate without some of the complexities of U.S. antitrust laws. In the U.S.A., ETCs are usually formed by the following entities:

Large companies, such as W.R. Grace, Sears, General Motors, Honeywell, and K-Mart, promote the sale of their own products and other companies' products. Some of these companies have not met with success and have ceased operations.

Trade associations, such as the American Film Marketing Association, have created ETCs to promote the exports of their members' products.

Bank holding companies have also formed ETCs.

Many ETCs also engage in imports and in the development of *counter-trade.* One of the most aggressive companies in the area of ETCs in the late 1970s and early 1980s was the former Control Data Corporation. Control Data was very active in counter-trade in order to sell their computer systems to countries that could not pay in hard currency but were willing to pay in product or by some other creative means. One of its most creative projects was in the attempted sale of a computer system to The Hermitage Museum in St. Petersburg, Russia (then Leningrad, USSR).

CDC was to provide the computer system required by The Hermitage in exchange for CDC obtaining rights to the sale of reproductions of paintings and art objects that would come from an exhibit owned by The Hermitage that was scheduled to tour in North America. A percentage of the profits derived from the sale of these reproductions was to be applied to the purchase of the computer system. The exhibits were arranged, and then cancelled as a result of the embargo placed on the Soviet Union in 1979 after that country sent troops to Afghanistan.

Attempts to develop ETCs in the United States, as illustrated by Control Data's experience, have met with limited success. The Japanese, however, have used trading companies with great success for a long period of time. The trading companies, called *sogo shosha,* are normally part of a much larger group centered around a bank or an industrial group. These groups are called *keiretsu.* In the *keiretsu* system, companies usually agree to become shareholders of each other to build stronger business ties. This is the primary reason for the U.S. Export Trading Company Act of 1982, which sought to level the playing field by removing certain antitrust law considerations that prevented U.S. companies from building *keiretsu*-type relationships.

Japanese trading companies are normally quite large. In recent years, these companies comprised six of the ten largest companies in the world in terms of sales (Mitsui, Marubeni, and Mitsubishi were the top three). This size allows the *sogo shosha* to provide extensive market coverage and allows a small company to access nearly the entire world without building a dedicated international function. In addition to their importing and exporting capabilities, Japanese trading companies have recently become involved in the full range of international business transactions, including the production of goods, the development of strategic alliances and equity joint ventures, licensing, and technology transfer. Korea has also developed several trading companies that are part of huge banking and industrial conglomerates called *chaebol,* which are similar to the *sogo shosha.*

78. Adapting Products for Export Markets

The best of all possible worlds would be to develop products that could be manufactured and sold in all markets with little or no adaptation. In reality, this is rarely possible. Products and services may be adapted to meet local conditions or they may have to be adapted to meet shipping and manufacturing requirements. The following are some of the factors that may arise in product adaptation:

Regional, national, or provincial factors

- ☐ *Tariff and non-tariff barriers*—For example, Denmark's refusal to allow the import of nonreusable bottles
- ☐ *Customer characteristics and desires*—Such as a culture's preference for juice in cartons rather than bottles
- ☐ *Purchase patterns*—Motorbikes for basic transportation in Thailand and as fun in the U.S.A.
- ☐ *Culture*—The importance of different colors in different cultures
- ☐ *Climate and geography*—Packing ice cream to withstand expansion in Mexico City's altitude

Product factors

- ☐ *Contents*—Lower fat content for the U.S.A. market, for instance
- ☐ *Packaging*—With regard to different systems of measurement

☐ *Functions and uses*—Circuit breakers are never turned off in the U.S. but may be turned off and on as a light switch in Europe
☐ *Quality and durability and need for after-sale service*
☐ *Country of origin*—Biases in favor of or against certain countries of manufacture

Business factors

☐ Costs of adapting products
☐ Number of adaptations needed
☐ Additional costs vs. profitability
☐ Ability to devote resources to adaptation
☐ Physical ability to adapt

79. Establishing Pricing Policies

Perhaps the major consideration of how you price your product abroad is where your products will be made (or services provided from). If you are primarily an international company which produces its products and services out of one or a few countries, you will probably need to develop a *world-wide pricing strategy*. On the other hand, if you are a global company where you are producing products (or providing services) in numerous locations you will probably need to develop *individual market pricing*.

A worldwide pricing strategy would be based on attempting to create average unit costs on fixed, variable, and export-related costs. Generally, the variable costs associated with additional product for export sales would be lower, resulting in lower unit costs for exported products. To this would be added the export-related costs (tariffs, taxes, shipment, insurance, political, and financial risks) that would result in a total export cost. The product would then be priced for each export market where the price would be competitive.

Individual market pricing allows you to also factor in the variables of local production and the achievement of revenues and profits designed to achieve the best global position of the business rather than achieving the company's goals in the home market.

80. Considerations in Export Pricing

Whatever pricing strategy a business chooses, the following considerations should be kept in mind:

Business objectives—Your business may decide in determining their pricing that they would prefer to gain market share at the expense of profits (at least for a limited period). If so, you need to be concerned about *dumping.*

Dumping—Selling goods abroad at either below the cost of production or at prices lower than in the home market. Sometimes dumping results in countries adopting counter tariff measures.

Transfer pricing—The price at which one company sells to related companies. Transfer pricing according to the laws of most countries must be at *arm's length price* to assure that income and taxes are distributed fairly. An "arm's length price" is a price you would give to a non-related party.

Gray markets—These are products that are legal but are not imported through the regular channels. This is often a problem of businesses that export indirectly (through others) and this may include export trading companies. It is also sometimes a problem for products bought in the local market and then imported illegally into other countries (e.g., from San Francisco to Asia or Miami to Latin America). Regular distributors do not desire to service such products as their profits are often undercut by such illegal importation. Such products may range from disposable baby diapers to laptop computers.

81. The Linkage Between Products and Services

It is rare today to acquire any significant product that does not require some level of service. Customer decisions are often made on the basis of service and often the selection of service dictates the type of products you acquire.

The more your products require service, the more complicated your entry into the international market could become. The first decision to be made is whether your business will provide the needed services

abroad or whether you will leave that job to your international partners. If you choose to select others to provide service, will they be the
organization that sells the products or a different organization alto-
gether? Finally, if there are significant revenues to be gained through
service, how can you find a way to acquire part of those revenues if
you don't directly provide the service?

The following table concerns the questions a business normally
faces when exporting.

Exporting Issues

Service	
Provide Yourself	**Provide Through Others**
Issues:	Issues
• Facilities abroad	• Same or different organization in
• People abroad	each country
• Traveling service forces	• Training issues
• Legal considerations	• Monitoring quality
• Tax considerations	• Monitoring the customer base
	• Revenue acquisition

82. Services Sought in International Markets

In addition to services tied to products, many businesses have been
successful in providing stand-alone services in the global markets.
Some of these services are tied to products, such as rental cars or leasing apartments, but many are direct services such as financial, human
resource, construction, and professional services.

Until recently, it was very difficult to provide services across borders. This started to change in the 1980s and governments began to
deregulate and to privatize some services which were open only to the
government or local nationals. Foreign interests acquired local telephone companies, natural resource providers, and airlines. Foreign
competitors were allowed into the markets. Today, almost every major
country has opened its borders to a wide variety of service professions.

Among the most sought-after services today are:

Franchising services of all types
Financial services including banking, credit card operations and
    mergers and acquisitions
Insurance services, which is an area that has opened up in recent years
Engineering and construction services, particularly management of
    projects
Information technology services in all areas of computers, software
    services and artificial intelligence
Educational services, particularly in distance learning and in all types
    of training

83. INCOTERMS

INCOTERMS[1] are the internationally accepted definitions of terms
of sales as they relate to the passage of the ownership of goods
shipped internationally. They are the product of the International
Chambers of Commerce which revises them every so often to bring
them up to date with new transportation techniques. Present terms
include:

Passage of ownership taking place in the home country:

Group E: Departure	EXW	Ex Works—The place of origin (factory, mine, warehouse)
Group F: Main Carriage Unpaid	FCA	Free Carrier—When placed with the inland carrier at either the point of departure or the port of shipment or some other designated point
	FAS	Free Alongside Ship—After unloaded at port of shipment
	FOB	Free On Board—Delivery of goods to an overseas vessel provided by the buyer

Passage of ownership taking place outside the home country:

Group C: Main Carriage Paid	CFR	Cost and Freight—To overseas port paid by seller to use port of destination
	CIF	Cost, Insurance and Freight—To overseas port paid by seller to the port of destination
	CPT	Carriage Paid To—Freight paid by seller until placed in the hands of the carrier at the port of destination
	CIP	Carriage and Insurance Paid To—Freight and insurance paid by seller until placed in the hands of the carrier at the port of destination
Group D: Arrival	DAF	Delivered at Frontier—Goods deemed for export at named point at the frontier, but not the customs border of the adjoining country
	DES	Delivered Ex-Ship—Same as above except goods are on board the ship
	DEQ	Delivered Ex Quay (Duty Paid)—Products at the wharf at the named port of destination, cleared for imports
	DDU	Delivered Duty Unpaid—Delivered at named placed of destination. Buyer responsible for duties, tolls and other charges
	DDP	Delivered Duty Paid—Same as above but duties, taxes and charges paid

84. "ISO" Requirements

In the past, one of the more difficult parts of international trade was producing products that could meet or exceed the quality management standards of various different countries. Whether in electrical products or in the gauge of railroad tracks, the standards applied by different jurisdictions were as great a barrier to trade as import duties and related charges. Among the organizations coming out of World War II was the International Standards Organization (ISO) which was established in 1947 and is located in Geneva, Switzerland.

The ISO represents about 90 member country organizations (for example: The American National Standards Institute (ANSI) is a member) covering the most important countries in the world. ISO developed the ISO standards (ISO 9001, 9002, 9003, etc.) in 1987 and revised them in 1994. By 1998, 127,000 companies in 150 countries held ISO certification. Adoption of these ISO standards is a virtual prerequisite for undertaking global business, and it is estimated that 100,000 additional U.S.A. companies will become ISO 9000-registered in ten years.

The ISO's role is to create standardization in all areas except electrical and electronic engineering. Those standards are the responsibility of the International Electrotechnical Commission (IEC). Examples of ISO Standards are in auto safety belts, steel quality, and medical products safety.

The ISO 9000+ standards are voluntary but most companies find they need to adapt to these standards to assure the global sale of products. In addition to the ISO standards, the exporter may also want to check local standards organization. ANSI, for example, publishes a guide to standards regarding package and container sizes which should be part of the standards used by freight forwarders and transportation companies.

In the year 2000, the standards will again be revised primarily for the purpose of simplification. ISO 9001, for example, which applies to companies that design, manufacture, install, and service products will be reduced from 20 elements into four—management responsibility; resource management; process management; and measure, analysis and improvement.

TRANSPORTING GOODS INTERNATIONALLY

Once you have sold your products, you need to take great care that they will arrive safely at their destination. In this section, we will examine how to find a good freight forwarder; how to document your exports; and how to ensure proper packaging, inventory, and storage.

85. Freight Forwarders

Given the additional paperwork involved in international sales, it is wise to involve a freight forwarder. Freight forwarders are specialists in international transportation who act as agents for the exporter in moving shipments to overseas destinations by contracting with the carriers on behalf of the shippers. Freight forwarders are familiar with import/export rules of foreign countries and with the export regulations of the shipping country, if any.

Typical services of a good freight forwarder are to:

☐ Advise exporter of freight costs, port charges, consular fees, insurance charges and other fees and charges
☐ Assist in preparing pro forma invoices
☐ Advise on packing and handling, and arrange for containerization
☐ Review letters of credit and other financial instruments
☐ Arrange space on carriers
☐ Assist exporter in working with customs brokers
☐ Assist exporter in undertaking a cost benefit analysis of the different modes of transportation

86. Developing an Export Documentation Checklist

What follows is a checklist of items necessary to export from the U.S.A. While some of the items mentioned on this checklist would be needed for any country, you should remember that the U.S., in particular, is one of the few countries in which exporting is a privilege and not a right, and therefore has some additional documentation requirements.

Documents Prepared Before Shipment

☐ *Commercial Invoice/Consular Invoice.* The commercial invoice is needed to prove ownership and to secure payment and must correspond exactly to the descriptions on the letter of credit or other methods of payment. Some countries also require a consular invoice which is prepared in the language of the destination country.

☐ *Export License.* In the U.S.A., all exported goods technically require an export license although most goods are shipped under a general license which does not require a separate application. Products subject to export controls require a validated license or a separate application and approval from the U.S. Commerce and/or Treasury Department. Validated licenses are required if goods might impact national security or foreign policy (e.g., embargo of Cuba) or if goods are in short supply. Validated licenses also require an Export Control Commodity Number (ECCN).

☐ *Shippers Export Declaration (SED)*—SEDs are required on all but the smallest shipments. These are required to enable the Bureau of Census to keep tracks of exports.

☐ *Certificate of Origin*—For countries that are part of free trade agreements to allow for preferential tariff treatment, or where otherwise required.

☐ *Export Packing List*—An export packing list itemizes the material in each individual package and indicates the type of package: box, crate, drum, carton, etc. It shows the individual net, legal, and gross weights and measurements for each package (in both U.S. and metric systems). Package markings should be shown along with the shipper's and buyer's references. A copy of the packing list should be attached to the outside of a package in a waterproof envelope marked "packing list enclosed." The list is used by the shipper or forwarding agent to determine the total shipment weight and volume and whether the correct cargo is being shipped. In addition, customs officials (both U.S. and foreign) may use the list to check the cargo. The original packing list should be forwarded along with your other original documents in line with the conditions of sale.

☐ *Insurance Certificate*—If the exporter is providing insurance, a certificate will be needed confirming the type and amount of coverage for the goods being shipped. Normal accepted practice for coverage is 110 percent of the cost, insurance, and freight, known as the CIF value. This certificate should be made in negotiable form and must be endorsed before submitting to the bank.

☐ *Inspection Certificate*—Many foreign purchasers request that the seller certify that the goods being shipped meet certain specifications. This certification is usually performed by an independent inspection firm.

Documents Used During the Inland Movement of the Goods

☐ *Shipper's Instructions*—As an exporter, you are responsible for providing your freight forwarder with the necessary information regarding your shipment. The more details you provide, the greater the chances of your goods moving problem free. Your freight forwarder can provide you with a commonly used form for noting instructions.

☐ *Inland Bill of Lading*—Inland bills of lading document the transportation of goods between inland points and the port from where the export will emanate. Rail shipments use "waybills on rail." "Pro-forma" bills of lading are used in trucking.

Delivery Instructions

This document is prepared by the freight forwarder giving instructions to the trucking or railroad company where the goods for export are to be delivered.

Dock Receipts

This document transfers shipping obligations from the domestic to the international carrier as the shipment reaches the terminal.

Bill of Lading/Air Waybill

Bills of lading and air waybills provide evidence to title of the goods and set forth the international carrier's responsibility to transport the goods to their named destination. There are two types of ocean bills of lading used to transfer ownership:

☐ *Straight (non-negotiable)*—Provides for delivery of goods to the person named in the bill of lading. The bill must be marked "non-negotiable."

☐ *Shipper's order (negotiable)*—Provides for delivery of goods to the person named in the bill of lading or anyone designated.

The shipper's order is used with draft or letter-of-credit shipments and enables the bank involved in the export transaction to take title to the goods if the buyer defaults. The bank does not release title to the goods to the buyer until payment is received. The bank does not release funds to the exporter until conditions of sale have been satisfied.

When using air freight, "air waybills" take the place of bills of lading. Air waybills are only issued in non-negotiable form, therefore the exporter and the bank lose title to the goods once the shipment commences. Most air waybills also contain a customs declaration form.

87. Packing Goods for Export

Goods shipped for export require substantially greater handling than domestic shipments. The exporter must pack the goods to ensure that the weight and measurements are kept to a minimum, breakage is avoided, the container is theft proof, and that the goods do not suffer the stresses of ocean shipment, such as excess moisture.

In addition to proper packing, the exporter should be aware that certain markings are necessary on goods transported internationally. Some countries require that the country of origin be marked on the outside of the container, and even have regulations as to how the mark of origin should appear.

The second type of marking with which the exporter should be familiar is labeling. Food and drugs must often carry special labeling as determined by the laws of the country of destination.

Third, certain "shipping marks" must appear on the outside of the package. The weight and dimensions should be visible and any special instructions should be shown, and you may want to repeat these instructions in the language of the importer's country.

If your business is not equipped to package your goods for export, there are export packaging companies that can perform this service for you. Ask your international freight forwarder for a list of export packaging companies in your area.

88. Issues in Selecting Transportation Modes

When choosing between the three major modes of transportation (air, sea, and land) or a combination of those modes, the exporter usually examines five areas. These are described below:

☐ **Cost:** Clearly the major factor in many shipping decisions. However, cost must be viewed from different perspectives. For example, a substantive export business has developed in Colombia for the sale of fresh flowers to the U.S.A. In this business, the least expensive mode of transportation has to be air given the weight and perishability of the products. However, one result of this has been that there is substantive space available on the flights back from Florida to Colombia. One of our clients takes advantage of this space by shipping athletic equipment by air at rates that are more-or-less the same as by sea since the airlines do not wish to return to Colombia with empty planes.

☐ **Reliability:** As more and more of the world moves toward "just-in-time" for inventory purposes, the reliability of transportation providers becomes even more an issue. There is some argument among shippers as to which mode of transportation is more reliable. Two ways found to greatly improve reliability are combining modes of transportation and selecting those providers who have created the best tracking systems. Sea-Air programs have developed where cities have both excellent sea and airports (e.g., Seattle, Singapore, Rio de Janeiro, and Dubai), so that shipments from Japan to Europe can take 14 days if shipped by sea to Seattle and then by air to Europe. Tracking is critical on global orders when sent to the same customer at different locations.

☐ **Time:** It is now possible to ship all but the largest or heaviest of products for arrival anywhere on the globe within a few days. This allows all businesses to make a cost benefit analysis. We recently counseled a major American ice cream producer on the possibility of selling finished product from the U.S. to South America. While air transportation was out of the question for normal shipments, it could be used occasionally to ship a special flavor to Argentina in time for the summer season (December through February).

☐ **Customer considerations:** Exporters sometimes forget that the customer will often drive the decision regarding choice of transportation. Part of your business planning for international sales should look at whether the potential customer in the territories to be entered may have different transportation needs. A smart exporter will offer its customers different transportation alternatives and make sure that its employees and providers remain flexible.

☐ **Miscellaneous factors:** The transportation decision is often influenced by factors outside the exporter's control. For example, if selling to a public agency, it may be necessary to ship on the national flag carriers. The American government requires all persons travelling on government business to fly only on U.S. airlines (unless service between the cities is not available). Exporters also need to be concerned that their shipments don't violate an embargo (e.g., Canadian shipments to Cuba passing through the U.S.A.).

89. International Packaging Requirements

A few years ago, a large mainframe computer being delivered to a remote site in the People's Republic of China (PRC) fell on a Chinese engineer while being unloaded. In no way was the accident the fault of the shipper (the computer manufacturer) which had packed the equipment properly. Nevertheless, the shipper (through its insurance) had to provide the customer a new computer and pay a substantial sum to the family of the engineer for his "wrongful death."

International law is fairly specific on where the fault lies as to substandard and insufficient shipping—it lies with the shipper and not the carrier or purchaser (unless the purchaser is also the shipper). With this in mind, the following should be considered regarding packaging:

☐ **Labeling.** Be sure the labels are such that anyone needing to read them can do so. The worst example of this was a shipment of seeds containing insecticides that was shipped to Pakistan with proper labels in English but not Urdu. The shipment was baked into bread (instead of being planted) and resulted in many deaths and injuries.

☐ **Climate.** Goods shipped to high altitudes must sometimes be specially packaged to avoid overflows. Shippers of ice cream to Denver, Mexico City, or Bogota sometimes have to ship more air and less product to keep the product from flowing over in its paper or plastic containers.

☐ **Containers.** In shipping large components of product, it may make sense to develop and use shipping containers designed to fit the specific needs of product packaging. Another benefit of containerization is that shippers are willing to lower their prices for containers which fit their respective modes of transportation.

90. International Inventory Issues

In a perfect world, your business would have multiple production and warehouse sites so that you could serve your international markets from various sources. This would allow for shipment from the lowest cost site and for protection in the case of strikes, wars, or natural disaster. That would give you a significant advantage over your competition.

For most businesses, the world is not perfect and they are faced with a number of issues associated with inventory. The first issue is whether to have multiple inventory sites. That issue and others are discussed below:

☐ **Financial issues associated with multiple sites.** With proper planning, a business can put itself at a financial advantage by a strategic placement of inventories. Inventories in countries with strengthening currencies allow the inventories to grow in value in relation to the home currency. The same might be true in countries undergoing rapid inflation where inventories become a hedge against that inflation.

☐ **Order cycle times.** With more and more companies moving to just-in-time delivery, the order cycle times have declined. Depending on whether the customer is willing to pay for rapid freight, the export business needs to decide whether it must keep local inventories close to the customer's sites. The ultimate decision might come down to increased inventory carrying costs versus additional storage and/or freight costs.

☐ **Customer satisfaction.** Customer service and satisfaction will differ from country to country. One such issue is the tradeoff between lower prices and immediate inventory. Particularly in some of the developing nations, it may be better to work from the price rather than service side. It is also a good idea to have some sense of the level of service of your local competitors and to try to be somewhat better. It may not make sense to be a lot better if the market does not demand it.

91. International Storage Issues

Most companies selling product abroad will try to have their local "partners" responsible for storage. One purpose for appointing distributors is to assure that the distributors keep sufficient local stocks. Distributors who only order when needed or ask the exporter to "drop ship" are not playing their proper role, and should soon be replaced by either better distributors or by the establishment of local or regional warehouses under control of the exporter.

If international storage is being considered, the first question to be addressed is the tradeoff between additional transportation costs and warehousing costs. That decision often is not simple and you might decide to go with a smaller warehouse for certain products that are in high demand while shipping directly those products that are not as much in demand.

Still another consideration is whether it would be more efficient to keep spares and disposable products at warehouse sites while deciding to ship the products themselves from the home markets.

In the end, whether or not you establish storage facilities will ultimately be dependent upon the nature of the product(s). If the products are large and cumbersome and can be serviced by a local vendor with some spares, then storage facilities may not be needed. On the other hand, if the products are commodities and/or disposables, then storage facilities (yours or someone else's) are a necessity.

PLANNING INTERNATIONAL OPERATIONS

International expansion is not likely to be successful unless your company develops and implements a global strategic plan. This section examines how such plans are created and examines some of the key variables in such plans. Also discussed are the means to control international operations and the issues that arise between headquarters, regional offices, and country subsidiaries.

92. The Components of a Global Strategic Plan

As companies increase their international presence, it becomes necessary to develop a global strategic plan, so that top management, wherever situated, can respond to both opportunities and threats on a global basis. In doing so, global managers usually look at seven components. These are:

Analyze Internal Variables. What are the strengths and weaknesses of the company in its global expansion? Which variables can be changed? Which can be controlled? Which cannot?

Determine External Variables. Potential and business risk analysis along with market and product studies.

Develop a Mission Statement(s). A mission statement is an attempt to describe the company's purpose in a broad general statement.

Determine Corporate Objectives. Examples might be to increase sales by 20 percent, or to become Number One in the market in three years.

Quantify the Chosen Objectives. Try to take the objectives one step further by showing how they may be accomplished.

Formulate Strategies to Achieve the Selected Objectives. Develop action plans to allow the company to reach its global objectives. This could include best-, middle-, and worst-case scenarios.

Develop Tactics to Implement the Strategies. Such tactics could be to increase the advertising budgets, have more staff, or introduce new products.

93. The Global Planning Process

Developing a viable global strategic plan requires the development of a planning process. This process can also be used in regard to individual country selection or for introducing a new product to multiple geographies. The planning process is normally completed in four stages:

Preliminary analysis and screening. An attempt to identify viable
  markets and/or products and to exclude those markets and/or
  products which are clearly unsuitable. Typical in this analysis is to
  look at company variables and host country constraints. In markets
  where exporting is a privilege (U.S.A.), you may also want to look
  at home country issues such as export controls and embargoes.
*Adaptation of the product and marketing mix to the selected
  markets.* Will the product have to be modified, repackaged, or
  relabeled? Can global products be developed or will indigenous
  factors prevent standardization?
Develop the product and marketing plans. Determine what needs to
  be done, along with where and when. Create specific actions to be
  undertaken.
Implementation and control of the planning process. Set standards,
  assign responsibility, and identify methods to measure
  performance. Establish a system to correct errors.

94. Strategic Planning Methods

Most American businesses think of strategic planning in terms of *top-down planning*—beginning at the highest level of the company and sent downward for implementation. Japanese companies, on the other hand, are said to favor *bottom-up planning* where planning begins at the lowest levels and then moves upwards for approval.

The advantages of top-down planning are that plans are made by the most senior people with a more global perspective. Additionally, if the planning is done correctly, there will not be a problem of discrepancies that may come from various sources at the lower levels. Conversely, top-down planning tends to stifle initiative and may not take into consideration the local nuances often so important in global business.

Bottom-up planning does not mean that decisions are made at the lower levels but that the process of planning begins at the lowest operating levels. This allows for significant local initiative and creativity, tends to improve job retention, and increases job satisfaction. If upper management accepts the plans, local managers are far more likely to work hard to implement them. Disadvantages of bottom-up planning are that it tends to take longer and runs the risk that the sum of the pieces don't fit together in the overall plan. Finally, bottom-up planning has a very negative impact on personnel if upper management tends to not implement it or to ignore it in making their planning decisions.

Some companies undergo both processes during the planning process and then try to reconcile the key differences to allow for unique local issues or particularly good ideas. This process, called *iterative* planning, is very popular by the truly global companies.

95. Total Quality Management

One of the most difficult words to define is quality. Many companies have found that their version of quality resulted in an over-engineered product which did not sell well in the marketplace. Others think they have developed quality products but they are not perceived as such by customers.

One attempt to define quality was the standards set by the United States Congress in determining the Malcolm Baldrige National Quality Award. This award is granted on the basis of three relatively equal criteria: quality assurance, quality results, and customer satisfaction.

Total Quality Management (TQM) is an attempt to manage quality on a global basis. The standard by which all products and services are measured by and to which a total effort is involved is:

☐ Superior products
☐ Zero defects
☐ Continued technological improvement
☐ Total customer satisfaction

This process dedicates a company to being a world leader in product quality. While zero defects normally can never be achieved, it is something that is continually sought. Also assumed is that the company dedicated to TQM will move away from the American expression "If it ain't broke, don't fix it," to the Japanese approach of *kaizen—*

or gradual and continuous improvement. Finally, TQM cannot be achieved without continued monitoring of customers to determine whether the products or services meet price considerations and quality standards.

96. Controlling International Operations

While some decisions clearly should be made at corporate headquarters and others in the field, there are many areas where the decision may not be so easy (e.g., what types of capital equipment or that subsidiary gets credit for the order). In determining the proper place for such decision-making, consider the following factors:

Global company or international company. In an international company that is structured to benefit the parent company (and its location), more decisions should be made at the headquarters level.

How subsidiaries are evaluated. If the subsidiary is judged by its "subsidiary or country contribution" where a lower profit or even loss for the subsidiary means a greater gain for the company, more decisions can be made in the field.

Degree of trust of subsidiary management. In a company that has a "foreign service" or at least moves people around, local decision-making is more likely.

Distance from headquarters. This can be physical distance or cultural differences. In "different" or "difficult" markets, local decision-making is essential.

Multicountry issues. If more than one subsidiary is involved in decision-making, the final decisions may have to be brokered or made at a regional or headquarters level.

97. Evaluating International Subsidiary Performance

One mistake often made by companies is to judge their foreign subsidiary solely on the basis of its financial results. This may fail to take into consideration the economy of scale it brings and also global treasury and tax strategies that may not be in its favor. Additionally, there may be more than just financial criteria by which to evaluate performance. Performance criteria may include:

Profitability—Based on some weighted analysis of a subsidiary's true financial contribution to the whole.

Market penetration—Judged often in relation to direct competitors.

Public and government relations—The degree to which the subsidiary contributes to the worldwide image of the company and is perceived as a good corporate citizen.

Human resource development—Is it developing good employees who can contribute technically and/or in broader, more global, management positions?

Productivity—What does the subsidiary do with the resources allotted to it?

Planning—Is the subsidiary doing a good job planning for its future development and growth? Is it developing models that can be used by other subsidiaries?

Total overview—Be sure not to overlook any tangible or intangible factors that contribute to a subsidiary's success or failure. For example, one company had a subsidiary that was below average on almost all performance criteria but was successful in developing an excellent group of tool and dye makers who were in short supply elsewhere in the company.

98. Issues Between Headquarters and Subsidiaries

Headquarters personnel see themselves as having a clear understanding of the totality of the company and control of its global strategic plans for the future. Subsidiaries, on the other hand, view themselves as the "doers"—those who are manufacturing the products, completing sales, and bringing in the profits. This often results in a number of issues that can result in considerable friction. Examples of these issues are:

Implementation of corporate policies. For a company to be truly global, headquarters will attempt to develop corporate policies with global application. This may become a difficult problem when such policies

are based on the culture and/or laws of a particular country. An
example of this would be an American company's policies on gifts
and sexual matters (e.g., U.S.A. laws on sexual harassment).

Allocation of head office expenses. Subsidiaries may sometimes
object to such allocations as a part of overhead over which they
have no control.

*Allocations for sample product, literature and intercompany
expenses.* Some of which the subsidiary will not deem that it needs.

Intercompany prices for products and services which could be
designed to meet global goals over local goals.

Headquarters supervision. The parties may differ greatly on the
amount of supervision needed, especially if subsidiary leadership is
constantly burdened by visits. One Mexican subsidiary found that
it received three times more visitors during January and February
than in the summer months from its parent company
headquartered in Minnesota.

Charges for technology and other intellectual property. Often such
items are transferred through intercompany agreements in which
royalties based on revenues are charged. This method, which is
normally used to transfer funds to the headquarters, is often
viewed with suspicion by the subsidiaries.

99. Opening Regional Offices

Companies often seem to be organized around regional lines (e.g.,
Europe, Asia, the Americas) and, given the proliferation of regional
trade pacts, trade within regions has greatly increased in recent years.
With the growth of regional influence, many companies now are
establishing regional headquarters that often become the buffer
between headquarters and the individual country subsidiaries. Deciding to open regional headquarters might be dependant upon the following factors:

☐ Does business exist (now or in the future) in a number of countries
within the region? If so, you may want to centralize control in a
single regional office. However, business in South Africa does not
justify a regional office in Lagos, Nigeria.

☐ Is there a logical regional headquarters? Miami, Florida (or
southern Florida) seems to be the "capital of Latin America" with

perhaps the exception of Mexico. Singapore might play a similar role for Asia, and Belgium and the Netherlands both try to provide the same at least for Western Europe.

☐ Does the following infrastructure exist to support a regional office?
  • Available quality personnel
  • Communications and travel
  • City amenities
  • Warehouse and office availability
  • Good living conditions

☐ Are there any tax or other advantages of using a regional office as a profit center? Regional headquarters in the Netherlands are common because of that country's network of favorable tax treaties.

International Financial Management

Every business runs on cash. If you are not managing your cash, you are not managing your business. If these statements are true about business in your home market, they are most certainly true in international business. However, you are likely to find new and more complex cash management challenges, the further abroad you go.

This section will give you practical clues and reminders that will help you meet these challenges and succeed in planning and managing cash flows generated by international business activity.

100. National Investment Incentives

Although it may be wise not to depend on them, it is often possible to vastly increase your return on investments abroad, or minimize your initial exposure, by taking advantage of incentives that governments have created to stimulate investment (and job creation) in certain sectors of their economies. Here's how to go about making the most of these opportunities:

☐ Contact the appropriate "investment promotion" agency of your target country.
☐ Investigate or subscribe to information services that track and report on investment incentive programs.
☐ Via the Internet, visit appropriate national government websites.
☐ Consult with your foreign service officer in charge of the "desk" for your target country.
☐ Consult with banks involved in trade finance within your target country.
☐ Study the goals and requirements of the incentive program, to determine if they are sufficiently compatible with your company's goals in that country.
☐ Engage an agent, a law firm, or other qualified and registered agent, to guide you through the application process.

101. Trade Financing Alternatives

Growing companies consume cash. Export and import growth is no different, in this respect. To maximize net trade cash flows, it is important to consider using some form of third-party trade financing—otherwise, either you or your counterpart will play the role of international banker. Here are some tips:

☐ Project probable financing requirements of your export/import program and do your research on the relative cost of money and trade financing in your home market versus the destination/origin market. Include in your analysis the financing requirements for:
  • Export receivables
  • Import payables
  • Finished goods or semi-finished goods inventories
  • Work-in-process inventories
  • Raw materials
  • Initial market development, promotion, and distribution
☐ Consult with your primary commercial bank and determine its trade financing capabilities and have it explain its policy for handling client foreign receivables.
☐ Consult with your country's or your state's export or import trade promotion office for leads to specific trade financing programs.
☐ Check with your country's primary trade finance bank or export-import bank for specific information on its programs and policies.
☐ Check with your industry association(s) to find out about possible industry-specific trade promotion financing.
☐ Investigate the import-financing capabilities of your destination country customer, distributor, or subsidiary.
☐ Investigate the export-financing capabilities of your supplier in the country of origin.
☐ Investigate trade-financing potential in the export-destination country or the import-country of origin.
☐ Investigate other "third-party" (not your company or your primary banker) trade-financing alternatives (in many parts of the world there is rapid growth, with many new entrants into this field):
  • Countertrade
  • Forfaiting
  • Factoring
  • Credit cards
  • Micro-lenders

102. Basic Forms of International Payment

Before engaging in transnational financial dealings, it is wise to know about the different forms of international commercial payment. Here's a quick summary:

☐ Cash "up front" (100 percent or some portion of invoice total)
☐ Open account—with varying terms (e.g., 30 days net)
☐ Open account—secured with a stand-by letter of credit
☐ Cash against documents (C.A.D.)
☐ Cash on delivery (C.O.D.)
☐ Letters of credit (L.C.)
☐ Bank bill of exchange—payment at fixed date
☐ Forfaiting
☐ Countertrade

103. Credit Terms: Cash Before Delivery

Credit terms vary greatly within American commerce and industry. In international commerce, however, given the added risks that pertain, it is often wise to begin with a commercial relationship based on cash. Here is an approach that may help you decide when to require cash before delivery:

☐ When just "breaking in" a new account
☐ When there is evidence that foreign exchange rates may fluctuate
☐ When the customer or distributor pays too slowly
☐ When predetermined open account limits have been exceeded
☐ When it is customary to do so

104. Letters of Credit

Letters of credit can be very expensive for both you and your overseas customers, but sometimes there is no choice but to use them. The security of a letter of credit can be very appealing to the financial people within a company, but it is important to understand the full and true cost associated with their use. Here are some points to consider:

☐ For some smaller shipments of relatively low value, if you take into account all of the application fees, confirming fees, and general inconvenience to both the exporter and the importer, the total cost of an export letter of credit may exceed the value of the shipment.

☐ For shipments of lesser value, it may be more cost-effective to require advance payments or some form of cash-on-delivery to manage the perceived risk.

☐ Some overseas customers, particularly state-owned enterprises may offer an export letter of credit as the only way they will pay you. Likewise, if you are importing, you may find that your overseas suppliers will insist on an import letter of credit—especially if you are a new account for them.

☐ Once your customer has opened up a letter of credit, he must comply with its often very detailed and exacting terms in order to get paid. Compliance is important; your company may have to use bank or other outside expertise to make sure there are no defects in compliance.

☐ When exporting to new customers or distributors in overseas markets, especially where the value of the shipment is high and you perceive the financial risks to be high, an export letter of credit confirmed by a trusted local bank might be the wisest method of payment.

☐ When requiring your customer to apply for a letter of credit, it is important to be mindful of the additional expense that your customer will have to incur and the effect this will have on the cost and the attractiveness of doing business with you, especially if you are in a competitive situation.

☐ Likewise, when requiring letters of credit, it is important that you be very clear about the terms and conditions for compliance. You must be satisfied that you will be able to comply with the terms stipulated in the letter of credit, when it arrives. It is very difficult, sometimes impossible, to change the terms of an already-issued export letter of credit.

☐ If your long-term goal is to offer competitive customer credit, it is important to remember that your customer's letter of credit payment performance is not a valid predictor of open-account payment performance. The only way to build an open account customer-credit relationship is to offer credit and monitor payment performance.

☐ As an intermediate step toward the use of open account terms with overseas customers, you may consider requiring a "stand-by" letter of credit, which will come due if the predetermined open account balances are not paid within the agreed-upon term.

105. Open Account Terms

Among the many methods for getting paid, an *open account* is the most flexible and the lowest-cost method—as long as you don't mind going into the banking business and investing your time to establish a solid, long-term relationship with the other party.

In some industries, the extension of open account terms to customers in some overseas markets may be necessary in order to be competitive. In many exporting countries, even smaller exporters enjoy the financial backing of a sophisticated international banking community and the support of government programs and policies that reduce the financial risk associated with the extension of credit to overseas customers.

Obtaining reliable credit performance information on credit applicants can be very difficult, in some countries. In the absence of reliable credit performance reporting, however, it is often possible to obtain adequate information from third parties such as other suppliers or local banks.

Open account terms can be tailored to credit and payment conditions within a particular overseas industry. This may be especially important if you are distributing merchandise through a dealer or wholesaler who serves an industry that customarily expects credit to be extended over 60, 90, or even 120 days.

Unless negotiated otherwise, open account payments are payable in the currency of the exporter's country or in another acceptable trade currency. Therefore, the overseas buyer assumes the currency exchange-rate risk.

Even though your export receivables may be payable in your own country's currency or in some other convertible international medium of exchange, it is important for exporters in strong-currency countries to remember that, by shifting the currency exchange-rate risk onto your overseas customer, they are increasing their customer's financial risk. It is important to continually monitor factors influencing exchange rates and to communicate frequently with overseas customers regarding the management of open account balances and their vulnerability to currency exchange-rate fluctuations.

106. Decreasing Open Account Exposure

If you decide that you must limit or decrease the financial exposure associated with the use of open account terms, there are a number of options open to you:

☐ From the beginning, it is important that both parties to the credit agreement share the same understanding of the marketplace and expectations with respect to the use of credit. The exporter should view the extension of credit as a tool for increasing revenues and profits; the customer using the credit should also be able to see the use of credit as a tool for reducing domestic financing costs and for increasing sales and profits.

☐ At the outset of the credit relationship, it is wise to negotiate reasonably conservative credit limits, along with the other key terms and provisions. Since you are the "banker," you will ultimately have to judge just how much credit the customer can reasonably manage.

☐ Particularly in the early stages of a new open account relationship, it may be possible to have your customer set up a stand-by letter of credit in your company's favor. These funds would become accessible to the exporter in the event the buyer failed to pay according to the established open account terms.

☐ By frequently communicating with the customer, monitoring the customer's credit performance, and observing pertinent economic and financial trends in both your country and your customer's country, it will be possible to adjust credit limits and terms to reflect current conditions.

☐ A proactive approach to overseas customer relationship management often creates a degree of loyalty and a strong commitment to honor your open account terms, even when the going gets rough in the customer's local economy.

☐ In some instances, the exporter may find it both desirable and practical to obtain export credit insurance, in order to shift some of the export credit exposure onto a third party.

☐ It may also be possible for an exporter to discount and sell export receivables to a third party and thereby reduce its export credit exposure.

☐ For exporters engaged in frequent high volume export transactions with receivables denominated in foreign currencies, it may be feasible to select among a variety of currency hedges, in order to cover the currency exchange-rate risk.

☐ An exporter can also reduce open account risk by:

- Providing training, customer service, credit management assistance, and technical support, when appropriate.
- Involving the customer in periodic business planning and assessment activities.
- Helping the customer increase its own exports and, thereby, increasing the customer's foreign exchange credits and its ability to withstand an exchange rate fluctuation.
- When anticipating significant changes in currency exchange rates, the exporter and the customer may be able to temporarily denominate the customer's transactions in the exporter's home currency. This would have the effect of insulating both the exporter and the customer from the effects of a change in exchange rates.

107. Forfaiting

There are a number of lesser-known methods for limiting trade credit exposure and risk. *Forfaiting* is one of them. Basically, forfaiting is selling medium- to longer-term export receivables, promissory notes and other amounts receivable from foreign sources to a third party who makes a business out of overseas collections. The "third party" surrenders (forfeits) its right to go back to the seller, in the event the overseas buyer fails to pay; hence the name *forfait*—French for *forfeit*.

This method is used primarily to finance export of capital goods where the buyer has a solid credit record or is backed up, in turn, by another third-party guarantor. Also, the buyer's payment cannot be contingent upon performance by the exporter. It must be a "done deal," as far as the exporter is concerned. This is because the forfaitor has no recourse to the exporter.

The banking system in Switzerland developed this method of "third-party" export financing to make export growth more attractive for client companies. At the time, there were no government-backed export financing programs available. Forfaiting is best used when no other satisfactory financing alternatives are available and, yet, solid export opportunities arise.

The relative cost of forfaiting can be relatively high, but the exporter gains by being relieved of a medium- to longer-term financing burden—along with all the pertinent risks, such as interest-rate fluctuations, exchange-rate fluctuations, and other political, financial or commercial risks.

108. Countertrading

The resourceful international trader knows there is always more than one way to accomplish his goals. Particularly for companies that are planning to export large quantities of merchandise, capital goods, or commodities to countries with relatively limited convertible foreign exchange reserves and/or heavy external debt-load, countertrade can provide the exporter with a very handy tool for getting paid in otherwise difficult trading situations. The term *countertrade* encompasses a wide range of export for import transaction.[2] Here's a general overview:

☐ From the exporter's standpoint, countertrade is like barter. Instead of receiving payment in cash or cash equivalents, the exporter enters into an arrangement whereby the importing country, in turn, is able to export merchandise, goods, or commodities in lieu of cash. For example, a company desiring to export cars to a given country might be required to accept the approximate value of the cars in orange juice produced in the importing country.

☐ *Counterpurchase* or *parallel barter* occurs when the parties enter into two separate agreements with different time frames. This form of countertrade is used when the outbound and the inbound merchandise, goods, or commodities will not be ready for delivery at the same time.

☐ *Buy-back* or *compensation arrangements* involve agreements to provide technology, equipment, services, as well as even financing, for a specific production project in exchange for product produced by the project, once completed and operational.

☐ *Clearing account barter* is a more sophisticated way of keeping track of an ongoing trade relationship and overcoming the requirement that each transaction be completely in balance (equivalent values exchanges). The importing country sets up accounts and tracks trade debits and credits, as a series of countertrade transactions (whether in or out of balance) are carried out over time. Ultimately, the parties are expected to achieve a "zero" balance in the account. Some such accounting systems also make it possible for the parties to sell or transfer clearing account credits to a third party (this is called *switch trading*).

☐ The defense sector of many countries use a form of countertrade known as *offset,* whereby the importing country will require the exporter to manufacture a portion of the product within the importing country. This is done to decrease the impact of the outflow of foreign exchange that would otherwise be required to pay for the product.

☐ *Debt swaps* are yet another form of countertrade, involving *debt-for-debt swaps, debt-for-equity swaps, debt-for-product swaps, debt-for-nature swaps,* or *debt-for-education swaps.* All of these "swaps" are forms of countertrade wherein less tangible, often negotiable, values are exchanged.

☐ Countertrade, in all its forms, is controversial in today's "open markets" environment. Free-trade purists see it as an interference in the marketplace where, ideally, the forces of supply and demand should operate without constraints and where transactions are paid for with some form of currency as the medium of exchange. Nonetheless, many developing countries, as well as numbers of developed countries, continue to foster countertrade as one of many means for facilitating trade and economic development.

109. International Scams

While most international business persons are honest, a number of scams have created problems for businesses throughout the world. These scams normally promise the foreign party the opportunity to

obtain a substantial fee for providing services to a person or company. In all cases, the foreign party ultimately winds up losing money.
The six most common scams are:

Money transfer and government contract schemes. The swindlers propose transferring a large amount to an overseas bank account owned by the foreign party who is to receive a percentage of the transferred funds as a commission. Such solicitations, as seen in Figure 3, request information about the company's bank, as well as blank and signed letterhead, and pro forma invoices. Once the above is obtained the scam artists will often request a "transaction fee" and continue to ask the victim for additional fees. The letterhead is also used to attempt to extract money from the bank account of the victim.

Charity scams. Same as above except the solicitation is to charities to which the scammers claim they wish to contribute.

Will scams. Another variation is that the swindlers claim that someone in the swindler's country has died, leaving the victim money.

Real estate scams. A "wealthy" scam artist proposes transfer of funds to purchase a mansion abroad.

Fraudulent orders for products. A large order is placed with a request for samples and registration and import fees. Once paid or sent, the order disappears.

Crude oil scams. The scam artists offer to sell crude oil at "special allocation" prices. Victims are asked to pay a bogus registration license fee.

Despite all the warnings that have been issued, including those by the swindlers' own government, these scams continue. The swindlers have developed more sophisticated techniques in recent years including official-looking government stamps and seals. If solicitations arrive from other countries and look too good to be true, they are. Figure 3, on the following page, illustrates a sample scam letter.

110. Fraudulent Transactions—Red Flags

Once you enter the international market, the number of opportunities to be involved in fraudulent schemes increases substantially. If a proposed transaction seems unusual, look for the following red flags.

Dear Sir,

Re: Business Proposal/Joint Venture

Your good business name was introduced to me by a business consultant in my country and by understanding the worth of your business and interest in your line of products, I deem it necessary to correspond and tell you about this business proposal. Based on this transaction, I have the same view of mutual understanding and trust to you pending when I hear from you.

I am director in the account department and member of contract award committees in the Federal Ministry of _____ of the Federal Government of _____. In collaboration with my colleagues, some senior officers in the Central Bank of _____ and Federal Ministry of Finance, have decided to transfer abroad some amount of money amounting to thirty million, five hundred thousand U.S. dollars (U.S.$30,500,000.00) which we realized from *over invoice contract* as per goods purchased/supplied from foreign company. These funds are now due for Federal Government payment.

As regards to your similarity of goods supplied, I have been mandated to arrange with you urgently for a possible transfer of this fund, into your personal or corporate account. And later go into a joint venture with you with some part of the money.

Meanwhile, be assured that the modalities have been worked out to effect a successful hitch-free money transfer. We as the owners have agreed to give out 30% of the fund as commission due to you, for your assistance, while 5% will be mapped out to offset any bill (expenses) incurred on the course of the transfer. This transaction is hoped to take place within 21 working days, as of the date of its commencement.

We await your immediate telefax to (fax number) on the private line, for further instruction and details. Should this transaction not appeal to you, do me a favour by getting back to me, for security reasons, so that we may know what to do, as the personalities involved are government officials, who have put many years of active service in the office and may not like their reputable images dented.

Urgent contact awaiting.

Yours faithfully,

(Name and important-sounding title)

Figure 3. Sample scam letter.

☐ Requests for a letter of credit to pay agents' fees or to guarantee a loan in advance
☐ Requests for blank letterhead and pro forma invoices
☐ Urgent requests for product samples as part of a large proposed sale
☐ Requests to ship product to a post office box
☐ Requests to ship goods by air freight upon receipt of a "certified bank draft"
☐ Vague or implausible explanations of how the sender obtained the company's name as a contact
☐ Unusual product requests—an example of which may be for a Mandarin language computer to be shipped to the island of Mauritius
☐ The passage of currency through another country, such as Egyptian funds passing through the Philippines on the way to the United States.

Should one of these red flags appear, it is best to avoid that transaction or at least request additional information before proceeding.

III. Transfer Pricing Alternatives

This method of minimizing tax impact and optimizing profitability among related companies should be familiar to anyone with profit responsibility in any enterprise with international operations. Here's what it is all about:

☐ Transfer pricing, or intracompany pricing, is the business of setting prices on products and services transferred within a company—e.g., between a company in one country and its subsidiary in another.
☐ Given the differing financial, competitive and tax conditions that often exist between parent company and a foreign subsidiary, transfer pricing is frequently used to minimize tax burdens and optimize overall profitability for the entire enterprise.
☐ Transfer prices can be established in at least four different ways:
  • Transfer at direct cost
  • Transfer at direct cost plus additional expense
  • Transfer at a price derived from end-market prices
  • Transfer at arm's length price

☐ These pricing decisions are usually based on an analysis of the following factors:
  • Corporate income taxes
  • Value added taxes
  • Import duties
  • Inflationary tendencies
  • Stability of governments
  • Regulations
  • Strategic concerns

Transfer pricing is not without controversy. Within a corporation, transfer pricing practices complicate internal control mechanisms to the extent that they manipulate reported costs and revenues. For the governments of the affected countries, transfer pricing other than "arm's length" pricing is something that requires scrutiny and is often limited or discouraged.

112. Foreign Credit

In an increasingly global marketplace, companies—large or small, multinational in reach or local start-up—have an ever-wider range of options for financing growth. At the same time, the existence of great differences in real interest rates, rates of inflation, currency exchange rates, and market regulation, create substantial risks that accompany many of these financing opportunities. Here are some of the most common means for obtaining foreign credit, along with a few tips to consider, before turning to these sources:

Foreign bank that is a correspondent of a domestic bank:
  A correspondent bank is a foreign bank—not owned or controlled by a particular domestic bank—that agrees to cooperate with that domestic bank in the administration of certain international financial transactions. These correspondent banks usually have superior knowledge of local financing opportunities and may, themselves, participate in the financing of import/export activities and overseas operations of domestically-based companies.
Foreign branch of a domestic bank: Some foreign countries permit foreign ownership of local banks that, in effect, operate as branches of domestically-based banks. Particularly if a company

already has a banking relationship with the domestic parent bank, the branch bank may be a very likely source of foreign credit.

Representative office of a domestic bank: A representative office is really an overseas sales office for a domestic bank. Although such an office cannot accept deposits or extend foreign credit directly, it can be helpful in arranging joint bank financing in support of domestic and international expansion.

Foreign bank: A local bank operating in an overseas market. If a domestic company owns assets overseas and has overseas operations, local banks may also become a source of local credit.

Foreign bank with domestic branches or representative offices: A bank whose parent is located overseas but is chartered to engage in commercial lending operations in a company's domestic market. Such a bank may be a source of domestic financing, as well as a source of foreign credit for overseas operations located in the bank's parent company market.

Euronotes, international bonds, and private (debt) placements: These are foreign credit instruments that may be open to larger, well known domestic companies with substantial assets and operations in those markets where these instruments are available.

Offshore banking: An offshore bank is a bank that has been incorporated and chartered in a foreign country and that engages in foreign currency transactions between and among parties not originating in the country where the bank is located. These banks are not usually a primary source of foreign credit but they may become involved in the facilitation of debt financing arrangements that are more easily carried out in the lax regulatory environment commonly enjoyed by offshore banks.

For smaller, entrepreneurial companies with export, franchising, or licensing operations overseas—but without overseas assets that might attract and secure foreign credit financing—it is sometimes possible to offer a combination of the company's domestic assets and creditworthiness, together with the assets and creditworthiness of a foreign partner, licensee, franchisee, or distributor to secure foreign credit through a bank located in the overseas market.

In evaluating options for obtaining foreign credit, it is also wise to investigate loan subsidies and guarantee programs offered by domestic government agencies.

113. Export Collections

Just as in the domestic market, overseas customers or distributors occasionally fail to stay current on their open-account payments. In today's shrinking world of commerce, new options are opening up for collecting balances created by export activity. Here are a few export collection strategies worth considering:

☐ Do some investigating. Find out as much as possible about the reasons that are driving the export collections problems. Before implementing any extraordinary collection measures, it is wise to make sure the problem has been brought to the attention of the highest appropriate level within your customer's or your distributor's organization and that your company is not contributing to the problem.

☐ Convert terms to *cash in advance* for future shipments. This measure not only helps the exporter immediately limit the growth of the export credit risk, but also creates an incentive for the importer/debtor to get back on a current basis.

☐ Require a *stand-by letter of credit* to secure future export receivables. This measure requires careful planning and thoughtful drafting of legal documents to determine under what conditions the "stand-by" funds will be paid to the exporter.

☐ Negotiate *extended terms* with negotiated financing charges, to take some pressure off the importer's current cash flow.

☐ Convert the balance due into a *promissory note* with a longer term and competitive interest rate. This can be secured or unsecured.

☐ Consider some form of *barter* or *countertrade* to convert the debt into a product or commodity that can be used or sold at a value satisfactory to the exporter.

☐ Initiate a *formal collection action* in the local courts or seek *arbitration,* if the balances are large enough to warrant the extra time and expense that may have to be incurred.

114. International Business Risks

Just as in any strictly "domestic" business activity, in international business activity there is usually some degree of risk associated with every sought-after "reward." Here's a list of recognized risks confronting any international business, along with some general suggestions for managing them:

Financial risk: In the financial world, they define *risk* as a value or result that is at present unknown. These values or results include *exchange rates, interest rates* and *commodity prices,* and changes in any of them may have either a positive or a negative impact on your overseas investment. *Risk management:* Become familiar with the risks that pertain to your company's line of business; monitor and plan for these risks—whether the expected value or result is positive or negative.

Commercial risk: This is the type of risk most companies face every day in their domestic markets. It is the risk of not getting paid, of being defrauded or "ripped-off" in some way due to illegal acts or to some form of corruption or unethical behavior by another party. Companies are increasingly vulnerable to these risks, the further they are from the markets in which they are doing business. *Risk management:* Know the people you are dealing with, whether you are facing a short-term transaction or building a long-term business relationship. Know the financial background of the people and the organizations you do business with; monitor these risks directly or via trusted intermediaries and/or third party sources (international credit bureau services).

Political risk: This is the risk of political change that might result in the adoption of policies unfavorable to your overseas business activities. There is some degree of political risk in every country in the world. *Risk management:* Read extensively and cultivate reliable sources of information.

Economic risk: This category of risk includes *exchange controls, tax policy,* and *price controls* that host-country governments implement to achieve some economic goal they deem important. *Risk management:* As with political risk, it is advisable to stay current with local political developments in your host country and make use of formal and informal sources of information and advice.

Cultural risk: This is the risk that cultural differences will adversely affect the acceptance of a product and organization, or a specific line of business activity. *Risk management:* Take the time to study the culture of the host country in which you intend to market your products or services. Seek expert advice from reliable sources— preferably, within the host country.

115. The Foreign Exchange System

The foreign exchange system is a fundamental part of the international trade "infrastructure." Here are some of the fundamentals and some insights into how it is used to create and/or protect financial values in foreign trade:

Foreign exchange: This term refers to currencies commonly used as a medium of exchange in the conduct of international trade. In the post-WWII era, the U.S. dollar, along with several other "strong currencies," has served as a medium of exchange, not only in support of trade between the U.S.A. and other countries but also between and among other countries.

Foreign exchange rates describe the comparative value that exists between one country's currency and that of another at any given moment. The forces of supply and demand usually determine this value but, in some cases, it is established by government decree and enforced by a country's central bank.

Users of foreign exchange include governments, companies, and individuals who purchase goods or services from overseas who need to use a medium of exchange other than the currency of their own country. In effect, such transactions involve two purchases: (1) the purchase of the goods or services, at an agreed-upon price usually expressed in the value of the foreign exchange (e.g., U.S. dollars); and (2) the purchase of the required amount of foreign exchange to pay for the goods or services. In most instances, exporters of goods and services expect to be paid in their home country's currency or in some other agreed-upon medium of exchange; however, they may become foreign exchange users if they accept payment in a foreign currency and subsequently engage in other transactions to convert the foreign-currency-denominated payment into their home country's currency.

Investors in foreign exchange: Companies that accept foreign currency in exchange for goods and services sold abroad become foreign exchange investors or speculators, in the sense that they become owners of an "asset" for which the value may increase, decrease, or stay the same—all depending on market forces that affect the relative value of the currency in question. There are also those who invest in currencies, or buy and sell currencies, to generate profits from the changes in these values.

116. Determining Exchange Rates

The exchange of currency is necessary for international trade. Whatever the exchange rate mechanism that may be in place, its purpose is to provide a market in which one currency can be easily exchanged for another. The market forces of supply and demand, as well as intentional and unintentional acts by governments, alone or in concert, determine exchange rates. Here are some tips for finding out what those rates are:

☐ *A moving target:* Given their lack of centralized control, their dynamism and their global reach, the foreign exchange markets that determine rates of exchange between currencies produce different rates in different markets at different times of the day. There is not just one rate of exchange for any given currency.

☐ *Sources of exchange rate information:*
  • Major financial markets around the world, in addition to making a market for stocks, also make a market for currencies and provide information on currency transaction prices.
  • Banks engaged in financing international trade
  • Tourist agencies and exchange kiosks located at international airports and transportation hubs around the world
  • Specialized commodities brokers
  • Other secondary sources: e.g., reference libraries, international trade publications, government agencies that monitor international trade, and, of course, the Internet.

117. Methods of Protection

Changes in the rates of foreign exchange can have a dramatic effect on the relative value of overseas assets and liabilities and on the relative value of international sales and profits. Here are some practical methods for protecting these values:

☐ *Avoid currency risk:* When possible, avoid dealing with foreign currencies. Do all of your international business transactions in your home country's currency. This is not an option for most foreign subsidiaries, or for importers in countries whose currency is not commonly used as a medium of exchange; nor is it an option

for many companies dealing in industry segments where
transactions are usually denominated in the local currency.

☐ *Hedge the risk:* There are several ways a company can offset the
risk of loss due to exchange-rate fluctuations:

• *Natural hedging:* Companies that have a substantial volume of
currency exchange activity can achieve a "natural" balance
between amounts payable and amounts receivable in a foreign
currency.

• *Contractual hedging:* Companies that end up "owning" cash or
other foreign-currency-denominated assets can enter into an
agreement that will assure the company of a pre-determined future
exchange rate.

118. Financing Business Activities

Methods of financing business activities vary greatly, from country
to country and sector to sector. It is important to understand the
methods of capitalizing business activities in your target market, in
order to negotiate all manner of business relationships. Without this
background, it may be difficult to craft a truly "win-win" business
arrangement in some countries. Here's what's important to look for:

Family ownership: In many countries, family-ownership is very
   common, even among larger enterprises. This means that very
   private family concerns may have to be carefully weighed, along with
   the more easily identifiable business decisions. It may also mean that
   your counterpart may have to involve a number of other people in
   key investment decisions, or before entering into agreements with
   other companies. Since the appetite for risk may vary among family
   members, these decisions may take time. When negotiating with
   family-owned businesses anywhere, it is wise to take advantage of all
   opportunities to become acquainted with family members and
   develop a level of trust with each of them. Family-owned businesses
   may often be perceived by family members as an important source of
   personal cash flow and this may color their attitude toward
   investment or re-investment in the enterprise.

Rate of inflation: In countries suffering a high rate of inflation, it may
   not make sense to invest equity anywhere in the country—let alone

in things like property plant and equipment, unless the payback is extremely fast and liquid. In highly inflationary environments, commercial loans are usually not available, and borrowing of any kind is extremely expensive. Business owners are often inclined to invest in overnight market transactions that enable them to preserve the value of their liquid holdings. These conditions will most certainly influence your counterpart's willingness to make longer-term investments.

Tax structure: In countries with highly complex, multi-layered tax systems, your counterpart may have to spend a lot of time planning ways to minimize tax impacts. In some countries, the tax system may discourage business owners from investing or increasing the taxable asset base in a particular enterprise.

Financing alternatives available: In many countries, the "financial infrastructure" may not offer many alternatives for financing a "start-up" or for the expansion of an existing business. Banking laws and the role of commercial banks in financing growth may also vary greatly from one country to another.

Labor laws: In some highly-developed countries, as well as in many lesser-developed countries, stringent labor laws make it extremely expensive and difficult to lay off or terminate employees. In such countries, your counterpart may be very cautious about taking on new business activities, which may require additional hiring. These differences in labor law often affect the way in which your counterpart capitalizes business activities. For example, rather than just adding shifts in order to increase production, in a stringent labor-law environment the business owner may choose to add more capital equipment.

119. Accounting Diversities

There is no one set of "generally accepted accounting principles" that applies to accounting practices everywhere in the world. Before attempting to analyze financial statements of any given company, in any country, it's important to first determine under which accounting standards the information was prepared. Here's a brief analysis on accounting principles, from an international perspective:[3]

☐ **Cross-cultural implications of accounting:** An overview of accounting principles and the practice of accounting in any given country will provide additional insight into its history, social and political organization and its predominant business culture.

☐ **Financial accounting systems and national values:** Financial accounting systems generally reflect the values and the needs of the users in the country in which they were developed. This means that financial statements prepared according to the rules of one country may not be easy to compare with those prepared in another.

☐ **Variables influencing national accounting environments:**
  • Needs of investors and lenders
  • Political and economic relationships with major trading partners
  • The legal system
  • Levels of inflation
  • Size and complexity of economic enterprises
  • Sophistication of management and the financial community
  • General levels of education

☐ **Progress toward adoption of international accounting standards:** Because accounting systems are as deeply ingrained as the cultural values they reflect, progress toward adoption of universally accepted international accounting standards and principles has been very slow. However, a number of international, national, and regional organizations are hard at work on this long-term goal:
  • **International Accounting Standards Committee (IASC):** Formed in 1973 by leading professional accounting bodies in Australia, Canada, France, Germany, Japan, Mexico, the Netherlands, the United Kingdom, Ireland and the U.S.A. to develop worldwide accounting standards. It is a private-sector organization that is trying to "harmonize" world accounting standards and eliminate the differences that cannot be explained by differences in environmental variables.
  • **International Federation of Accountants (IFAC):** Formed in 1977 to develop a worldwide accountancy profession. Its focus is on the development of accountancy as a profession, rather than on accounting standards. However, it does issue *International Standards on Auditing (ISA)* to harmonize the way audits are conducted worldwide.
  • **United Nations (UN):** The UN's interest in international accounting has much to do with its interest in the effects of the growth of multinational corporations that, in effect, transcend

national jurisdictions. The UN pursues its interest in accounting standards through its *Intergovernmental Working Group of Experts on International Standards of Accounting and Reporting* which meets annually and reports on international accounting and reporting developments in member countries around the world.

- **Organization for Economic Cooperation and Development (OECD):** Made up of nearly all the industrialized countries in the world, its primary purpose is to foster economic growth and development in member countries. It creates a vehicle for member countries to consult with one another on general economic issues. The OECD also attempts to serve as a catalyst in the development of international accounting and reporting standards, and has issued a code of conduct promoting certain voluntary financial disclosures by multinational corporations.
- **European Community (EC):** The EC has been working to harmonize the generally accepted accounting principles of its member countries.
- **African Accounting Council:** Formed in 1979 to harmonize accounting practices, upgrade accounting education, and exchange ideas on accounting standards between member nations. It is made up of representatives from 27 African countries.
- **Association of Accountancy Bodies of West Africa:** Formed by professional accounting institutes in the Gambia, Ghana, Liberia, Nigeria, Senegal, and Sierra Leone regions.
- **Asociación Interamericana de Contabilidad:** Made up of representatives from 21 nations in North and South America. It solicits papers and holds conferences every two or three years.
- **ASEAN Federation of Accountants:** Made up of representatives of the six member-nations of the Association of Southeast Asian Nations, its purpose is to advance the status of the accounting professions in its member nations; it also intends to work on harmonization of standards among its members.
- **Confederation of Asian and Pacific Accountants:** Made up of representatives of accounting organizations in 20 Pacific Rim nations.

- **Fédération des Experts Comptables Européens:** Established in 1986 as a successor to earlier groups—one EC-related, the other Europe-wide. Its focus is on the accounting professions, but it also intends to become involved in the process of harmonizing standards throughout Europe.
- **Financial Accounting Standards Board (U.S.A.):** The principal body that writes the "generally accepted accounting principles" (GAAP) by which the financial statements of American companies must be prepared. The FASB deals with the immediate effects of globalization (e.g., currency translation standards) and is committed to full consideration of international perspectives in all of its work.
- **Securities and Exchange Commission (U.S.A.):** An American government agency that oversees and ensures the adequacy of accounting and reporting standards of companies whose securities are traded publicly. Since SEC accounting and reporting standards apply to both U.S. and non-U.S. firms, it exerts influence on the development of accounting standards in the countries from which the non-U.S. firms originate.
- **American Institute of Certified Public Accountants:** Made up of about 300,000 certified professional accountants, it publishes standards for performing audit examinations. Again, like the SEC, it exerts influence by virtue of its influence on the practices of non-U.S. firms doing business in the U.S.

120. An International Accounting Checklist

If you have a frequent need to translate, analyze, and compare financial information on companies in several foreign countries, it helps to have a checklist that reminds you of the differences in key accounting rules. Here's how to go about it:[4]

☐ **Introduction:** Keep in mind that, in many countries where smaller family-owned-and-operated businesses dominate, where even relatively large enterprises are private and closely held, and where it is not common for ordinary citizens to own shares in publicly-held corporations, the tradition of accounting and reporting to outside investors or other stakeholders may be rather weak.

☐ **General:** The accounting and reporting traditions of most countries can be grouped and categorized according to the following models:

- *British-American Model:* Also referred to as the *Anglo-Saxon Model,* it really should be known as the *British-North American-Dutch Model,* because the models in each of these regions are quite similar. This model focuses on the information needs of investors and creditors—a reflection of the fact that they developed along with the growth of their financial markets.

- *Continental Model:* This model focuses on legal and regulatory requirements of governments and banks and is designed to help govern compliance with government or bank-imposed requirements. This model is also prevalent in many French-speaking African countries.

- *South American Model:* Like the Continental model, it focuses on government regulatory requirements but also includes special features designed to accommodate persistent high rates of inflation.

- *Mixed Economy Model:* This model developed in the wake of the political upheavals that occurred in Eastern Europe as former state-centralized economies began adopting market-oriented economic policies. The model retains some of the features of statism, while incorporating new features—largely from the British-American Model. Companies operating under the jurisdiction of this model often have to maintain dual accounting systems.

- *Islamic Model:* Some countries have fostered the development of an Islamic model with a theological basis that, for example, prohibits the recognition of interest on money. This model has not yet fully evolved to encompass all elements of financial accounting.

- *International Standards Model:* In some emerging economies around the world, government and industry are promoting the development of accounting rules that conform to and adjust to evolving international standards. By studying the history of a particular country and the possible colonial influences in its background, it is often possible to determine at least the origins of a given country's accounting model.

☐ **Key Differences:** The following are the key accounting differences that you should look for as you go around the world and attempt to interpret, analyze, and compare financial statements.

• *Definition of cash and cash equivalents:* In some accounting systems, this includes the gross amount of all *cash, demand deposits, and highly liquid investments*—all monetary assets; while, in other systems, this definition includes all of the same assets but requires that *bank overdrafts* be deducted, thus generating a *net* figure. Elsewhere, *short-term* borrowings must be deducted—in effect, reporting a *net monetary asset* figure.

• *Goodwill:* There is a lot of debate around the world and varying practices with respect to the recognition and accounting for any reputed values that would add to or charges that would reduce *fair market value.*

• *Pensions:* In many countries around the world, the government is the main provider of pension benefits and it is uncommon for private enterprises to offer such benefits to employees; therefore, only a few countries have well-developed private-industry pension accounting and regulation systems. In those countries with tighter pension accounting standards, enterprises are required to accrue pension obligations at a higher rate and this will have the effect of understating the enterprises' earnings.

• *Recognition of inflation and other price changes:* In most countries, the accounting system is based on the *historical cost principle,* i.e., assets are reported at the lower of cost or market value. However, in countries where inflation is persistent and high, the accounting model has been adapted to include the concept of *General Price Level Accounting (GPL)* according to which items recorded at historical cost are uniformly and systematically updated over time. Alternately, some countries employ *Current Value Accounting* or *Current Cost Accounting (CCA)* which updates the value of items based on their current values and/or the costs of obtaining equivalent values.

121. Foreign Currencies

Understanding foreign currencies, their history and the forces at work that affect their relative value can give you a significant advantage in planning and carrying out international operations, as well as give you insight into the economic and political life of the countries that stand behind the 200-plus "listed" currencies. Here's a simple approach to understanding the world's currencies:

☐ *"Strong" currencies:* The relative strength of some currencies, e.g., the U.S. dollar, can also be enhanced by their wide use as an international medium of exchange. In the common parlance, a *strong* currency is one that:
  • Is backed up by a relatively large economy that attracts substantial foreign investment
  • Has little or no consumer price inflation and relatively stable interest rates
  • Is from a country where the government has a fiscal surplus or a fiscal deficit that is only a small percentage of the country's gross domestic product (GDP)
  • Is from a country where the accumulated government debt, if it exists at all, is less than half of the country's gross domestic product (GDP).

☐ *"Weak" currencies:* Obviously, a *weak* currency is one that does not meet one or more of the *strong* currency criteria. It is a currency backed up by a relatively small economy that suffers relatively high inflation and/or is backed up by a government that incurs large fiscal deficits.

☐ *Convertibility and liquidity of currencies:* Some countries do not have a central banking infrastructure that provides a market for their currency or they do not permit trading in their currencies and, therefore, if one receives payment in these *soft* currencies, there is little chance of converting the currency into *hard* currencies for which there is a ready market. Along these same lines, *liquidity* is a comparative concept referring to the relative ease with which one is able to exchange the currency for another, within a reasonable time frame.

122. More on the Euro Currency

As discussed in tip #47, the majority of the European *Economic and Monetary Union* (EMU) countries joined in the creation of a European Currency called the *euro*. If the EMU achieves its goal of creating a strong trading currency that can compete with the U.S. dollar, the Japanese yen, and the British pound, it will influence the conduct of trade finance and regional competition throughout the world. It is important for anyone involved in international business to understand this new currency and know how to use it.

The euro became the medium of exchange for all participating countries on January 1, 1999. Initially, only Germany (deutsche mark), France (franc), Austria (schilling), Belgium (franc), Finland (markka), Ireland (pound), Spain (peseta), Italy (lira), Luxembourg (franc), Portugal (escudo), and the Netherlands (guilder) participated in the conversion to the euro.

Over a period of three years, the euro will gradually replace all of the participating countries' currencies so that, by 2002, it will be the only medium of exchange within these participating countries. EMU members Britain, Sweden, Denmark and Greece have "opted out" of the initial euro conversion process, but they may consider joining in at some future date.

At the end of 1998, the EMU established irrevocable, fixed rates of exchange between each participating country's currency and the new euro. The *European System of Central Banks (ESCB)*, which is made up of the European Central Bank and the central banks of the other participating countries, will take over responsibility for monetary policy in Europe.

Some experts anticipate little or no immediate effect on other trading currencies. Others warn that, over time, the euro will compete with the U.S. dollar and decrease worldwide demand for the U.S. dollar. These experts argue that the U.S. Federal Reserve Bank will have to be more concerned about the effects of external currency accounts deficits and a weakening dollar. If successful, the euro will be much in demand as a medium of exchange for international trade and may grow to play a role similar to that played by the U.S. dollar during the post-World War II era.

123. Influences on Currency Values

The relative value of currencies can vary greatly from one moment to the next, and the apparent success of your international operations will vary right along with these changes in relative value. It is important to continually monitor the background factors which may influence the value of a particular currency. Here is a simple list of factors to review when you are sizing up a currency and trying to foresee probable changes in its value:

The size and strength of the economy it represents. The bigger and stronger the economy, the greater the stability.

The relative stability of prices and interest rates. The higher the consumer price inflation and the higher the interest rates, the higher the probability of continual change.

The degree to which direct foreign investment is flowing into the country. The greater the inflow of foreign investment in property, plant and equipment, the greater the stability of the currency.

The relative size of a country's foreign exchange reserves. A measure of a country's ability to cover its current account obligations (if any). The greater these reserves, the stronger and more stable the currency.

The existence and relative size of the country's fiscal deficit and debt. The higher the fiscal deficit and the accumulated debt in relation to the gross domestic product (GDP), the more likely that inflationary pressures will de-stabilize the currency.

The existence and relative size of a current account deficit. Often, the greater the current account deficit in proportion to the gross domestic product (GDP), the less stable the currency.

Government policies or actions affecting political and social stability within the country or relations with neighboring countries. Changes in the tax system, as well as changes in discounts and interest rates controlled or influenced by a country's central bank, can have an immediate impact on currency values—as can outbreaks of social unrest or political and economic disruptions that might prompt investors to sell the currency in question and invest in some other currency or investment medium.

124. The U.S. Dollar as the Medium of Foreign Trade

As the U.S.A.'s economic "empire" has grown throughout the 20th century, the U.S. dollar has increasingly been favored as a medium of exchange in international trade all around the world. It is important to know how this has come about and to discern what forces are at work that may challenge the preeminence of the U.S. dollar as the world's trading currency:

The relative size and strength of the economy backing the U.S. dollar: After World War II, the U.S.A. emerged as, by far, the world's largest industrialized economy. This status increased the perception that the U.S. dollar was both strong and stable.

The appeal of U.S.A.-made technology and goods in overseas markets: As more people overseas purchased U.S.-made technologies and goods, this created increasing world-wide demand for dollars with which to pay for these technologies and goods.

The attractiveness of the U.S.A. market to foreign investors: As more overseas investors purchased U.S.-dollar-denominated equity or debt, this further increased demand for dollars.

Historical events during World War II and in the post-war period: Not only did World War II project U.S. trade and economic influence further into the rest of the world, but the U.S. economy was the only industrialized economy that remained largely intact at the end of World War II. This, more than any other factor, reinforced the use of the U.S. dollar as a medium of international trade. It became a convenient common denominator of trade value.

125. Your Country's Export Bank

Almost every country in the world views exporting as an activity that is desirable. In some countries, exports are seen as essential to economic well-being. Frequently, national governments create specialized banks to support and facilitate exports. It's important to understand how these banks work and to know how to make use of the resources they have available.

Typically, a country will pass legislation creating a special purpose bank to facilitate trade—both export and import of merchandise and raw materials. In some countries, these banks are branches of the national government; in others, they are afforded a great deal of autonomy to pursue the growth of trade. These banks are funded by national governments but they also derive revenue from banking operations.

The Export-Import Bank of the United States, for example, often provides loans to foreign buyers interested in purchasing American-made goods. They also often provide stand-by loans, loan guarantees, and export credit insurance. Usually, an individual business can request these export/import services through the international department of a local commercial bank or by going directly to local offices or representatives of the national government.

126. Product Nationality and Export Financing

Not every industry or product manufactured in a given country can expect to receive export financing. Most governments and the export banks they have created are interested in creating employment within their national boundaries and they usually favor those products that have a high "local" content of labor and also raw materials.

"Local content" simply refers to the national origin of the raw materials, direct labor, and other value added in the manufacturing of a particular product. Most governments and export banks require that local content be above a certain minimum to qualify for government-subsidized export financing. These local content minimums may range from 20 percent to 100 percent.

127. Benefits of "Foreign Trade Zones"

Governments create "foreign trade zones" to increase the efficiency of import/export activities, to ease the customs/duty-related cash flow of importing companies, and to promote local employment by making it attractive to certain manufacturing and/or assembly operations within the zone. Many foreign trade zones are specific, limited-access areas into which raw materials may be imported and finished goods exported, and from which a range of manufacturing and finishing processes may be performed—all with favorable tax treatment (duties). The financial benefits of "free trade zones" can be substantial for some companies. For example:

Deferred payment of import duties. Companies that must import materials or components for products to be manufactured or consumed with the host country may warehouse these items in the FTZ and not pay import duties until withdrawing the products or components from the FTZ.

Exemption from import duties on materials that are destined for export. Companies wishing to reduce the cost of goods destined for export may bring raw materials and components into the zone—free of import duties, manufacture the goods that require the materials or components, and then re-export from the FTZ.

International Tax Planning

Proper tax planning is often critical to the success or failure of international operations. Some companies, particularly early in international expansion, will try to structure their operations to assure that taxes are paid only in the home market. Longer-term oriented global companies, however, will try to minimize their tax liabilities by strategies that attempt, to the extent possible, to move profits into lower tax jurisdictions.

In this section, we will explore these strategies and offer some analysis on the issues of permanent establishment, value-added taxes, and using tax treaties and/or tax havens.

128. Management Impact of Taxation

How important are the tax aspects of making critical business decisions? The first critical decision might be whether to create an international or global company. An international company could be defined as one that may have many offshore operations but is still managed to maximize the company's optimal position in the home market. This company will attempt to make the bulk of its income in the home market and pay tax in that market. A global company, on the other hand, will attempt to minimize its taxes on a global basis and therefore make decisions that would move income toward lower tax jurisdictions in order to achieve a greater global profit.

The following management issues may have tax considerations:

☐ Ownership structures of affiliates, branches, and subsidiaries
☐ Location of plants
☐ Allocation of production
☐ Market selection
☐ Intercompany pricing
☐ Personnel decisions—particularly expatriate decisions
☐ Financing decisions—particularly short-term financing
☐ Research & Development (R&D) locations

129. International Taxation

Once your company has income in one or more jurisdictions, you need to consider the approach that countries take to international taxation. On the most basic level, the two approaches taken by nearly all governments are a residential approach or a territorial approach.

The *residential approach* taxes the income of its residents without regard to where the income is earned. Note that we used the word resident as distinct from citizen. The *territorial approach* taxes all parties, no matter what their resident country is, on income earned within its territory.

Many countries apply both approaches depending on the circumstances. For example, the U.S.A., Mexico, and Japan subject resident taxpayers (corporate or individual) to taxation on their worldwide income, while nonresident taxpayers (corporate or individual) are taxed only on their local source income. France, on the other hand, is completely territorial in its approach to taxation.

130. Permanent Establishments

One way to avoid direct taxation (income taxes) in most countries is not to create a permanent establishment or, as some would call it, a fixed base. Typical business transactions that do not normally create a permanent establishment are direct sales from the home country, catalog sales, and contracts involving agents and/or distributors, franchising or licensing from the home market.

For income tax purposes, the term "permanent establishment" means any place in which business activities are wholly or partially carried on (e.g., a fixed base). This would subject the owner of the fixed base to taxation on the income of the fixed base. Permanent establishments normally include branches, agencies, subsidiaries, offices, factories, installations, mines and other places of extraction of natural resources.

In most countries, however, the following activities will not constitute a permanent establishment:

☐ Facilities used solely for the purpose of storage or display of goods belonging to the non-resident

☐ The maintenance of a stock of goods or merchandise belonging to the nonresident for the purpose of storage or display, or for processing by another company

☐ The maintenance of a place of business solely for the purpose of acquiring goods or merchandise, or for the collection of information

☐ The use of a place of business solely for the purpose of carrying on activities of a preparatory or auxiliary character such as advertising, supply of information, scientific research, and loan preparations

☐ The deposit of goods or merchandise in a bonded warehouse

If the countries involved have a tax treaty, that treaty will normally define what constitutes a permanent establishment in a manner which is the same for both countries.

131. Direct and Indirect International Taxation

Companies with permanent establishment in any jurisdiction will pay direct taxes in those jurisdictions. These taxes are normally on income and are levied on domestic and foreign corporations and shareholders. Companies without a permanent establishment may still have to pay taxes of an indirect nature. These are normally imposed on dividends, interest and royalties.

Direct Taxes

Direct taxes are normally imposed on income derived from business profits, intercompany transactions, capital gains, and sometimes interest and dividends. In some countries, companies may also be taxed on increases resulting from inflation. Taxes may also be imposed on the acquisition of real estate, conversion of currency and other negotiable instruments. A percentage of income (usually after tax) may be reserved for profit sharing.

Indirect Taxes

Companies who license or franchise products and services or who charge interest may be subjected to certain indirect taxes which are collected on behalf of the foreign jurisdiction by withholding. In effect, if a royalty due to a foreign source is U.S.$100,000, and the withholding tax is 15 percent, the payor of the royalty would pay $85,000 to the payee and $15,000 to the government on behalf of the payee, then the payee would probably have a tax credit in the country in which they pay taxes.

The amount of the royalty withholding can be reduced by careful tax planning and the use of tax treaties. For example, the U.S.A. does not have a tax treaty with Brazil, but the Netherlands does with both the U.S.A. and Brazil. American companies may then run their royalty-baring licenses through a Dutch company to take advantage of favorable withholding terms.

132. Value-Added Taxes

The Value-Added Tax (VAT) is a one-time tax payable by the ultimate user on all types of products (and in some countries services), which is very common in Canada, Europe and Latin America. However, each business entity involved in the process—from the sale of raw materials, to the production and distribution of finished products, to the ultimate user—is required to bill the tax to its customers and to pay the tax on its purchases and crediting the amounts so paid against the amount due on its own activities. The net amount payable by each entity is considered to represent a tax on the value added by each.

Countries which apply VAT to services (e.g., Mexico) do have a large number of exemptions (public services and medical services, but not legal services). Rent and lease payments may also be taxable.

The VAT has been the primary source of revenue for the European Union as distinct from income and sales taxes in the U.S.A. It also presents a significant problem of tax equalization between countries. Germans, for example, will normally pay income taxes and are more concerned with what they pay, so Germany has high income taxes and low VATs. The French, on the other hand, don't like to pay taxes, so in France income taxes are low while VATs (which are added at purchase) are very high.

VATs are not payable on exports, and if you are traveling abroad and purchasing products that you intend to export, you may be eligible for a refund of VAT taxes paid.

133. Transfer Pricing

The *transfer price* is a price for products and components that are sold within and among units of an international company. Normally this includes the parent, subsidiaries and affiliates, or any organization which is controlled by the company.

Free to charge what they could, global companies would price their products in the following manner to their controlled companies:

☐ Charge high transfer price to the German subsidiary which would then make little or no money and therefore not pay high German taxes

☐ Charge low transfer prices in countries with high tariffs (e.g., Brazil) in order to reduce the actual financial amount of the tariff and thereby reduce the landed price to the customers

☐ Charge high transfer prices to a country where it may be difficult to repatriate profits

☐ Charge a low transfer price to countries with low tax rates

In order to combat global companies using transfer prices to largely avoid taxation, many countries now have developed complicated rules for determining transfer prices. The basis of these rules is that transfer prices must meet an *arms-length standard*—that of an uncontrolled buyer dealing arms-length with another uncontrolled seller.

Tax authorities will look at the following "red flags" in attempting to determine whether companies are abiding by the transfer price rules:

☐ Significant operations in low-tax jurisdictions

☐ Patterns of losses in the home country

☐ Patterns of lower profits than the industry norms

☐ Payments of management fees to subsidiaries and affiliates

☐ Payment of intercompany royalties in excess of five percent of sales

134. Foreign Sales Corporations

Every country in the world wants to encourage exports. One manner used is to limit or eliminate VAT and/or income taxes associated with the sales abroad. European and other countries which use VAT taxes rebate the VAT paid on products and services which are exported. In the U.S.A. (which does not have a VAT), the favored government method is the Foreign Sales Corporation (FSC).

The FSC is a shell company located in a designated foreign country or U.S. possession. The U.S. parent supplies the goods directly to its export customers and runs the sales through the FSC. The specific amount of taxes saved depends on the calculation applied, but in general the savings is usually about 15 percent of the tax liability—that is, 15 percent of the effective tax rate. If the effective income tax rate is 34 percent, the FSC rate would be 28.9 percent (34 percent × .15 = 5.1; 34 percent − 5.1 = 28.9 percent).

FSC makes sense if the amount of tax savings from international sales exceeds the costs (money and time) of establishing the FSC. For example, U.S.$1 million in sales generating $100,000 in profits would generate $5,100 in tax savings. Given the costs of FSC in the area of $4,000–6,000 per year, it probably would not be cost efficient to establish an FSC. If you are close to a breakeven point, however, you might consider sharing an FSC with other companies. There are additional restrictions on the type of companies that can establish FSCs (e.g., "S" corporations cannot—or companies where all shareholders of the parent are individuals).

Overall, the FSC offers a significant benefit to companies reaching a certain level of exports.

135. Tax Havens

Tax havens remain, under the right circumstances, a viable method of avoiding or delaying the imposition of certain taxes. They are usually small countries or territories that grant foreign companies and individuals the use of their company structures and financial systems without the imposition of tax or at a very low tax rate.

The most popular tax havens usually have a combination of benefits, including limited taxes and the absence of exchange controls, political stability, nice physical amenities, and a good support system.

Common uses for tax havens are:

☐ Captive insurance companies (those tied to one company only)
☐ Managing offshore security portfolios
☐ Collecting royalties from licensees and franchisees
☐ Regulating earnings from foreign operations

In the past, tax havens had been used to hide money as these jurisdictions did not have agreements to reveal financial information. In recent years, however, their role has changed from hiding assets to assisting companies and individuals to avoid or delay taxation from the profits of legitimate businesses.

136. Tax Treaties

Treaties to avoid double taxation exist between most countries that have significant trade. From a government's perspective, a tax treaty will help it to better control the activities of its residents and nonresident companies to assure that it receives its fair share of taxes. From the tax payers' point of view, tax treaties offer certain benefits which make it more profitable to operate in the treaty countries—such as lower withholding taxes on royalties, dividends and interest, and clear rules on the repatriation of profits and investment.

Tax treaties attempt to offer a common definition of permanent establishment. They may also deal with shipping and air transport, capital gains, personal services, athletes and artists, students and pension funds. Finally, tax treaties provide the mechanisms for the exchange of information between the tax authorities of the government.

Tax treaties have also become a precondition to entrance into free trade agreements and common markets. The U.S.-Mexico Treaty went into effect in 1994 with the beginning of NAFTA and was a condition for entry imposed on Mexico.

MARKETING AND SALES

Everything starts when the customer says "yes"! Today, even for smaller businesses, that customer may be saying, "ja," "da" or "sí" as likely as "yes." For persons charged with responsibility for marketing and sales, the oportunities are immense—and so are the challenges.

This section will offer you quick insight into the fundamentals for planning, organizing, and executing effective marketing and sales programs in a global market.

137. Customer Service Functions

The support services required for entry into foreign markets can be provided by your own employees or can be contracted out to professional freight forwarders, brokers or other third parties. No matter who provides these services, it is important to remember that the cost of human error tends to increase in proportion to the size and weight of your product and the distance it must travel. No matter what the size of your company, when you are organizing to serve customers and support distribution in foreign markets, consider the following tactics to ensure high quality service and avoid costly errors.

☐ Share your company's global vision, mission, goal, and strategy with the people who will be providing customer service to foreign markets. They must know where their department fits into the company's mission.

☐ Assess the readiness and the training needs of the current department. Are all members thoroughly familiar with your company's product line? Is there anyone already on board who has had experience with export/import administration, overseas work experience, foreign languages, and bank letters of credit?

☐ Identify the requirements and expectations. Involve department members in a study and comparison of the procedures and special requirements unique to export administration. Employees need to understand why special skills and knowledge are needed.

☐ Provide initial training, hire skilled personnel, and benchmark "best in class." Whether through training, hiring, or outsourcing (to forwarders), make sure you have all necessary knowledge and skills available to the department. Arrange for a site visit to an experienced, successful international customer service operation, or find other ways to expose your department to models of excellence in international customer service.

☐ Listen to customers. Have your international sales or dealer personnel meet with your international customer service personnel to discuss requirements and expectations that may be unique to your particular industry.

☐ Make a plan which includes performance measures that are meaningful to your overseas customers. If it's not planned, and measured, it probably won't happen. Establish clear, measurable goals, adopt a plan to achieve them, and make sure everyone agrees on the measurements to be used.

☐ Evaluate and adjust frequently. If possible, include your international sales force, dealer support managers, and your overseas customers in a periodic performance evaluation. Export requirements and competitive conditions change frequently. A successful customer service program should be geared for frequent procedure changes.

Where domestic markets are huge and where anticipated export sales volumes are relatively small, it may appear that the export "tail" is wagging the domestic sales "dog," but the company that achieves excellence in serving its foreign customers will very likely do a much better job of serving the domestic customers as well.

138. Foreign Market Expertise

To find attractive opportunities for growth in foreign markets and to prepare to compete effectively once you enter them, it is important to develop a system for quickly gaining the expertise you need.

Know your own market first. It will be a lot easier to size up a foreign market if you already have a good understanding of your own. Ask yourself:

☐ Who are your customers? Who are your most desirable/profitable customers? What makes them desirable/profitable?

☐ What is your product/service and how is it delivered? Do your sales force and/or other distribution channels add value for the customer?

☐ Roughly, how big is your present market?

☐ What drives growth in demand for your product or service in your present market?

☐ Who are your competitors and from where do they originate? Are they all local or regional ? Do you have any international competitors? What is your share of the present market?

☐ Who are your suppliers? Where are their sources?

☐ Historically, where has the best technology in your industry come from?

☐ What are the factors most critical for success of your product or service in your present market—product quality, unique features, technical support, distribution, financing, inventory, delivery, etc.?

139. New Markets

In today's global market environment, it is reasonable to expect that successful products in one market will be successful in another. However, it is important to size up the new market, to determine acceptance and demand, and to identify ways in which the existing product may have to be adapted to new requirements. Here are some steps you might want to consider:

☐ Update your knowledge of governing patent and trademark laws and rules in the foreign markets you are considering. This will help you determine some of the costs of entry and also assess the "knock-off" risks associated with your particular kind of products. In some markets, it is very easy to lose patent and trademark protections, unless you follow procedures that may be quite different from those that apply in the U.S.A.

☐ Get input on product acceptance, special requirements on features and labeling from industry regulators, customers, distributors or agents in the selected foreign markets. By soliciting a broad range of end-user and regulatory input, you may be able to avoid costly customs delays as well as re-work or retrofit expenses.

☐ Anticipate features that will make the product easier to adapt to special requirements in the overseas markets you intend to serve.

Especially in those markets where special standards sometimes serve as arbitrary, or non-tariff, barriers, it is important to consider responding to those requirements in this early stage.

☐ Well before launching the product, determine which customs classifications will likely apply, anticipate customs duties, and plan the export and foreign distribution process. It is sometimes possible to avoid excessive duties by carefully selecting the product classification. This is also a good time to consider such things as a total or partial "breakdown and reassemble," in order to lessen the impact of duties.

By considering these four steps, you will increase the probability that your product will be profitable in the new market of your choice.

140. Good Advertising Practices

Good advertising is good communicating. In order to successfully communicate with customers in foreign markets, it is important to account for even the most subtle differences in language and culture. Here are some tips:

☐ Although the English language accompanies many successful products into foreign markets, it is wise to remember that, ultimately, *the international language of business is the language of the customer.*
  • Do your homework to determine which language or languages will best communicate with the customers you have in mind.
  • Keep in mind that, in many markets, the local language is not only essential for communication but a national treasure that must be "handled with care."
  • Listen carefully to the responses of native speakers who represent the market segment you wish to communicate to. It is important that they be representative. In most countries, different dialects and language habits may determine the effectiveness of your communications, even if you communicate in the "official" language of the country in question.
☐ It is wise to research the local laws and rules governing the visual appearance and the written content of your advertising messages.

Some countries impose severe limits on what can be said about a product or about a competitor's product.

☐ Investigate for cultural differences that may affect the successful reception of your intended message. This investigation should cover such things as specific social values, rules and laws; importance of national identity; and purchasing practices.

☐ Research the availability and effectiveness of local advertising channels and advertising placement costs and practices. Some channels may provide more efficient access to your intended customers than others, and these may not be the same channels you are accustomed to using in your home market.

141. International Trade Shows

In some industries, participation in trade shows provides excellent opportunities to consummate additional sales and build an overseas business presence. "Scout" the show, or consider using the opportunity in other ways, before registering as an exhibitor.

☐ Attend shows to gather intelligence on your competitors.

☐ Monitor external trends affecting your industry and/or your customers' industry.

☐ Monitor new product developments and new technologies in your industry and in related industries.

☐ Evaluate merger and acquisition prospects.

☐ Build relationships with key customers, original equipment manufacturers (OEMs), suppliers, and potential strategic allies.

☐ Recruit talent.

☐ Achieve "visibility" through participation in related industry association events.

☐ Use on-site or off-site hospitality suites or recreational events as lower-cost methods for gaining visibility and making contact with customers.

☐ Inspect and evaluate advertising media and other support services.

☐ Make sure you have carefully considered the cost/benefit ratio for show participation, in comparison with other alternatives for achieving similar purposes.

☐ Are there some activities that can only be efficiently carried out at shows? Can you quantify the benefit derived from those activities?

☐ Will there be an "opportunity cost" created by the diversion of resources that could have been spent on other, similarly-directed activities?

☐ Make sure an exhibition in the chosen show will clearly support your company's mission and strategy.

☐ Will this show give you an opportunity to "differentiate" your company from its competitors?

☐ Will you have the resources and the opportunity to project the relative size and importance of your company in relationship to your competitors in the industry?

☐ Establish a "bailout" date based on projected attendance, so if attendance estimates drop too low, you can pull the plug before incurring major expenses.

☐ Make sure you have a realistic budget and a detailed plan for getting the highest possible return on your exhibition dollar.

142. Global Pricing Strategies

Increasing globalization of world markets and integration of regional trading blocks creates new opportunities and new challenges for those charged with pricing products and services.

☐ Know where pricing fits into your company's basic business strategy. In other words, are you:
 • Pricing for value?
 • Pricing to gain market-share?
 • Pricing to differentiate your product, service, company image?

☐ When considering pricing in specific foreign markets, first determine whether your basic business strategy will be sustainable in the destination market.
 • If you are pricing for value, will customers in the destination country perceive value the same way?
 • If you intend to quickly gain market share, will you face more or less direct competition in the destination market?
 • If you are pricing for differentiation, will you be able to influence perceptions of your company in the same way you have in the home country?

☐ Identify all the non-controllable factors that will influence the price of your product or service in your destination country through:

- Pre-export product adaptations
- Expediting, freight, and insurance
- Financing costs
- Inventory costs
- Port-of-entry, warehousing, and transfer costs
- Import duties and taxes
- Post-import product adaptations
- Advertising and distribution costs
- Local transfer and value-added taxes
- Exchange rates
- Local rates of inflation
- Local inventory and distribution financing costs
- Competitor pricing tactics
- Perceived or demonstrable value to the end user

143. Direct and Indirect Marketing

Successful introduction of any product or service depends heavily on selection of the appropriate method of distribution. Since distribution patterns and practices vary widely around the world, it is always wise to approach this question with an open mind as you consider each new market. Some factors to consider:

☐ Understand your home-country distribution system
  - Sales subsidiaries (decentralized)
  - Direct sales (centralized management)
  - Branch offices (centralized management)
  - Distributors (acquire ownership of product or service)
  - Agents
  - Original equipment manufacturers (OEMs)
☐ Understand why it works for your product or service
  - Does your product or service have high brand recognition and is it important to control the use and association of the brand name?
  - Does your product or service have a high "proprietary" content that must be protected and controlled?
  - Does your product or service require substantial technical support at the time of installation or initiation?
  - Does your product or service require after-sale support of any kind?

- Do your customers depend on your sales force or distributors for problem-solving and applications development?

☐ Study distribution practices in your destination country to take into account any differences that might influence your choice of distribution channels.
  - Are there differences in the customer base that should influence your choice of distribution channels?
  - Do comparable distribution channels exist?
  - Are there differences in distribution costs and capabilities that might influence your decision?
  - Are there local laws or rules that affect the costs and the risks associated with different distribution channels?

144. Selling to the Public Sector

In many markets around the world, the public sector not only makes policy and funds priorities but also directly implements many services, as well as major industrial and infrastructure projects. In some countries, the state may be the primary purchaser of your goods or services. Here are some things to consider when selling to the public sector:

☐ Just as you would for any potential customer, know your market and study what it is that will motivate key people to buy from your company. When dealing with the government, however, there may be other considerations:
  - What national goals or policies will the purchase of your product or service fulfill?
  - What warranties or guarantees are available to minimize risk to the purchaser?
  - Is your product or service and your company willing and able to meet all the registration and financial disclosure requirements of the host government?
  - Is your company willing to risk disclosure of proprietary information to competitors in the host country?

☐ Choose a reputable local agent or representative who is appropriately registered with the government entities you wish to sell to.

☐ Be prepared to meet rigid minimum inventory and performance bonding requirements.

☐ Be prepared to take on substantial accounts receivable financing requirements caused by slow government payment practices.

☐ If you are an American company, be prepared to insulate your company from practices that may violate the U.S. Foreign Corrupt Practices Act.

145. Selling to Governments

While the 1990s have been characterized by governments getting out of activities they have been involved in in the past, governments are still the leading purchaser of goods and services in most countries. Dealing with governments requires different skills and styles than dealing with private industry. What follows is a partial list of those unique aspects:

☐ *Distinct purchase and payment cycles.* Governments tend to be more rigorous about when they can purchase and sometimes when they can pay. For example, historically, Mexico's federal government has not paid its bills in the months before and after national elections. These bills will eventually get paid but there is an interruption in payments that bothers many credit managers.

☐ *Local sourcing requirements.* Some governments require that a certain portion of a larger purchase (e.g., components or labor) must be locally sourced. This is often called offtake requirements. When local product is unavailable, sometimes requirements of the use of local labor are applied.

☐ *Use of local infrastructure.* Governments may want purchases brought to their country on local air or shipping lines.

☐ *Qualification process.* Foreign suppliers may have to economically qualify as providers before being able to bid on government tenders. This is normally true for local vendors, but foreign vendors may be required to have a local office or a local partner.

☐ *Tenders and Requests for Proposals.* Tenders and Requests for Proposals are often the manner in which governments seek to purchase. These require bonds and lengthy responses to documents, and, because of the high costs, require companies to take into consideration the likelihood of winning the bid versus the costs of bidding.

☐ *Formal Negotiations.* Government negotiations are normally more formal and consist of a large number of negotiators. Therefore, a team approach would be required over using a few negotiators.

☐ *Sovereignty considerations.* A government is not likely to have another government's law apply to the agreement or to have the selection of foreign courts or arbitration.

146. Creating an International Image

In order to instill in your customers the confidence that you are committed and capable of conducting business internationally, it is important to convey the proper image across borders. Customers will not take you, your product, or service seriously, unless they perceive that your company is capable of sustaining a long-term position in international markets.

Identify your home country in the address on your letterhead and your business cards (are you from Bangor, Maine, USA—or Bangor, Northern Ireland?). Consider also using logos, titles, or brief mission statements that communicate your company's intention to serve customers worldwide.

Create either an international subsidiary, an international division, or other organizational structure that is visibly dependent on success in overseas markets. Provide international managers with appropriate titles and ample authority to negotiate and commit resources to overseas ventures. Place employee expatriates in visible positions in your international headquarters, and select advertising imagery that is universal in its meaning, in the sense that it is not tied to just one culture.

Communicate in the language of your customers. Encourage overseas employees to learn the local language and avoid living in expatriate enclaves.

147. Selling Globally on the Internet

With usage increasing 10 percent per month, the Internet offers a significant vehicle to market and sell products and services across borders. While true for all companies large and small, a well-conceived website can be a significant advantage to the smaller company.

Websites are used for a combination of advertising, company visibility, public relations, name recognition, press releases, direct sales, referrals to in-country intermediaries, customer support, and technical assistance. A good website would have the following characteristics:

Information with constant updating to encourage repeat visits
Clear navigation paths for movement within the site
Interactivity to reader feedback
Connection to other sites
Simply written yet culturally sensitive information
Language-sensitive wordage

The global character of the World Wide Web does create some unique problems in cross-border selling which includes the cost and availability of international shipping, customs/duties, usability of credit cards, and currency conversions. It may also be wise to have several languages on your website.

148. Internet Implications

The Internet, which began in the 1970s but has only been available to the general public since the early 1990s, is expected to have (according to IBM) over 500 million active users by the year 2000. As such, it will have a profound impact on international business in the 21st century. Four major implications are worth noting:

☐ *The Internet will speed up the process by which companies enter international markets.* Traditionally, companies enter international markets incrementally, testing first a few foreign markets and approaches and increasing their global presence when their knowledge base increases. The Internet now provides businesses with the technological prowess to gather knowledge and international access. The policy of first trying a few similar countries does not work with a website generating business throughout the world.

☐ *The Internet will make it easier for smaller companies to enter international markets.* The following benefits of the Internet will level the playing field between larger and smaller companies: the Internet will reduce the cost of marketing research, and it will allow "niche" product and service providers greater access to the broader market. Costs of global advertising will also be reduced and the general costs of communication will be significantly reduced.

☐ *The Internet will change the manner in which international intermediaries (e.g., agents and distributors) are used.* Distributors normally purchase products for resale setting their prices at what they think the local market will bear. The Internet will make this more difficult as customers become aware of different prices in different countries and seek those which are lower. Many of the traditional marketing and sales functions will also be replaced. The role of these intermediaries will then become more agent-like and more customer service oriented. Value-added customer service will then replace physical distribution as the role for international intermediaries.

☐ *The Internet will bring a larger role to governments that are trying to increase export sales.* Most governments have introduced incentives designed to foster export promotion, particularly for small- and middle-sized businesses. Some of these incentives (e.g., information, overseas contacts, financing sources) can often best be provided on the Internet through a government services webpage.

149. Cross-Cultural E-Mail

E-mail has become one of the most valuable tools for intercontinental communications. When using e-mail across borders, keep the following in mind:[5]

☐ Remember, other cultures may be communicating in their second language.

☐ Try using their language in salutations or closings. End with a personal closing.

☐ Don't judge intelligence based on their grammar or their language skills (when they are communicating in your language).

☐ Don't use acronyms (e.g., FYI, ASAP, etc.).

☐ Watch for abbreviations: "nite" (night); "u" (your).

☐ If the message evokes a negative emotion, defer immediate response (or call them for some personal communication). Avoid "nasty-gram" warfare.

☐ If in doubt, use a formal writing style, rather than informal.

☐ Know the hierarchy of the organization and who is appropriate to copy. Ask, if you don't know.

☐ Try to arrange a face-to-face conversation if at all possible. Video conferencing is a good alternative to international travel.

INTERNATIONAL HUMAN RESOURCES

Excellent employees are a precondition for successful global expansion. This includes people who may office in the home country but who are critical for understanding the needs and desires of their global customers. It also includes people who will actually move abroad and work with local employees to merge operations to create global synergies.

Selection, care, and retention of your "international" people requires understanding of many facets of human resources. This section looks at the key issues and concerns of international human resources.

150. The True Cost of Manufacturing Labor

In deciding where to manufacture, it is useful to examine eight components that help to determine the true cost of labor.

☐ *Compensation.* Clearly salary is a major issue but also consider government-mandated benefits and those that are necessary to attract and retain employees. In Mexican *maquiladoras,* for example, it is usually necessary to provide transportation vouchers, day care centers, and one or two meals to the workers.

☐ *Infrastructure.* To get lower cost workers, is it necessary to build a plant, acquire capital equipment and take on a union? Do you still have capacity elsewhere?

☐ *Worker productivity.* This must be considered in relation to compensation and other factors.

☐ *Transportation and logistical costs.* What do you have to ship to the workers and where does it have to go after it is finished?

☐ *Component costs.* Are major components available in the local markets? If not, are there significant tariff or nontariff barriers to get those components to the place of manufacture?

☐ *Government requirements.* Will the government require any special considerations as to labor, environmental, safety, or other like considerations?

☐ *Management/technical availability.* Even if low-cost, productive, direct laborers are available, what is the availability of technicians and managers? If available, what do they cost and can they be retained?

☐ *Getting out.* How difficult would it be to leave the jurisdiction if you no longer, for whatever reason, wanted to be there?

151. International Human Resource Management

Companies entering into global markets need to consider the human resource (HR) implications of their actions. Below are steps all corporations should consider:

☐ *Determine how HR considerations fit into the entire global development plan.* The critical issue here would be whether the company will establish operations of its own abroad or work through intermediaries (e.g., distributors, franchises); and, if it does establish operations abroad, will it place locals or expatriates in critical management positions?

☐ *Understand your workforce needs.* Determine whether staffing levels will be different in other countries because of cultural and/or legal considerations. Decide whether unions are acceptable, and, if so, under what circumstances. Look at the issue of compensation versus efficiency. Decide how much work you want to outsource.

☐ *Decide if and how you will globalize your workforce.* Will you attempt to apply global standards of recruitment, training, compensation, and termination? Will personnel policies (particularly those concerning employee behavior) be applied worldwide?

☐ *Decide whether you desire a company "foreign service" or whether international assignments will be filled on another basis.* Some companies have attempted to develop a type of foreign service where employees are selected or moved toward international career positions. Such a policy might also include the opportunities for all company employees—wherever situated—to serve in international assignments including corporate headquarters. Other companies prefer to look at overseas assignments as "seasoning" and would, for example, generally limit their French employees to opportunities in France or the French-speaking world.

☐ *Understand the cost of global employment.* Determine what an expatriate might cost instead of a local and don't forget the costs of training and repatriation. Be sure to understand the real costs of compensation in each market and what the HR costs might be if you have to leave a market, especially in a civil law country.

☐ *Develop selection processes which help you consider both the person's temperament for international assignments and business skills.* Be sure to factor in the role of the family and determine whether the total family is suitable for the overseas assignment. The worst of all possibilities is to have an excellent candidate fail because his or her family was not suitable for the assignment.

☐ *Determine what you will offer expatriate employees and explain those terms up-front.* Do you provide mobility bonuses, cost of living, salary premiums, housing allotments, cars, and country clubs? How often will they receive home leave? Will they be required to train their successor? Will a job be guaranteed upon their return?

☐ *Determine the degree of training to be given to international employees.* Those employees who operate out of their home countries but have global activities require one type of training. Expatriates may need training in language, intercultural communications, and general orientation to everyday living in their new assignments.

☐ *Design a repatriation process.* Explain repatriation upon selection. Recognize the possibility of reverse cultural shock and the likelihood of needed financial assistance upon return. Decide whether guaranteed employment will be granted upon repatriation.

☐ *Consider the ethical dimensions of international management.* Does your company want or need to take an ethical position which crosses geographical boundaries? If so, determine your reasons and the manner in which the policy will be implemented. Studies have shown that foreign employees will usually adapt well to the organizational structure of a business, but there is no compelling evidence that ethical behaviors in business cultures will converge in the near future.

152. Global Management Styles

In determining how management styles differ from country to country, it is useful to look at three key variables. These are:

☐ *Degree of organizational planning*—the extent to which the organization must have everything planned carefully, or to merely set organizational goals and allow managers considerable latitude in day-to-day decision-making.
☐ *Degree of organizational hierarchy*—the extent to which the organization is somewhat military in character, where decisions are made in a centralized style, or a situation where decisions are made in a participatory manner with consideration of all points of view.
☐ *Degree of personal involvement in organizational decision-making*—the extent to which "who you know" and how well-connected you are prevail over "who you are."

Using these three parameters, we could arrive at the following generic management styles:

☐ U.S.A.—Lower degree of organizational planning; some hierarchy but more oriented to "who you know"
☐ Japan—High degree of organizational planning and hierarchy, but also highly participatory
☐ Germany—Moderate degree of organizational planning, centralized style and "who you are" rather than "who you know"
☐ Brazil—Low degree of organizational planning, centralized style, and extremely important "who you know"

153. Employee Definitions

The Brazilian labor code defines an employee as any *person* who renders *services* on a *regular basis* to, and *under direction of,* an *employer* in return for a *wage.* This is a fairly standard definition of an employee but how it is interpreted differs from country to country. For example, in Brazil, usually all six of the underlined terms must be present before an employee relationship is said to exist. In the U.S.A., however, no one factor is determinative. The decision is based on whether or not the individual is dependent upon the business for which they work for continued "employment." If they are so dependent, then an employee relationship will be found.

In all business, but particularly in global business, there are three categories that are often used which may not be considered as employees. These are:

☐ *Consultants*—Those who work on their own account and initiative and assume their own risks of success or failure of their business. Consultants normally are not covered by the labor laws and all issues with them are normally a matter of contract.

☐ *Sales representatives and distributors*—Sales representatives obtain a commission for assisting in the sale of products and services. Distributors purchase from the exporter for resale. Neither are considered employees but many countries, states, or provinces provide one or both with "employee-like" protection upon unjust termination.

☐ *Foreign employees*—Foreign employees who are paid abroad and spend limited time in the foreign subsidiary may not be considered local employees. Two factors, however, need to be considered:
  • The immigration laws and regulations that may create worse problems than whether someone is an employee or not
  • Definitions of residency that may give the foreign employee the right to be covered under local laws even if he or she is paid from abroad

154. Hiring Issues

Whether or not a formal written agreement or labor contract is used, the employer must determine the following in the hiring process:

☐ *What is considered salary and what is considered remuneration?* Conventional wisdom indicates that remuneration is salary plus all benefits the employee receives by reason of employment. However, the employer must be sure which benefits count toward determining an employee's compensation as the overall compensation calculation may be the basis to determine disability, retirement, and termination benefits.

☐ *Which benefits are mandated, which are incremental, and what benefits are not allowed?* For example, in some countries, overtime is not allowed unless it is part of a written agreement. The cultural consideration in this case is paramount. While, in the U.S.A., overtime may be viewed as a benefit, in other countries it may be perceived as a detriment.

☐ *Employee tenure is also a consideration.* In some countries, an employee becomes permanent after only 30 days. That means they cannot be terminated thereafter except for "just cause." In other countries, employees of long tenure (10+ years) cannot be fired at all.

☐ *Non-competition and confidentiality are also issues.* To what extent can you preclude your employees from working for a competitor? How confidential must they keep the information of the company or third parties? For how long?

☐ *Invention rights are also a consideration, particularly if the employee is technically oriented.* In some countries, the rights to inventions assigned to the company revert to the employee(s) if the company does not exploit the invention.

155. Termination Issues

While the U.S.A. and a few other countries have modified versions of "employment at will," most countries require that "just cause" for termination be shown for anyone terminated after a short probationary period. If "just cause" cannot be shown, the employer is required to pay termination indemnities. The basic principles are:

☐ Most laws are based on residency not nationality. Foreign employees are likely to be covered while locals working abroad may not be covered. In some cases, the local courts may add up *all* time spent by the employee with the company to determine termination benefits. In one case, an employee was awarded 32 years of benefits even though he had only worked the last two years in that country (and 30 in the previous country).

☐ Labor law and codes set minimum standards that cannot be waived by contract.

☐ Many countries recognized union and strike rights in their legal systems.

- By law, the worker is almost always considered the weaker party. Therefore, ambiguities are viewed in favor of the worker.
- Some countries require workers councils (Germany) or profit sharing (Mexico).

156. Termination: Just Cause

In all but the most extreme cases, a worker can be terminated if "just cause" exists. Unfortunately, the definition of just cause is pretty narrow. Normally included are:

- Death or permanent disability
- Worker resigns on his or her own
- Hired for a short term in a written agreement (usually less than one year) and the term expires
- Terminated within the probationary period
- Incompetence, negligence, theft, and disclosure of confidential information. In some cases, failure to show up for work is not just cause unless it goes on for a long period.
- In some countries when the company is closed or the position is eliminated

Where no just cause exists, the following would be the typical payments due from the employer in most jurisdictions:

- Notice period—usually 30 days
- Seniority pay and interest on same
- Legally mandated bonuses
- Severance pay based on length of service (one month per year is common)
- Any accrued benefits

Finally, the employer should plan for special situations usually related to salary versus remuneration. These include:

- Augmented salaries—e.g., bonuses, automobiles, etc.
- Change of duties—e.g., a "harder" sales territory
- Employees with dual positions—e.g., are they entitled to two full indemnity packages?

157. Globalizing Your Workforce

Sometimes problems arise within international operations because the workforce in the home country lacks the intercultural skills necessary to understand their counterparts in the foreign subsidiaries and affiliates. Examples of areas where such problems are common are:

☐ Degree of identification with the company and its goals
☐ The true number of work hours
☐ The degree to which risk taking is allowed and/or encouraged
☐ To whom and how to explain problems
☐ Direct versus indirect communications
☐ The degree to which one socializes with co-workers
☐ The use of expense accounts
☐ Consequences of poor performance

In addition to those potential issues, there are those "behaviors" that may be mandated by law. The U.S.A., for example, has tough laws protecting workers against racial discrimination and sexual harassment, while other countries' laws are more favorable toward such things as pregnancy and birth issues, worker participation in management, and workers' rights upon termination.

To deal with these intercultural issues, companies have attempted two general approaches. Some larger companies attempt to develop global standards of behavior which they apply in all areas where they are legally free to do so. One example of this would be the U.S.-headquartered company that adapted its policies of corporate ethics for all employees no matter where located.

Most companies rely instead on various degrees of intercultural training for both their home company employees and those abroad. This is often accomplished by attempting to bring those employees together for short periods of time where areas of culture differ significantly (e.g., American vs. Japanese styles of communication).

158. Overseas Assignments

Choosing the right people for international tasks is difficult at best, but failing to make the right decision could be very costly in many ways. In selecting expatriates, consider the following five factors:

Personal motivation. The biggest mistake that could be made would be to send someone abroad who lacks the personal motivation to succeed. This is often done under the guise of "seasoning" a fast-track individual to give that person some international experience.

Family factors. Overseas assignments are often turned down because of family reasons. Three common reasons for turning down an expatriate assignment are family adjustment, spousal resistance, and spousal career.

Personality traits. The three most important personality traits for the expatriate employee are: flexibility and adaptability, interpersonal skills, and entrepreneurial skills. Other related skills include objectivity, imagination, and self-discipline.

Country skills. Knowledge of the local language and culture and, if there is an existing company operation, knowledge of that operation would be helpful.

Company skills. Knowledge of company policies, products, and markets. Technical competence and company loyalty. Knowledge of the industry and of the competitor's modes of operation.

159. Culture Shock

Culture shock relates to a series of reactions to psychological disorientation that most people experience when in a markedly different culture for an extended period of time. Almost all travelers, even the most experienced, experience some form of culture shock. Visitors and successful expatriates usually experience an initial euphoria from the novelty of the situation. This is normally followed by a period of irritation and sometimes hostility for the new culture. This period is the most critical for the family as they are less likely to have the level of activities and the feedback of the expatriate.

Another period of culture shock—often called reverse culture shock—occurs upon repatriation. Particular care should be taken at this point, especially if the expatriate is leery of returning or if conditions have changed dramatically in the home country (such as a large increase in real estate prices).

Coping with culture shock is ultimately the responsibility of the employee and his or her family, but the company can provide some resources to allow the employee to cope with culture shock by:

☐ Providing a corporate contact at headquarters from which the expatriate can be kept informed and can get questions answered.

☐ Providing resources for and access to information about the place of assignment.

☐ Providing substantial feedback to the expatriate. The advent of e-mail has made this much easier.

☐ Allowing for pre-visits to begin the acculturation process.

☐ Allowing liberal home visit policies for the expatriate and his or her family.

☐ Providing tastes of home wherever possible. This could be through local ethnic restaurants, home language movies, and clubs designed for expatriates.

160. Preparing for Assignments Abroad

Preparing for an assignment in another country can be a complex and often frustrating experience. To prevent oversights and errors, consider the following checklist:

☐ *Geographical*—The places of origin, the overseas assignment, and the destination for home leaves

☐ *Duration*—The date the assignment will begin and end, and approximate home leave dates

☐ *Compensation*—
  • Salary and premiums, if any
  • Benefits
  • Position on tax equalization

☐ *Transportation*
  • Class of travel—to and from destination, and home leaves
  • Destination—Automobile, chauffeured limo, other forms of transportation

☐ *Living arrangements*
  • Temporary—Duration and reimbursement, company-approved location required
  • Housing—Type of housing permitted, housing allowances, policies regarding the shipment and reshipment of household goods, use of long-distance telephone privileges

☐ *Documentation*
 • Passports, visas, work permits
 • Vital documents—copies of birth and marriage certificates
 • Medical records
 • Credit card and other needed numbers and PINS
 • Letters of introduction
 • Business cards
 • E-mail site
 • Expense reports
☐ *Medical physicals and vaccinations*
☐ *Special preparations*
 • Language training
 • Intercultural communications training
 • Readings on the history and culture of place of assignment
 • Emergency instructions

161. Expatriate Packages— Salary-Related Issues

Sending employees abroad is expensive, especially if they desire to live in a similar lifestyle to the home country. While companies want to minimize their financial exposure, paying too little or failing to tax equalize could also be a recipe for disaster. Consider the following in constructing your expatriate compensation package:

Base salary. This is normally the same as paid at home and becomes the statistical basis for any premiums to be paid. One mistake often made is to use the base salary of the current place of location. If an employee is located in Omaha but will return after the assignment to Manhattan, then it might make more sense to use Manhattan as a base salary.

Cost of living allowances (COLA). These are normally provided to expatriates based on some cost of living index (e.g., if New York is 100 and Tokyo is 200, the cost of living allowance would be an additional 100 percent). Be sure to use an index that has some relevance to the expatriate's personal situation (e.g., with spouse and children).

Mobility bonus. A simple bonus, usually in one lump sum, may be paid to the employee as an incentive to move. It may also be paid at the time of repatriation to ease the movement back to the home country.

Foreign service premium. A percentage, usually 10–25 percent added to the base salary and/or COLA which is paid as an incentive throughout the assignment. The foreign service premium often creates problems upon return as the employee is used to more money and has difficulty adjusting to the base salary.

Hardship allowances. Still another incentive paid to expatriates are allowances for moving to less than desirable places or where it would be difficult to provide for spouses and children (e.g., lack of suitable schools).

Housing allowances. One of the trickiest of all allowances because often the expatriate has to keep up two residences, and even if the expatriate sells his or her property at home, the employer may have to provide the difference between inflation on real estate and inflation on savings accounts. Another consideration is the cost of utilities and who (especially in the case of long-distance telephone calls) pays for them.

Tax equalization. When an expatriate's taxes are higher than what they would pay at home, should the company tax equalize the employee? This seems like an obvious thing to do especially to get expatriates to take assignments in higher tax jurisdictions. However, the cost of doing so could be very expensive for the company when one considers that all the additional allowances and premiums are taxable, and tax equalization is so complex that the company will have to hire an accounting firm to complete all the tax forms.

162. Expatriate Packages—Non-Salary Issues

In addition to the salaries and various premiums, expatriate employees enjoy a number of other allowances. Included in many packages are:

☐ Moving allowances
☐ Housing allowances (e.g., real estate commissions and closing costs, storage, rental company)
☐ Transportation allowances—everything from a chauffeured limo for top executives down to metro fare with weekend car rentals for lower level employees
☐ Travel expenses to and from assignments

☐ Home leaves
☐ Rest and recreation leaves (e.g., a person in Beijing may get leave in Singapore or Hong Kong)
☐ Education allowances for children in grades K–12 to attend special schools and, in the case of university students, air fare to and from their university
☐ Health and country club memberships
☐ Additional medical care
☐ Use of intercultural communications services

163. Staffing Issues: Expatriates vs. Locals

Once your international branches and subsidiaries are established, you need to consider how to staff the key positions. Some companies opt to staff these positions with expatriates who are normally trusted employees who are familiar with the company's ways of doing business. Other companies prefer locals who would be familiar with the ways of doing business in the country and are usually better connected. A normal approach is to begin new operations with expatriates and then as the business grows and matures to train locals to take their places.

When deciding which approach is best in any given situation, keep the following points in mind:

Degree of headquarters control. The more international operations are to be run from the headquarters, the more logical it would be to choose trusted expatriates over locals.

Newness of the organization. If the foreign organization is new, it is logical to fill a few of the key positions with expatriates—most common are the country executive, financial director and technical personnel. The most popular expatriate position for new companies is the financial director as most companies feel most comfortable with financial decisions in the hands of a trusted employee.

Nature of the organization. If the branch or subsidiary is mainly for marketing and sales, then locals with their knowledge of the market and contacts would be preferable over expatriates. The situation might be different if the business consists of R&D and manufacturing facilities.

Cost factors. Expatriates, particularly those with families, cost up to three times their U.S. salaries in Europe and up to four times their salaries in certain Asian countries. Cost factors are the largest single reason to select locals.

Sophistication of the organization/products. The more sophisticated the organization and its products, the more expatriates might be called for.

Availability of local talent. Local talent may be more available in the U.K. and Japan than in Bulgaria and Bangladesh. Expatriates are often used simply because there is no local talent available.

Availability of expatriates. Simple technical competence, loyalty, and product knowledge does not necessarily make a good expatriate. Independence, resourcefulness, resilience, and tolerance are also necessary—and sometimes those kinds of "talents" cannot be found in the organization.

Importance of local culture/connectiveness. In countries where being connected is paramount to doing business, the local is almost always better than the expatriate. In some situations, however, (e.g., long-term projects) you are better off with a person who is better connected to the company itself.

Employment law considerations. An expensive expatriate may be considered a bargain in countries where it is difficult to terminate the local without paying massive indemnities. Make sure, however, the expatriate doesn't wind up in the same situation because employment laws generally apply to "residents"—not "nationals."

164. The Role of Labor Unions

Occasionally, it is advisable for a company with no unions in its domestic market to use unions abroad (e.g., a house union in a country with high union membership). In other cases, your company will be required to work through unions. Whatever the situation, when working with labor unions, you should remember that it is in the interest of labor unions to cooperate with each other across national boundaries to equalize compensation and benefits for workers employed by the same company in different geographies. To accomplish this, unions are up against some considerable difficulties. Globalization has given management the power to move production from market, thereby weakening local unions.

Once activities are centered out of various countries, it becomes more difficult for unions in any one country to obtain the data they need to determine their bargaining positions. Unions also find it more difficult to identify the decision-makers when there are multiple jurisdictions involved.

Management can choose to use a "divide and conquer" strategy with labor unions, but it also might consider attempting to coordinate its labor relations on a global level which, if handled properly, could be far more efficient. This cooperation may also help global companies in obtaining the information they need to make informed global human resource decisions.

165. Workforce Reductions

Workforce reductions are difficult in any situation but they become even more difficult if they are necessary in one or more foreign jurisdictions. Labor laws and the strength of unions and other employee associations differ from country to country, but generally workforce reductions outside your home market are more costly and time consuming. To lessen needs for workforce reductions, consider the following tips:

☐ Understand local laws and regulations regarding dismissal including advance notice and costs. Reserve some funds to cover these costs.
☐ Work with customers and production people to improve scheduling and to flatten out manpower needs.
☐ Refrain from hiring large numbers of employees during periods of expansion. Consider other alternatives—part time, job services, consultants.
☐ Before downturns become too serious, institute hiring freezes.
☐ If downturns will be six months or less, consider keeping all existing employees in place.
☐ Consider outsourcing more parts and components.
☐ Fill vacancies from within which may allow you to eliminate the lower-level job without any workforce reduction.
☐ Keep workers informed on the company situation during good and bad times.
☐ Look at retirement as an alternative to workforce reduction. In some countries, termination payments are taxable but retirement

distributions are not. Additionally, retirement would come from a fund which is already established while terminations may have to be paid out of existing operations.

166. Repatriation Issues

Repatriation, or returning home after an expatriate assignment, can be a serious problem for both the company and the employee and his/her family. Yet until recently, few companies paid attention to repatriation issues. The conventional wisdom was that,
   since these individuals are returning to a familiar way of life, they should have little problem adapting to the home environment. This conventional wisdom has proven time and again to be wrong as repatriation can be a complicated issue with many variables.

The largest problem faced by the returning expatriate is the readjustment to the home office. Additional problems faced by the employee and his or her family are the general readjustment to the home country's way of life and the issues associated with personal finances.

Readjustment to the home office could be a problem in a number of different areas. Many expatriates are "promoted" to a higher position when they go abroad—perhaps a country executive position in a new market only to go to a perceived lower level upon their return. Even if the compensation is not an issue, the returning employee often feels a sense of loss of authority and longs for being the bigger fish in the smaller pond.

Related to this issue is the degree of autonomy. Foreign assignments tend to provide more autonomy. While this may first be a problem for many, good expatriates often find the ability to make many more decisions on their own to their liking and feel lost when they return to the normal corporate decision-making process.

In today's world, rapidly rising corporate employees need mentors. Often during the expatriate assignment, the mentor may leave the company, retire, change jobs, or lose power. To the expatriate, it can be devastating to return to corporate headquarters to find him- or herself outside the existing power structure. Often, this may mean there is no distinct job to come home to. An example of this is one employee who was sent from his position in the corporate legal department to the position of country manager in Russia because of his language and cultural skills. After returning from a successful term in Moscow, he came back to the legal department to find that his contemporaries had passed him by and that the only positions available did not suit his skills or temperament. He resigned shortly after his return.

167. Repatriation—Family Considerations

Often the person being repatriated is bringing his family back with him. While the family probably hasn't "worked," they will feel many of the same concerns as the repatriate (e.g., lack of autonomy, decline in status). Additionally, family members often have expectations that they will easily adapt to their return "home." The reality, however, is often different.

Family members may have become accustomed to the fringe benefits often given expatriates that include country club memberships, private schools, and, in some cases, domestic help. When they return home, they find none of these available. Also, classmates and friends may have moved on and even the neighbors (or the neighborhood) may be different. The returning family may suffer a form of reverse cultural shock.

Often repatriates also have financial problems. If they sold their home, they may find that values have increased to the point that they can no longer afford a similar home. If they rented their house while they were gone, they may come back to find it in poor shape and needing considerable work. Finally, repatriates may have become accustomed to living at a higher standard of living than they can currently afford. All of these can make the adjustment more difficult than the expectation.

168. Solutions to Repatriation Problems

To lessen the problems associated with repatriation, the following suggestions are offered:

Up-front knowledge—Be sure that both the company and the expatriate have some understanding of the problems of repatriation before they accept the assignment. Use that knowledge to prepare for as many eventualities as can be dealt with.

Keep connection with home—Keep in contact with the expatriate (e-mail, as well as audio and video conferencing are excellent). As part of the expatriate package, allow home visits which require some time at headquarters and allow for home visits for the family. Begin repatriation counseling at least six months before the scheduled date of return.

Compensation—Many companies pay a foreign service premium (an additional sum paid each month while on assignment). This leads to rising expectations. Instead, pay a lump-sum mobility bonus when they go and when they return, along with the employee's standard compensation (adjusted for cost of living). Also, provide for some level of financial assistance upon return.

Counseling. Provide the repatriate and the family with financial and psychological counseling (if needed).

Temporary assignments. Do not allow a repatriate to return without a definite new assignment (even if you continue to pay them). Be creative and attempt to find temporary assignments that could serve as a link between the old and the new (e.g., the former French country executive preparing a report on European operations for the home office team). Be sure to consider the repatriate's former status in determining his or her next assignment.

169. Global Labor Strategies

A company with the potential of having multiple assembly and/or manufacturing facilities abroad needs to determine whether it is possible to develop a global strategy which applies to direct labor. In considering this strategy, keep the following points in mind:

☐ Give one person in the corporate headquarters the responsibility of reviewing the labor relations policies in the various subsidiaries. Give that person the responsibility of developing global policy.

☐ Set up a regular reporting system regarding labor developments.

☐ Develop a company position toward direct employees and determine to what extent it can be implemented worldwide.

☐ Anticipate worker concerns and demands and check to see if they are similar in most or all locations.

☐ Standardize training and development programs. Use trainers from one location to train in other locations.

☐ Take a proactive approach to letting your direct employees understand your side of the story.
☐ Be aware of potential political issues behind labor problems or unrest.
☐ Determine which worker requests can be fulfilled without too much cost or trouble and grant those requests whenever possible.

170. Global Compensation Policies

HR professionals are constantly dealing with the dilemma of finding the best employees and consultants while responding to constant pressure to keep costs down. Additionally, more and more companies are looking at developing global compensation policies. The following factors should be kept in mind:

What is the respective position of the employee in the company? Are they viewed as essential to the company's success or as necessary appendages? If the former, the HR department is far more likely to obtain the attention of top management and global compensation policies are more likely.
Expatriates or locals? If the company would prefer to use expatriates rather than to develop local talent, it is going to be less interested in developing global compensation policies and will be more interested in adjusting to local policies.
Interrelationship of the Research and Development functions. If R & D comes from the interrelationship of the home office and the subsidiaries, then a global compensation system is probably in order. If most R & D is done in the home country and/or through third parties, then globalism is less critical.
Developing global employees. More and more companies look to create international employees. One example of such an employee might be a foreign student who is recruited in the headquarter's country, learns the business through "practical training" and/or work visas, and then returns to a position of authority in their home or other country. This method of recruitment requires global policies.
Simplifying salary administration programs. While more difficult initially, once global compensation programs are in place, they are easier to administer than a hodgepodge of local policies. This does not mean that fixed salaries should be administered centrally, but

that the company should develop basic policies toward compensation; e.g., they will pay in the top third of salary scales of each jurisdiction to attract the best employees.

171. Motivating International Employees

Effective international employment practices require an understanding of the motivational processes, including an understanding of human needs and the hierarchy of needs. This hierarchy differs from country to country and therefore so do motivation techniques.

In the U.S.A., people were largely motivated by compensation and companies acted accordingly. However, in the past decade, Americans' need to compete in the global market has caused a major reassessment of motivation policies based largely on compensation. These policies look more at the employee who is "being" rather than "becoming." They are more oriented toward present needs and more oriented toward community rather than individual needs.

A few years ago, the *Financial Times* looked at what values societies placed on different types of professions. Based on purchase power, the results differ greatly from place to place as illustrated in the following table.

Purchasing Power of a Primary School Teacher in Relation to a Production Department Head

North America	New York	37%
	Toronto	61%
Europe	Paris	43%
	London	81%
	Geneva	100%
Asia	Singapore	32%
	Tokyo	54%

The country that is perhaps the most oriented toward financial compensation as a motivational tool is Japan. This applies even to direct workers and middle management (salarymen). The average Japanese worker receives 25 percent of his compensation through bonuses, while U.S.A. direct laborers rarely receive any bonuses which they can control through specific performance. The Japanese compensation system, however, requires that bonuses (like most else) be earned through teamwork. Additionally, the Japanese have less "perks" which come with being at the top of the hierarchy (executive lunchrooms, large offices, and covered parking).

172. Labor Participation in Decision Making

The manner and degree of labor participation in corporate decision-making differs greatly throughout the world. In some countries, like the U.S.A. and Korea, labor decision-marking participation is limited even where labor unions are present. On the other end of the scale are countries like Germany and Sweden where worker participation in management decisions is legally mandated.

In countries like Japan and Sweden, labor plays a significant role in decision-making on the shop floor where teams are involved in quality decisions and sometimes even the configuration of the factory floor. This type of decision-making power is growing rapidly in many countries.

Labor participation in management, often called codetermination, is important in many of the European countries. In large companies in Germany, a supervisory board made up equally of management and labor runs the company on a day-to-day basis and reports to the company boards of directors. The Netherlands also uses codetermination but labor has minority participation and therefore less participation in day-to-day management.

In countries like the U.K., worker participation is often even at the board level. British work councils provide workers a say on corporate boards and give them access to documents normally reserved only for board members, making employees privy to important information that often changes the nature of the discussion. Many European companies have some form of work councils.

Risk Management and Corporate Security

Safety of your people and corporate assets is a major consideration in these days of unstable countries and organized terrorism. In this section, some valuable tips are provided on how to deal with some important security issues.

173. Country Risk Assessment

Country risk assessment is an important factor in making foreign investment decisions. Traditionally, companies tended to look at country risk from the point of view of nationalization and expropriation but, in recent years, country risk assessment has become more complex. The following issues should be looked at in any analysis of country risk:

Financial

☐ Tariff barriers
☐ Nontariff barriers including such items as packaging, marking, and labeling
☐ Currency stability and convertibility
☐ Price controls
☐ Policies favoring local business—mandated or cultural
☐ Role of state enterprises in business

Political

☐ Military's role in government
☐ Corruption
☐ Religious/ethnic pressures
☐ Power relationship between executive and other branches of government
☐ Fairness of the legal systems and the courts
☐ Regional issues

174. Governmental Instabilities

While the 1990s brought a larger number of countries under democratic rule, one must still be aware of the telltale signs of a possible coup—whether from the military or "revolutionaries." The following are these danger signs:

Elections about to take place. This is especially likely if the elections are perceived to be close or where a major shift of ideological power is likely.

Emergence or strengthening of extremist groups. This normally indicates displeasure with the existing government.

Disputes among the armed services, where one branch may attempt to take over the government.

Economic problems and the institution of International Monetary Fund (IMF) or other austerity programs. These often cut essential government services and lead to protest.

Outbreak or increase of terrorism, which may either destabilize a government or force it to take unpopular actions.

Problems among minority groups or minority regions.

Crackdown on the free press or other areas of expression.

In some countries, like Colombia, these problems are endemic and do not directly destabilize governments. In fact, Colombia has one of the best traditions of uninterrupted democracy in South America. On the other hand, the endemic instability does increase the risk of doing business. In other countries, governments fall frequently but an underlying elite and/or bureaucracy make them lower political risks than countries that are more politically stable.

175. Employee Safety in High-Risk Areas

Kidnapping is big business and has become more prominent in recent years. Additionally, high-profile business travelers are subject to other forms of criminal exploitation such as bombing, robbery, and assault. The best single method of protection is to convince such employees to adopt a lower profile, but this is not always desirable or possible. Enclosed are some ideas to help keep employees safe:

☐ Attempt to keep photos of key employees and their families out of the press and television.
☐ Keep out of the social pages of the newspaper.
☐ Don't use limousines or other high-profile vehicles.
☐ Employees' schedules should only be given to people on a need-to-know basis.
☐ Housing should be unpretentious on the outside and have proper security devices.
☐ Provide security training to all needed employees.
☐ Keep telephone listings private.
☐ Use different routes to get to and from work.

176. Kidnapping: Do's and Don'ts

While being kidnapped is a traumatic event that happens very fast, you can significantly increase your chances of survival by remembering some logical points:

Do:

☐ Attempt to remain calm and develop mental disciplines that will allow you to maintain that calm. Develop routines (mental and/or physical) that you can undertake on a daily basis.
☐ Attempt to convince your captors that you are not as important as they may think. Be humble but not subservient.
☐ Communicate special needs, particularly medical needs.
☐ Note your surroundings and details of your captors to the extent possible.
☐ Expect to be kept for some time.
☐ Try to earn their respect.

Don't:

☐ Attempt to negotiate your own release.
☐ Antagonize your captors in any way but particularly by arguing against their cause.
☐ Let your captors dominate your mind.
☐ Become too hopeful or too depressed. Strive to keep a steady state of mind.

☐ Give up on those who will be trying to get you released.
☐ Attempt to escape unless you are reasonably sure you will succeed.
☐ Give your captors any information on your company or other members of your family.

177. Security in International Air Travel

The following general tips will increase your security when travelling internationally:

☐ Check with your travel agent or government agent to determine which areas are not deemed safe to travel.
☐ Do not use company business cards on your luggage.
☐ Do not openly display your passport, visa, or other travel documents.
☐ Arrange to be met at all destinations.
☐ Take the most direct routes. Consider spending a bit more to obtain these routes.
☐ Use executive clubs and lounges whenever possible.
☐ Avoid smaller airlines and smaller aircraft (which are easier to hijack).
☐ Consider meeting in a safer mid-route location—such as New York travelers meeting Colombians in Orlando, Florida, for instance.
☐ Understand ground transportation alternatives if you can't be met. Avoid "gypsy" taxis.
☐ Travel as light as possible.
☐ Avoid wearing expensive jewelry and watches.

International Legal Management

Legal issues and concerns can make a difference between success or failure in international operations, and the selection and use of good counsel can often save a company considerable time and costs. In this section, we will review how to organize your legal function for the optimal efficiency, as well as the legal issues and concerns that you are most likely to face in your international expansion.

178. Legal Differences

Businesspersons create problems for themselves because they or their lawyers often fail to understand the differences in the legal systems in the countries they are dealing with. For example, Americans often try to obtain approval for lengthy contracts covering every eventuality in societies where most eventualities are covered by codes so that legal agreements need only cover the basic terms and conditions—such as price, delivery, and warranties.

While every legal system is different, they can generally be divided into four categories:

☐ *Common law*—the U.S.A., Great Britain, and some former members of the British Commonwealth (including Australia, Canada, and to some extent India). Some of its major characteristics are:
  • The importance and quantity of lawyers.
  • Relative freedom of contract, often resulting in longer, more detailed agreements.
  • Laws and statutes tend to be general and can often be altered by agreements, bureaucratic agencies, or judges.
  • The importance of precedence—judicial decisions can become current versions of the law. Judges determine both facts and laws.
☐ *Civil law*—Common to continental Europe and has been adopted by many former European colonies including all of Latin America. Civil law is characterized by the existence of written hierarchic norms (a constitution, laws, regulations, decrees and directives)

that courts must apply to the resolution of conflict. Some of its major characteristics are:
- Lesser number and status for lawyers and judges
- More formal—important role for notaries
- Shorter, less detailed contracts—if details are already in the codes, there is no need to cover them in the contract
- Specific codes include—civil, commercial, tax, property and labor
- Judges determine facts but must apply the codes. Former judicial decisions are not binding on the judge(s) hearing a particular case.

☐ *Islamic law*—While many Islamic countries have developed aspects of civil and/or common law, they continue to require that these laws be interpreted in harmony with God's rules and the Koran. The area of greatest interest to foreign businesspersons operating in Islamic countries would be the charging of interest which is in moral conflict with Islamic Law. While the individual Islamic countries have developed some alternatives such as certain accepted "service charges," one must be careful on how these are applied. One solution is to build interest charges into the price of the product.

☐ *Socialist law*—While the number of socialist countries is declining, one must still consider socialist law in dealing with the People's Republic of China, Vietnam, North Korea, and Cuba. Additionally, remnants of socialist law exist in Eastern Europe and the former Soviet Union. Since socialist law is based on codes, it is most similar to civil law. However, this law tends to be more mechanical and cumbersome than the civil law one might find in France or Mexico. Some examples of the differences are:
- All contracts must be in writing—in most civil law countries, a contract can be proved by the oral acts of the parties.
- There can be no gaps in the contract.
- Contracts must state exact price(s).
- Material breach of contracts more closely resemble quasi-criminal violations for breaching one's obligation to the State.

179. The Extraterritorial Impact of U.S. Law

Coming out of the Cold War and the Watergate eras, the U.S.A. developed a series of laws that have extraterritorial effect—that is, they are deemed to apply to U.S. companies and their partners and U.S. products *outside the United States*. While not all laws are covered (e.g., environmental and occupational safety), one should be aware of the laws that do apply and how they may impact your ability to do business.

The following laws have been deemed to be extraterritorial:

☐ *Exports and export administration*—In the U.S.A., exporting is a privilege, not a right. To obtain that privilege, an export license is needed for all U.S. products and, in most cases, for products coming out of the U.S. Most products are licensed through the Shippers Declaration but certain products require validated licenses. Additionally, most exports to some countries (e.g., Cuba, North Korea, Libya, and Iraq) require such licenses.
  - U.S.A. products are deemed to be those with 25 percent or more U.S.A. content, although a product which passes through U.S.A. jurisdiction may be deemed a U.S.A. product.
  - Services and technology are included in the law in addition to products.
  - The law applies to anyone dealing with U.S.A. products. A distributor in France cannot sell a U.S.A. product to Cuba without a license from the U.S.A. government, and the manufacturer and/or exporter has the ultimate responsibility for adherence to U.S.A. law.
  - U.S.A. laws can also be violated by telephone, fax, and e-mail.
  - The U.S.A. government uses a "red flag" concept that identifies obvious items which exporters are encouraged to take notice (e.g., an Arabic language computer sold to Bolivia). In such a circumstance, the exporter must determine whether such shipments receive validated licenses.

☐ *Bribery/foreign corrupt practices*—Passed in the aftermath of Watergate, the Foreign Corrupt Practices Act (FCPA) of 1977 remains law partially because no politician wants to come out in favor of corruption. Designed to deal with foreign bribery, it also applies domestically. The FCPA makes it illegal for any company to bribe any "foreign official for the purpose of obtaining business."
  - The law applies to foreign subsidiaries and to foreign agents, distributors, or parties of U.S.A. companies.
  - A foreign official is anyone in power and any member of a political party whether or not in power.
  - Obtaining business also includes retaining business.

- The FCPA excludes small payments that are to expedite or to secure the performance of a "routine government action"—the so-called *facilitating payments*.
- The red flag concept also applies.

☐ *International boycotts*—The purpose of two laws passed in the late 1970s is to prevent American companies from assisting in the Arab Boycott of Israel. The first law (the "Ribicoff Amendment") provides for the loss of certain tax benefits for companies participating or cooperating with the boycott. The second law provides severe monetary penalties and loss of export privileges for companies who furnish information about business dealings with Israel to Arab countries, and for those who fail to report such requests.

- Foreign subsidiaries of American companies are covered by the laws.
- If you are asked about Israeli business dealings, you simply cannot answer about your relations or non-relations with Israel, although you can answer other requests (e.g., size, color, quantity, price).
- You must report all requests to the Office of Antiboycott Compliance (OAC).

☐ *Antitrust laws*—While American antitrust laws have extraterritorial impact, these laws are designed to benefit the American consumer. Therefore, some provisions may simply not be applied in international transactions. Those that might apply abroad are:

- Boycott—An agreement of two companies not to do business with a third.
- Monopolies—Those actions leading to monopolies or near monopolies.
- Reciprocity—"If you will not buy my goods, I will not buy yours."
- Tying agreements—"If you want product A, you must also take some product B."
- The Robinson-Patman Act—An act that grants lower prices to large buyers.

☐ *Labor and employment*—Provisions of various laws concerning employee discrimination and other labor laws do apply to American citizens and permanent residents of U.S. companies abroad.

180. Managing International Legal Affairs

Since legal departments are normally cost centers, it is essential that the company's lawyers manage their affairs with a minimum of disruption and cost. The following tips are intended to help you meet those goals:

For Companies With No Internal Legal Function

Have the selection of and interfacings with all lawyers come through one checkpoint. This function is often performed by the Chief Financial Officer (CFO) because of budget control.

If the volume of work allows, have an internal employee perform as many of the paralegal functions as possible.

Establish a relationship with a local lawyer (or law firm) with international expertise. Use this person (firm) to develop your global standard agreements and to answer general strategic questions.

Work with your outside attorney to establish a list of contact points in each country you are doing business.

Concentrate on preventive legal strategies.

For Companies With An Internal Legal Function But No International Lawyer

Determine if one of your existing lawyers would like to play that role. Provide encouragement and training.

Decide how much of the international work you can actually do and how much the Legal Department will act as traffic cops.

Develop a solid contact with an international lawyer and law firm in your home community. Give them some work from time to time so you can get their attention when you really need them. Use these attorneys as a sounding board.

Develop a list of in-country attorneys to use as projects develop.

Establish a set of guidelines for outside attorneys to follow. Don't make them so onerous, however, that good attorneys will lose interest in representing your business.

For Companies With One Or More
International Attorneys

Have these attorneys responsible for their own budget.
Use these attorneys to perform preventive law training on
    international issues.
If you have more than one attorney, have them specialize either by
    division or geography depending on their expertise.
Consider having these attorneys report both to the head of the
    division or geography and the General Counsel.

181. How Foreign Investment is Regulated

Almost every country in the world provides for some regulation of
incoming investment. Some countries do everything they can to
encourage foreign investment, including financial incentives, restrict-
ing markets, and tax holidays. Other countries, concerned about promoting national plans and protecting local industries place more negative restrictions on foreign investments including limited percentages
of ownership, restrictions on repatriating of investments and profits,
R&D, and local employment requirements.

Most countries, including the U.S.A., have a mixed foreign investment regime. American states often provide excellent incentives to foreign companies providing investments and jobs in their markets, while
the U.S.A. federal government attempts to preserve certain industries to
American companies (e.g., mass media, airlines, and nuclear power).

When contemplating investment abroad, consider the following
points:

☐ Will your investment be complementary to national investment?
☐ Will it replace local businesses that have been performing
    satisfactorily?
☐ Will it have a positive effect on the balance of payments of the
    country in which it is invested?
☐ Impact on employment including job opportunities and wages paid?
☐ Will it help develop higher level employment?
☐ If including manufacturing or assembly, will it integrate domestic
    components?
☐ Will it contribute to the technological base of the country?
☐ Will it improve prices, quality, or both?

If your investment meets some of these criteria, it is likely to be welcomed. Make sure that the local authorities are familiar with what you are bringing into their countries.

182. The Operational Code

Even a mediocre lawyer may know the written law but it takes a good lawyer to understand the *operational code*. The operational code is the combination of written and unwritten rules and practices that determine what can and cannot be done at any given point of time. In a foreign environment, knowing the operational code can place you at a distinct advantage.

Virtually all laws, decrees, regulations, and directives are subject to some interpretation. The degree of interpretation will depend on the subject matter of the law and the country. While many developing countries will develop liberal interpretations of nearly all commercial laws, some countries like the U.S.A. are known for the broad authority to make exceptions to their tax and immigration laws.

In 1980, a major computer company asked the Mexican government for an exception to the 49 percent foreign ownership rule. The government eventually said yes but only after requiring the company to locate its plant in a rural area and an agreement that they would sell part of the company to Mexicans within five years. In 1985, another major computer company asked for the same exception and received it without any requirements.

Both companies had good lawyers and other professionals. The difference was that, in 1980, oil was over $30 per barrel and Mexico was undergoing a major expansion. By 1985, oil had declined to $14 per barrel and Mexico was mired in the global monetary debt crisis. Look for lawyers and other advisors who know the operational code, and remember that knowledge of the written law is only the beginning.

183. The United Nations' Convention on the International Sale of Goods

Billed as an international version of the Uniform Commercial Code (UCC) in the U.S.A., the United Nations developed the Convention on the International Sale of Goods (CISG) to standardize international terms and conditions governing international sales. The CISG began on January 1, 1988, and now has been ratified by more than 40 countries, including the U.S.A., Mexico, Russia, France, Germany, Canada, and China. Great Britain and Japan are not signatories.

The CISG is a mixture of common law and civil law and may be somewhat confusing to an attorney who is trained in only one type of law. It covers only goods (not services); consumer goods (if sold directly to the customer) are excluded.

Our advice would be to build a specific "opt-out" of the CISG statement into all international contracts that deal in whole or in part in goods. Reasons:

☐ If the contract is between two signatory states (e.g., the U.S.A. and Canada), the CISG will automatically apply unless there is definitive language opting out of the CISG. Therefore, an agreement between companies in the U.S. and Canada—two common law countries—might be governed by some aspects of civil law.
☐ CISG covers only the "formation of the contract" and "rights and obligations" of the parties. It does not cover contract validity, title issues, and the rights of third parties. Therefore, many disputes might have to be resolved as a mixture of the CISG and local law.
☐ Judges in most countries don't know the CISG and don't seem to want to learn it.
☐ The CISG has not been adequately tested in the courts of the signatory nations.

While the CISG is a definite step forward in international business law, you are normally better off with your local commercial law than being the test case for new laws.

184. Selecting International Legal Counsel

The choice of foreign lawyers can be critical to the success of your business because often such individuals represent an independent sounding board between the agendas of your own people and those of your suppliers and customers abroad.

When selecting foreign attorneys, keep in mind that these attorneys should have:

Technical knowledge. It is essential that the attorneys have good technical knowledge of the law and your industry.

Operational code knowledge. In addition to technical knowledge, good lawyers know how laws and regulations are being interpreted and what projects are likely to be approved.

Government contacts. Such contacts are needed to facilitate government approvals.

An understanding of your culture. A good foreign lawyer understands your culture and such things as your negotiation styles and sense of timing. When things are not going your way, they should be able to explain why in ways you can understand.

An understanding of your language. Unless your people are fully capable in dealing in the local language, the attorney must be fluent enough to interpret local laws in a manner understandable to you.

Knowledge of your legal system. The lawyer may not be familiar with your country's specific laws, but he or she should at least be familiar with your legal system.

Assurance of complete confidence and trust.

Availability for the long run. Chances are the lawyer will be needed after the agreement is signed to make sure that it is implemented and to be kept informed to provide observations and advice on the continuing conduct of business.

A clear explanation of their legal fees. Some lawyers bill monthly, others will not bill until a project is done. Some explain everything they do while others might send you a very large bill for "legal work." To avoid unpleasant surprises and unbudgeted expenses, make sure you know what, how, and when in relation to legal fees and expenses.

185. Protecting Intellectual Property

One particularly large, and often forgotten, cost of international expansion is the protection of intellectual property. Patents and trademarks are territorial and without taking action to file overseas, your protection will be limited to the home country. The good news is that there are a series of international conventions to protect intellectual property. The bad news is that, with the exception of the EEC for community registration, you must register in each country individually. In that case, intellectual property considerations and costs must become an important consideration in the decision to enter into or expand international markets.

To provide some sense of the issue, suppose your company has three trademarks and wants to appoint distributors in 15 different countries. To fully protect the trademarks, it would require 45 registrations. Assuming this cost is around U.S.$1,000 per registration (fees and legal costs), the company has a U.S.$45,000 up-front cost to enter these markets. If the trademark already exists in the name of another entity or person, the costs of challenging it or buying it out might considerably increase the cost of entry.

Patents and trademarks are protected by the Paris Convention that includes virtually every important country except Taiwan, Thailand, and India. Under the Convention, patents are protected for one year from the date of first registration while trademarks have six months. "Famous" marks can be protected even if not registered.

It may not be necessary to register patents in as many jurisdictions as other intellectual property. In registering patents, the chief considerations are the size of the country market and the capabilities of production of the patented goods in those markets. Even very large companies may not register their patents in countries like Mongolia and Somalia.

186. Alternative Dispute Resolutions

In preparing your agreements, you should consider whether you would prefer to litigate or provide for some other form of dispute resolution in the event that major problems arise between the parties. What follows are some general considerations regarding when you should litigate and when you should seek other forms:

Litigate:

☐ When the parties have chosen your law and your courts
☐ When the key issue which might arise is payment and you have⁻ provided for promissory notes or other like procedures which could lead to executory proceedings in the courts
☐ Where you might seek remedies other than financial (e.g., injunctions or specific performance)
☐ Where the enforceability of arbitral awards might be difficult in the country where they need to be enforced (e.g., lack of treaties)

Seek Other Forms of Dispute Resolution:

☐ When you perceive the local courts may be biased
☐ When you will need to defer issues to experts in your business
  rather than a judge
☐ To avoid courts with little international experience
☐ When you would prefer a decision with no right to appeal
☐ When you want representatives of both parties actually involved in
  making the decision(s)—That is, each party has the right to pick
  the mediators or arbitrators

187. International Arbitration

The differences between a trial and an arbitration are significant and should be considered as part of the decision regarding the best method of dispute resolution.

☐ Arbitration is usually initiated by a simple demand and if both
  parties are willing to arbitrate, the arbitration will commence in a
  number of months. Since a trial will be in one party's favored
  courts, the other party may issue procedural and other challenges
  to delay the court hearing for years.
☐ Arbitration hearings will be episodic while trials tend to be
  continuous.
☐ Arbitrations will have less discovery and almost no use of depositions.
☐ Arbitrations in civil law countries are less likely to have live
  witnesses and the discourse will take place between the arbitrators
  and legal counsel.
☐ Arbitral awards are rarely challenged and almost never overturned.

While arbitration may not be cheaper than litigation (particularly if there are multiple arbitrators), it is likely to be faster and not subject to appeal. However, to achieve those goals it is important to have your attorney draft arbitration language that is clear and concise.

188. Key Items for International Agreements

One of the biggest mistakes of companies entering the international arena is to use their domestic agreements for the international suppliers, marketeers, and customers. That approach fails to consider differences in language, cultural orientation, business practices, and the applicable local law. While it would be both time-consuming and expensive to draft a different agreement for each country, here are a number of areas that must be covered in all international agreements.

- [ ] Choice of law—law of one of the parties or a third country
- [ ] Choice of forum—courts of one country or, in some cases, the courts of a neutral third country
- [ ] International dispute resolution—you are much more likely to choose arbitration in an international agreement to avoid local biases
- [ ] Clearly define territory and, if appropriate, customers
- [ ] Delivery terms
- [ ] Payment terms—letters of credit or other forms popular in cross border transactions
- [ ] Currency issues—particularly currency of payment and exchange rate conversion and timing
- [ ] Responsibility for achieving local government approvals
- [ ] Term and termination—consequences of same
- [ ] CISG opt-out statements

189. Application of Law

Whenever reasonably possible, you should have the laws of your home country apply to your international agreements. Besides the obvious reason of understanding these laws, international issues also need to be considered.

Even if the foreign party disregards the choice of law and enters into litigation in its local courts under the local law, the judgment may have to be enforced in your home country. In the enforcement hearing, your local courts will have a chance to then apply the law agreed to in the contract and, if necessary, amend or overturn the earlier decision.

If you are entering into a contract in a country where you feel very uncomfortable with the local law, but the other party refuses to accept your law, then consider a third country's law. Many developing or unstable countries will accept U.K. or Swedish law. If you must accept the foreign local law, however, consider either arbitration under that law or compromise so that the foreign law may be selected but all cases must be arbitrated or tried outside that country.

When the U.S.-Iran Claims Tribune was first established, it needed to decide which cases it had jurisdiction over. The decision was that if the parties had elected Iranian law that the cases should be adjudicated in Iran. Companies who had designated other than Iranian laws had their cases heard by the tribunal and a chance at the more than U.S.$1 billion set aside to resolve those claims.

190. The Controlling Language of the Agreement

English is almost universally accepted as the language of international business. In fact, it is also becoming the compromise language among non-native speakers of different languages. However, the issue often remains which language will control the Agreement. This is especially true when the agreements are drafted in two or more languages. In resolving this issue, here are some do's and don'ts:

Do's:

☐ Whichever language is used, make sure the agreement is written in as simple language as possible. Avoid legal boilerplate.
☐ Use the language that will be the most applied in the day-to-day operations.
☐ If you must choose the foreign language (often for legal purposes), add a provision that day-to-day communications will be in your home language.
☐ Provide clear definitions of any major terms used in the agreements.
☐ Use charts and other illustrations whenever possible.

Don'ts:

☐ Have the agreement written in both languages, each of which are equally binding. This doesn't work.
☐ Provide for different languages for commercial versus technical terms.

MARKET ENTRY STRATEGIES—GLOBAL BUSINESS WITHOUT LEAVING HOME

Going international can be accomplished by several methods, one of which is being an importer of goods, services, or capital. A company that only imports is also an international company that must be concerned about cultural differences. They need to be savvy in negotiating across borders and, like exporters, may be involved in adapting products and services for local markets. Finally, importers need also to develop the personnel and management tools necessary to undertake international trade and finance.

In this section, we will explore the following concepts:

☐ Sourcing foreign components and labor
☐ Representing a foreign business or selling foreign products into the domestic market, agents and distributors, and licensing foreign technologies, including franchising
☐ Exporting from the home country using catalogs or traveling salespersons

191. International Sourcing

In order to remain competitive in both home and foreign markets, many companies are now choosing to acquire some of their products, parts, and/or components from abroad. Additionally, even companies that produce a large portion of their products through their own facilities are now finding, for a number of reasons, that it is better to begin to move to suppliers, both domestic and foreign, in order to reduce costs and labor commitments and to protect the interests of their shareholders. This is commonly known as outsourcing.

When a company is considering replacing domestic suppliers with foreign suppliers, or in moving from direct production to foreign suppliers, it will do so for the following reasons:

Price: Can a company reduce costs by moving production to countries where labor and/or productions costs are lower?
Quality: Can quality be improved or retained in a lower-price environment, or can quality be significantly increased with no, or only slight, price increases?

*Unavailability of domestic product or lack of consistency of local
production.*

Faster delivery. U.S. companies on or near the Canadian and Mexican
borders sometimes find faster turnaround from companies in
Northern Mexico or Canada than from companies in parts of the
U.S.A. In fact, many large Japanese companies established final-
assembly operations in Tijuana, Mexico, to be close to their
customers in California.

Better technology or technical services, such as just-in-time inventory
management.

Competitive factors. Source abroad as a vehicle to keep the prices of
domestic suppliers low, and to assure continuity of supply.

However, international sourcing also has its share of problems.
Some of these are:

Difficulties in evaluating and selecting foreign suppliers. Sourcing
abroad requires additional resources to locate and qualify foreign
suppliers. Buyer's agents must sometimes be sought. Once selected,
the management process can be difficult.

Quality. More efforts have to be made to assure quality control and
to limit the percentage of rejects.

Delivery time. The potential importers must consider the additional
variables which could extend delivery times. Even the best
production and inventory management techniques can be defeated
by customs problems.

Political and labor problems

Currency fluctuations and payment problems

Paperwork and extra documentation costs

Marking and labeling issues

192. Agents

Agents are independent companies (and sometimes individuals)
who represent foreign exporters and take orders on the exporter's
behalf. Agents normally work on a commission basis and are paid
when the exporter makes a direct sale to the customer. They do not
take title to, or possession of, the goods or services they represent and
the prices to be charged are agreed to between the seller and the

buyer. Normally, agents do not stock products, nor do they provide pre- and post-sales support to the customer.

Companies will normally appoint foreign agents if they are not ready to establish their own operations but wish to deal directly with distinct individual customers, or to seek customers on a Request for Proposal (RFP) or project basis. The skill requirements for agents are normally personal contacts and some industry experience. Technical skills will not be sought except in particular cases.

The biggest single area of disputes involving agents, both during and after the relationship, is over commissions and the commission structure. The following issues are typical:

☐ *Commission payments.* Some agents will need a nonrefundable up-front payment, particularly if up-front expenses may be high and/or the possibility of success may be limited. Additionally, it needs to be determined whether commissions are due upon completion of the sale or whether the agent's responsibilities will be tied to collections.

☐ *Methods of resolving disputed commissions.* Disputed commissions arise when there is more than one agent involved, when the principal feels that he has "handled" the sale, or when the relationship between the principal and agent has ended before the work is completed and/or the customer has made all payments.

☐ *How long will commissions apply?* Once an agent has introduced a customer to the principal, how long is the agent entitled to a commission for products and services sold to the customer? This will depend on a number of circumstances including the agent's continual involvement with the customer. Additionally, is an agent who has introduced a prospect to the principal entitled to a commission (full or partial), even if the sale is made after the relationship between the principal and agent has finished?

☐ *Effects of price reductions on commission structure.* Agent commissions are often set with the assumption of a sales price to the customer within a certain range. Disputes arise when customer negotiations result in considerable price reductions. Often the agent is then requested to decrease his or her compensation to make the sale and/or to increase the principal's margin.

☐ *Whether the agent will obtain commissions on products or services sold directly by the principal in the agent's territory (with or without the agent's involvement).* To a certain degree, this relates to whether the agent is exclusive or nonexclusive, but even when nonexclusive there may be some reasons to give the agent at least a partial commission on direct sales.

To resolve such issues and avoid problems, it is necessary to define these issues as clearly as possible in a definitive legal agreement. In deciding to become an agent, you should look for a principal with the following profile:

Principal's Profile

1. International reputation as a fair and honest business operation
2. International experience and knowledge, especially in working with agents
3. Truly needs agents
4. Willing to sign an agreement that clearly specifies territory, commission structure, and payment
5. Willing to give exclusivity in certain markets, or in regard to certain customers
6. Willing to provide training and marketing materials
7. Offers clear guidelines on the agent's discretionary authority, if any
8. Willing to take sufficient time to develop the local market

193. Distributors

Distributors are independent companies that purchase products (take title) from the foreign manufacturer or other importers to sell in the distributors' markets. The products purchased are intended for resale to the distributors' customers which can be either the actual end-user or another intermediary.

While sometimes it is necessary to make alterations to the products, distributors normally sell what they purchase. Distributors assume the risks of buying and stocking the products in the local markets and normally will also provide product support and other after-market services. Distributors establish and maintain their own contacts with their customers, including setting prices they will charge to those customers. They are also normally responsible for local advertising and promotion.

The biggest areas of concerns in becoming a distributor for a foreign company are *territory* and *pricing*. Your company should not take an appointment unless you are absolutely sure that the *territory* will be sufficient to support the business. What is a reasonable territory is ultimately a business decision based on a multitude of factors. However, your company should resolve, beforehand, how many other local competitors the importer will allow into your market, and whether the importer desires to sell direct or will refer all contracts in the territory to your company and/or others appointed in the territory.

You should also be sure that the importer's *pricing* to you is sufficient to provide your company with a reasonable rate of return. Since you will control the price in your local market, you should determine whether you will be able to price the products to be competitive in the marketplace. For example, a 25 percent discount off an importer's international list may be sufficient if you can charge a premium in the marketplace, but may not be enough in an extremely competitive environment. Throughout the entire relationship, you will need to work with the importer to achieve the optimal price that provides for competitive flexibility while maintaining a volume of sales.

As a local distributor of a foreign company, you should develop a relationship with a foreign manufacturer/importer who has the following profile:

Importer's Profile

1. International reputation as a fair and honest business operation
2. International experience and knowledge
3. Reputation for quality products and services
4. Has, or is developing, a distributor relations function in its corporate or regional headquarters
5. Willing to designate a contract person or function who is responsible for dealing with your operations
6. Committed to using distributors in your territory for some time in the future
7. Willing to offer a balanced and realistic legal agreement
8. Willing to provide sufficient marketing materials
9. Willing to offer training on a regular basis
10. Recognition of the unique characteristics of your marketplace (e.g., local marking and labeling requirements)
11. Willing to provide you with sufficient territory and allow expansion if you are successful
12. Offers pricing that is realistic and suits the vagaries of your marketplace
13. If applicable to your industry, offers good opportunities to make additional profits in after-market activities

194. Licensing

Licensing is normally a contractual arrangement in which the *licensor* (granting company) grants access to its technology, patents, trademarks, copyrights, trade secrets, know-how, and other intellectual property to a foreign *licensee* (receiving company) to be used by the licensee in exchange for a fee and/or other considerations. This grant may be in the form of a direct sale of rights or is limited to a certain period of time. International licensing can be tied to sourcing, joint ventures, distributors, and agents, and can be part of intercompany agreements between the parent and subsidiary.

From the licensee's perspective, the following points should be kept in mind:

☐ *To what degree will the licensor attempt to become involved in the licensee's activities?* If the technology transferred is complicated, the licensee may seek the licensor's assistance early on to understand and implement the technology. At that point, it may be important to assure the availability of foreign technicians. However, if the licensor continues to insist on close monitoring of the licensee's activities, make sure the reason for this is not to learn the local nuances and customer base so that the licensor will be prepared to enter the market directly at some later date.

☐ *Apply the fairness principle.* From the licensee's perspective, high royalties and component prices will have to be adjusted downward if the licensee perceives and can show the licensor that it is not receiving its fair share of the profits. However, licensors will soon lose interest in licensees who are not providing it with sufficient revenues and/or profits to justify the relationship.

☐ Include some mechanism for resolving misunderstandings short of the standard legal mechanisms. The licensee should assure that the licensor will assign one individual (normally one of its employees), who will stay with the project throughout completion. This individual should attempt to understand the workings of the licensee and to "represent its views" before the licensor. Additionally, communications should be regularized and problems not allowed to fester.

To assist in finding the proper licensor, the licensee might look at the characteristics cited in the licensor profile in the following profile.

Licensor's Profile

---

1. Experience in licensing, particularly international licensing with high quality technology
2. Fairly-priced services and components
3. Available and willing to provide continuing assistance, either included as part of the royalties or at reasonable fees
4. Willing to allow for licensee innovations
5. Willing to provide updates, enhancements, and new products
6. Willing to consider granting exclusive rights, or to allow licensee to earn exclusive rights
7. Willing to allow for increased vertical integration, that is, allowing more of the product to be produced by the licensee as it learns the technology
8. Willing to consider reasonable territorial expansion
9. Desires a long-term relationship
10. Considers your territory a valuable one
11. Willing to protect the licensee from encroachment from other licensees
12. Willing to protect the licensee against challenges to the licensor's intellectual property

---

195. Franchising

A franchise operation is a contractual relationship between the franchisor and franchisee, in which the franchisor offers, or is obligated to maintain, a continuous interest in the business of the franchisee in such areas as know-how and training, wherein the franchisee operates under a common trade name, format, or procedure owned or controlled by the franchisor, and in which the franchisee has made, or will make, a substantial capital investment in the business from his own resources.

To take advantage of franchise opportunities, the franchisee (the company who takes the franchise) should consider the following about their ability to be a franchisee:

Business experience, knowledge, and acumen in one area does not necessarily equate to the same in another area. An international banker may not have the acumen to run a restaurant. Likewise, a former executive from a major food corporation may not do well in tire sales and related services.

Lack of business experience in the subject matter of the franchise can be overcome if the franchisee is willing to accept advice and guidance from the franchisor. However, if you belong to the "can't teach an old dog new tricks" school, you should refrain from being a franchisee.

Many franchises fail because of a lack of financial and/or human resources. If the estimate to start a franchise is U.S.$250,000, be willing or able to place an extra U.S.$75,000–$100,000 in reserve. If you will be involved in the direct management of the franchise, consider whether this is really what you want to do with your time. If you will turn the management over to others, be sure to provide for sufficient financial resources to cover these needs and consider that, at times, you may need to manage the managers.

In finding the optimal franchisor, consider the characteristics found in the following profile.

Franchisor's Profile

1. Successful in franchising in its home market and other markets
2. Good and workable procedures and operations guides
3. Willing to adjust both its up-front and continuing costs to reflect market size and conditions
4. Viable training programs with sufficient staff to develop them
5. Products and services that are viable in your market
6. Availability of products and services at reasonable costs, willing to assist franchisees in obtaining local products, as relevant
7. Recognizable intellectual property
8. Desires a long-term relationship
9. Ability to provide financial assistance or delay payments for problems that are not the fault of the franchisee
10. Willing to allow some independence in local operations
11. Desires to expand and willing to include franchisee in that expansion
12. Advertising techniques and programs that are suitable for your territory

196. Trading Companies and Other Export Intermediaries

Suppose someone comes to your office and offers to buy your product "right off your loading dock" and take charge of re-selling it in foreign markets. Is that a good idea?

Export intermediaries who are set up to do this include trading companies, export houses, original equipment manufacturers who might incorporate your product in theirs, and purchasing offices for foreign governments, or corporations, and other agencies that buy product in your domestic market and re-sell it in a foreign market. Before going further, consider the pros and cons of using export intermediaries.

PROS:

☐ No muss or fuss. The intermediary buys the product from you and takes responsibility for its distribution in overseas markets.

☐ No market research required.

☐ No diversion of resources into developing export channels in overseas markets.

☐ No foreign commercial risk. The transactions occurs in your own domestic market, making collections easier and avoiding direct and indirect working capital costs.

☐ No special logistics requirements. Intermediary handles export shipping and insurance.

☐ No export documentation requirements (usually). Intermediary handles export documentation, licenses, etc.

CONS:

☐ No way to add value. It is not possible to assure provision of services such as installation or maintenance.

☐ No control over placement.

☐ No control over use of trademarks.

☐ No customer contact.

☐ No benefit from additional market knowledge.

☐ No avoidance of manufacturer's liability, yet no control over the conditions that might create a liability action.

☐ No assured consistency in marketing and sales effort.

☐ No assurance that the product will be competently marketed.

☐ No assurance that the export/import process was handled properly.

If success for your product requires "valued added" service to the end-user, then you might have to consider a more direct method of exporting, such as agents, distributors, sales branches, or sales subsidiaries.

MARKET ENTRY STRATEGIES— DIRECT MARKETING FROM THE HOME COUNTRY

Because of a combination of changing lifestyles, technological innovations, and the movement toward more favorable government regulations, the possibility of selling your products and services directly to the end-user without the use of local intermediaries is one of the most rapidly growing areas of international business. This is particularly true with the growing use of the Internet and in the area of catalog sales of consumer products, but is also important for those industrial products that must be individually designed to meet unique customer specifications.

197. Catalog Sales

This approach to the international market should be considered when:

☐ *The consumer desires or requires purchasing the product and services directly from the manufacturer or retailer.* Catalog sales are now an accepted manner of doing business in North America (including Mexico), Western Europe, Australia, New Zealand, and Japan. In fact, the changing lifestyles of those countries have increased the interest. More and more, consumers desire to purchase products and services in the leisure of their homes. The availability of phones, faxes, computers, improved delivery services, and internationally valid credit cards also increase desire and capability. Finally, catalog sales can reach small towns and rural areas that are not served by major retail outlets.

☐ *The manufacturer or retailer desires to increase its revenues and profits while perhaps providing its products and services at a lower cost to consumers.* Even with the additional costs associated with catalog sales (credit card charges, freight, and packaging), it may be possible to provide the products and services at a lower cost to the consumer. A recent study showed that because of high retail prices in Japan, a U.S.-based mail-order company was able to provide such items as audio equipment, cameras, kitchen appliances, watches, and perfumes at 50–80 percent of the prices charged in Tokyo. Even more interesting is that some of these discounts were applied to products manufactured by Japanese-based companies.

For almost a century, catalog sales have been a significant part of the American market. Now, direct sales are increasing dramatically outside the U.S.A. Sales to consumers through mail, telephone, or door-to-door canvassing have increased tenfold in Japan between 1980 and 1990 and over 300 percent in Germany during the same period. Products now sold frequently through direct marketing are books and magazines, home furnishings, clothing, housewares, and cosmetics. Services include financial, travel and tourist services, and various forms of insurance.

A whole support infrastructure has been developed for those who desire to sell direct. This includes excellent globally-oriented packaging and delivery services, the availability of good customer lists in almost every major city in the world and the telecommunications systems we have already discussed. While not inexpensive, the continued declining costs of these infrastructure services, coupled with the savings made by avoiding indirect exporters, now makes catalog sales a viable alternative for many companies to enter global markets.

198. Traveling Sales Forces

Companies, particularly in the industrial products area, should consider the use of direct sales forces located in the home countries to develop international business. Where products are expensive and/or where they have to be individually designed for each customer, these sales forces could be far more effective than agents, particularly where the number of sales per year is limited.

Under these circumstances, even a fairly large company may be able to address all of Asia, Europe or Latin America with one, or a few, persons per territory. These positions, even with the cost of travel, can be more cost effective than having to establish an overseas organization or relinquish some of your margins to agents or distributors. Additionally, these jobs become effective training grounds for the development of international expertise and savvy, which would be required when the exporter decides to expand its international operations.

The home country exporter should be concerned as to whether its traveling sales forces might subject its goods to taxation in the foreign jurisdictions. If the sale is made abroad, certain countries may try to tax a portion of the sale, although this will often depend on the volume and regularity of the sales. If the exporter's employees are subject to foreign jurisdiction (as service personnel or as traveling salespersons), the exporter should be aware of the possibility of taxation of the individual. This often depends on the amount of time spent in the country and on the immigration status afforded by the country to the employee. Venezuela, for example, taxes individuals visiting that country for commercial purposes. These taxes are based on where the services are performed rather than on the place of payment, and the employee may not be able to leave the country until the taxes are paid.

Market Entry Strategies—Selling Through International Agents and Distributors

Many companies open global markets with agents and/or distributors. While not risk free, these methods allow businesses with limited resources to operate in major markets and companies with significant resources to offer their products and services in smaller markets.

This section defines terms and discusses the advantages and disadvantages of using agents and distributors and provides selection and retention techniques. Finally, this section describes effective methods for terminations.

199. International Distributors

Distributors are normally used when a company wishes to establish sales of completed products in a foreign market, but the company determines that market size and other variables preclude its direct involvement in the particular market.

For a company to consider appointing distributors in a particular market or as a general international strategy, it should consider the following *internal company characteristics:*

☐ The company does not have, or is unwilling to commit, sufficient management or financial resources to establish its own sales force or marketing subsidiary, but the company is willing to commit those resources necessary to develop a viable distributor relations function, to train distributors, and perhaps to take limited financial risks in the area of currency exposure, collections, and termination payments.

☐ The company does not have, or is not willing to acquire, the experience level to allow it to establish its own local operations, but it has, or is willing to acquire, experience necessary to evaluate and select potential distributors, retain and motivate them, and evaluate their performance.

☐ The company has developed, or is willing to develop or contract for certain international services such as export administration, international traffic, credit and collections, and legal services.

200. International Agents

Agents are normally used when a company wishes to establish sales to distinct individual customers, or to service customers on a *request for proposal* (RFP) or project basis. For a company to consider appointing agents in a particular market, or as a general international strategy, it should consider the following *internal company characteristics:*

☐ The company must be willing to deal with the customer. While an agent may be used to find and qualify the customer, and perhaps to even make the deal, the exporter will ultimately have to deal with the customer in terms of providing the products, collections and pre- and post-sales services.
☐ If agents are used in requests for proposal (RFPs), or on a private project basis, the company will have to develop the expertise needed to respond to RFPs (e.g., qualification as suppliers; bid, performance, and warranty bonds; technical negotiations).
☐ On the other hand, agents do not require the level of training and constant motivation as do distributors.

201. When to Use Distributors and Agents

Distributors

If its internal characteristics lead toward using distributors, the company must then consider its *product characteristics*. Distributors may not be suitable for products that are perishable. Additionally, products that are project-oriented, high in price, or designed individually for each customer are not suitable for distributors. While millions of personal computers are sold each year through distributors, it would be very difficult to convince a distributor to stock a multimillion dollar supercomputer that would have to be specifically configured to meet the needs of the customer, and has a selling cycle of two years. However, the right distributor could be used to handle products of a highly technical nature if it has the right service equipment and properly trained sales and service staff.

The products most suitable for distributors are those sold in short sales cycles, have regular customers, require limited maintenance, and are at prices that will convince a distributor to handle a sufficient local stock. The more commodity-oriented the product is, the more likely it will be suitable for international distributors.

Market characteristics also help determine the viability of using distributors. Is the market size sufficient to allow for local stock? What type of entities would be the customers for the products? For example, if the market consists of only large customers or public entities, it may not be suitable for distributors because the customer would most likely prefer to deal directly with the exporter. In that case, a local agent may be more suitable. What is the competitive situation in the selected market? How price- and quality-sensitive is the market? Finally, is the market ready for your company's product?

The next area a company would explore is the *availability of quality distributors* in the selected market. Selecting good distributors requires careful consideration and not all markets will have suitable distributors. Normally, a company will look for a distributor in a complementary line of business with an established reputation and with suitable knowledge of market conditions.

The distributor must be able to stock—and continue to restock—sufficient inventories, handle installations, and cover warranty and other after-sale functions. Distributors must also have trained staffs or be willing to have their people trained by the exporter. Finally, although it is difficult to enforce requirements that a distributor carry only your line of products, it is possible to require that the distributor *treat your line as its primary line.* One of the biggest problems faced by small and middle-sized companies is the case where the distributor adds your line to competitive lines, overprices your products, and then effectively locks you out of the market in favor of your competitors.

Finally, a company should pay careful attention to unique legal and financial considerations in the target market. Many countries have distributor termination laws, which make it very costly to terminate distributors. Such laws are common in Europe and Latin America. In a few countries (like Chile), because of anti-monopoly laws, it is illegal to appoint exclusive distributors. Additionally, some countries use their tax laws to discourage distributor appointments in favor of agents (India).

Financial considerations may also impact whether or not you use distributors. Countries with soft currencies and/or poor balance of payment conditions may require approval of certain agencies (normally a central bank) before granting foreign exchange payments in hard currency. Payment terms and cycles may be longer, which may require your company to consider whether to offer better, or different, payment terms. Typically, if a company does offer better terms (e.g., 60-day net), they will increase the cost of the products (or lower the discounts) to cover their exposure.

Agents

Agents are more useful when the company has certain *product characteristics*. Products that are designed for projects are individually configured for each customer, are expensive, difficult to stock, or have long sales cycles, seem more suitable for sale through agents.

The most appropriate *market characteristics* for agents are the opportunity for a few, but larger, sales, and marketing to public agencies. A blanket manufacturer, that essentially provides a commodity, uses agents in most of the world because it serves two essential markets. The first are the governments that prefer direct purchasing from the manufacturer; the second are the large retail outlets (department and discount stores), whose economies of scale would price most distributors (with their mark-ups) out of the market.

The *availability* of quality agents is equally important, but quality agents have different characteristics than quality distributors. In the case of agents, product knowledge and training may be less important than personal contacts. Sales to the military are often arranged by retired officers and sales to large companies are arranged by people who belong to the right clubs, sometimes more than the right professional associations.

The appointment of agents has its own unique legal and financial considerations. In addition to the termination laws that may apply also to agents, a company must be concerned, in some countries (including the U.S.A. to some extent), about the benefits provided to employees. Special care must be taken to assure that your agent is not considered to be an employee of your company. To prevent this problem, some countries require agents to register with public authorities as commercial agents. Agents may also raise certain ethical issues, and in the case of the U.S.A., may raise concerns under the Foreign Corrupt Practices Act. While agents do not raise collection issues (because you pay them), a company must be sure that they have established appropriate payment terms with the customer.

202. Advantages and Disadvantages of Distributors

Distributors represent a relatively low-risk strategy to enter into international markets. Properly selected and motivated, distributors provide you with the following **advantages:**

☐ A good distributor will provide you with knowledge of the local market, which includes how to import into that market and how to sell within it.

☐ Because the distributor buys and sells for its own account, the exporter does not have to carry local inventories, nor is it involved in credit and collections with the end-user customer. The exporters should be very concerned, however, with the payment terms offered to the distributor.

☐ Distributors allow the exporter to avoid, or limit, commitments to unexplored markets, or market segments.

☐ Distributors allow the opportunity to test new products, or to harvest old products.

☐ With proper training, good distributors will install, service, and provide direct warranty service to the end-user customer.

☐ With a distributor relationship functioning, the exporter should receive forecasting competitive information and solid reports on political and economic conditions in the territory.

☐ Use of distributors normally does not subject the exporter to taxation in the country of sale.

☐ Distributors can assist the exporter in advertising the products in a manner that conforms to local laws, industry standards, and local customs.

Despite the numerous advantages, there are several **disadvantages** that must be considered before appointing distributors:

☐ Distributors can lower your overall gross profit and limit your ability to achieve revenues and profits from after-sales services. To motivate distributors to sell, you must provide them with a discount from your net export prices. If, or when, the amount of this discount exceeds the cost of other forms of international business transactions, then distributors may not be the best format for international sales. Additionally, revenues and profits, which normally may come from after-sales services (e.g., extended warranty contracts or service calls), could be lost because distributors normally assume this function.

☐ Distributors limit your control of distribution resale prices. Theoretically, distributors can underprice your products or, more likely, price your products so high that market share and goodwill are lost in the name of short-term profits.

☐ In a similar vein, distributors limit your communications with the users of your products. Distributors will not want to provide you with customer lists to avoid you dealing directly with their customers.

☐ The last two points may make it more difficult to obtain direct knowledge of the foreign market and significant developments in that market.

☐ Market opportunities may be missed if the distributor is spread too thinly or doesn't carry the inventory and support personnel to service the market.

☐ Finally, the relationship may be subject to dealer protection legislation that makes it difficult and costly to terminate distributors.

203. Advantages and Disadvantages of Agents

The major **advantages** associated with using agents are:

☐ A properly selected agent can provide you with key contacts and intelligence in achieving business in the territory. All the product knowledge in the world, solid local stocks, and a top-notch service organization will not result in much business unless the individuals representing your product have the contacts to introduce the customer to your company and its products.

☐ Agents require less training and background than distributors. Therefore, your initial time and financial commitment is lower and you do not have to invest resources unless you are close to an actual sale.

☐ Agents do not purchase for resale, therefore you have more control over pricing and direct interface with the customer.

☐ The proper agent allows you to reach markets that cannot be met through distributors. As previously stated, an agent is a better choice for large, public, or project sales.

☐ The use of agents normally does not subject the exporter to taxation in the country of sale.

The key **disadvantages** in using agents are:

☐ Poor product knowledge and lack of understanding of your market could result in poor performance by the agent.

☐ Agents are more difficult to evaluate than distributors. A distributor normally has stores, employees, and a track record. Agents may be only as good as the most recent government or private company leadership. It is more difficult to evaluate claims of agents, and longer-term relationships are less likely.

☐ Once a sale is about to be made, the company may have to make a larger commitment to the customer. It will assume collections, installation, maintenance, warranty, and other pre- and post-sales activities.

☐ The company may have to provide a local stock of product and spare parts, and it may have to commit its own sales and technical personnel to the territory or hire local companies to provide those services.

☐ Agents may be more difficult to control and may tend to create additional termination problems in the areas of labor and commissions. One of the biggest problems associated with agent termination is to determine whether a partial commission may be owed if the business closes shortly after termination.

204. An International Distributor's Profile

If you have decided to use distributors as a means to enter international markets, it is probably wise to develop a profile of characteristics you might seek in a good distributor. The following profile illustrates these characteristics.

International Distributor's Profile

1. Local reputation as a fair and honest business organization
2. Assertive sales organization
3. Financially able to carry adequate stocks and to expand to match the growth of your industry
4. Knowledge of the marketplace; ability to inform you regularly on current market conditions
5. Handles complementary products, but does not handle products that are directly competitive
6. Able to forecast market changes
7. Has well-trained sales and support staff and is willing to seek additional training, where necessary
8. Willing and able to think longer-term by being competitive whenever economically possible
9. Advises the exporter on any customer resistance encountered in the marketplace
10. Sells features and quality in addition to price
11. Informs exporter of safety requirements, specifications, and the requirements imposed by governments or industry standards
12. Pays on time
13. Establishes relationships with other suppliers necessary to offer customers complete solutions
14. Considers your line of major importance, and devotes primary effort to it
15. A candidate for future technology transfers and/or an equity joint venture (that is, be able to grow with the exporter)

205. An International Agent's Profile

If you have decided to use agents as a means to enter international markets, it is probably wise to develop a profile of characteristics you might seek in a good agent. This profile might consist of the following fourteen characteristics:

International Agent's Profile

---

1. Local reputation as a fair and honest business organization
2. Registered with the appropriate professional associations and governments as an agent; incorporated
3. Does not demand advance commissions
4. Knowledge of the marketplace and customers it would solicit
5. Experience in the customer's industries or activities
6. Able to assist the exporter in qualifying for government projects and other RFPs
7. Has language translation capabilities which are available to you as part of the agreed-upon commission
8. Able and willing to assist in post-sales problems and opportunities
9. Able and willing to assist in collections
10. Does not handle competitive products
11. Advises exporter on any customer resistance encountered in the marketplace
12. Sells features and quality in addition to price
13. Considers your line of major importance and will devote considerable effort to it
14. A candidate for future technology transfer and/or an equity joint venture

---

206. A Distributor/Agent Application

The purpose of the application is to screen and qualify potential candidates. These applications can be prepared with your word processing and desktop publishing capabilities. The application should be kept simple as seen in Figure 3. Any prospective distributor or agent who does not complete the application is clearly not willing to devote significant efforts to your products.

The distributor and agent applications help you with the selection process in the following ways:

☐ It forces the prospective distributor or agent to put his or her intentions in writing.
☐ It helps identify the geographic focus. You would certainly question a distributor who wants all of South America but only has offices in Bogota, Colombia, for instance.

(text continued on page 211)

Distributor Application

Thank you for your interest in our company. Please complete the following application for consideration as a distributor of our products. In addition, please provide a copy of your most recent financial statement and a company brochure or annual report.

Upon completion, please fax to: _____ Fax: _____

You will be contacted by our office after we have reviewed your materials.

Date: _____ Territory: _____

Company Name: _____

Contact Name: _____

Telephone: _____ Fax: _____ E-mail: _____

Complete Address: _____

_____

_____

Owner of Company: _____

Type of Company: Corporation/Partnership/Other: _____

Subsidiary—Parent: _____

Type of Company: Manufacturer _____ Sales _____

When did you begin operations? _____

Total number of employees: _____

      Number of Sales Managers: _____

      Number of Sales People: _____

      Number of administrative staff: _____

      Other: _____

Annual Sales (US $)

      1996: _____

      1997: _____

      1998: _____

      1999: _____(projected)

How big is your warehouse/distribution center (square feet or meters)? _____

Describe your truck fleet:

Number of trucks	Size	Owned	Leased

Do you represent any other imported lines?

Company name:	Products:

(continued)

Do you represent any products competitive to ours?

Company name:	Products:

Principal Clients

Identify your principal clients and their type of business:

Client	Type of business	Number of sites

What level of sales do you require in order to add a new product line?

Year 1: _____

Year 2: _____

Year 3: _____

How do our products fit into your current product lines? (Complementary, additional sales, enter new market segments, etc.) _____

_____

_____

Sales projections for our products: _____

Year 1: _____

Year 2: _____

Year 3: _____

How are you promoting your current product lines?

Newspapers:	_____	Radio:	_____
Television:	_____	Trade Shows:	_____
Magazines:	_____	Catalogs:	_____
Billboards:	_____	Store announcements:	_____
Other:	_____		

_____

(continued)

Define your sales territory: _____
_____
_____

Define how you are positioned to reach all the major cities in your market: _____
_____
_____

In your market, what are the costs for imported foods, as a percentage added to the manufacturer's price?
Transport: _____   Labeling: _____
Distributor margin: _____   Retail margin: _____
Taxes: _____   Customs costs: _____
Other: _____

Define your consumer base:
　Annual income: _____
　Per capita spending on the products: _____
　Other factors: _____

Are there any special characteristics or product modifications necessary for your market? Explain: __
_____
_____
_____

What are the major obstacles that you see for the sales and marketing of our products in your market? _____
_____
_____

Bank reference:
　Bank Name: _____
　Address: _____
　_____
　Contact:_____
　Telephone: _____
　Fax: _____

Please indicate two (2) foreign companies that you have represented that we may contact as a reference:
Company name: _____
Address: _____
_____
Contact: _____
Telephone: _____
Fax: _____

Company name : _____
Address: _____
_____
Contact: _____
Telephone: _____
Fax: _____

Is there anything else you would like to mention? _____
　Please attach a recent Financial Statement and a brochure or Annual Report for your company.

Figure 3. Sample distributor application.

(text continued from page 207)

☐ It provides knowledge of their banking relationships and some credit history. Do not appoint a distributor or agent who will not provide banking references.
☐ It helps to identify inventory requirements.
☐ It helps to determine fit business practices.
☐ It provides information on support personnel.
☐ It helps to determine advertising capabilities.

207. An International Distributor/Agent Procedure Guide

If at all possible, you should consider developing a distributor or agent brochure. We recommend a marketing approach to your legal agreements. This approach combines an export-oriented, user-friendly brochure with a more limited, plain-language legal agreement. The brochure, which is incorporated by reference into your agreement, might include the following points:

☐ A cover page with a picture of your corporate headquarters or products, which may be entitled "The XYZ Company and Its Distributors: A Global Discussion of Policy and Procedure."
☐ A description of your company.
☐ A description of your ideal distributor (agent) requirements, e.g., qualifications.
☐ A description of the responsibilities of the exporter and of the distributor (agent) with regard to such items as stocking, sales promotion, and being competitive.
☐ A discussion of your company's general policies on such things as minimum billing, profit margins, competitive products, conditions of sale, use of trademarks, and allowable product alterations and modifications. This could be done in a Question and Answer format. For example, your Q and A on minimum billing might read as follows:
Q. Why do we have a policy of minimum billing?

A. Our policy of minimum billing was established to help us pay the cost of the invoicing and clerical work associated with processing each individual order. We encourage our distributors (agents) to place orders of economical size to help us give them better service. For further information on minimum billing, see the applicable Conditions of Sale.

208. Locating Good Agents and Distributors

Finding good distributors and agents is not easy, but the contacts mentioned below can assist you in your search:

☐ If you are a U.S.A.-based company, start with the U.S. Department of Commerce (DOC), which has services such as the *Agent/Distributor Service (ADS)*, a personalized overseas search for interested and qualified distributors and agents in a specific country. The DOC also has the *Trade Opportunities Program (TOP)*, which provides sales leads, and the *National Trade Data Bank (NTDB)*, which provides trade and export promotion data. Other countries have government agencies which provide similar services. Consider, also, state or provincial trade offices.
☐ Contact and use international chambers of commerce. For example, the U.S.-Mexican Chamber of Commerce in Mexico City can provide leads for both U.S. and Mexican companies.
☐ Check with in-country trade and professional associations.
☐ Advertise in foreign trade association publications.
☐ Participate in trade shows.
☐ Contact companies in related businesses. For example, computer software companies can check with hardware suppliers. Suppliers of equipment to banks and financial institutions can check with other suppliers.
☐ Check, if possible, with competitors. Sometimes they are willing to tell you who not to choose.
☐ Check business directories and yellow pages, which are available at most major libraries in your home country.
☐ Check with international banks, accounting and law firms, and other service providers.
☐ Develop your own list of personal contacts.

209. Maintaining and Motivating Distributors and Agents

Once you have appointed your distributors and agents, you need to consider how to go about maintaining the good ones and motivating them to do a better job. Our experience has taught us that this is better done with a whole lot of "carrots" and only an occasional use of the "stick." Here are some of the key considerations for retention and motivation:

Develop Loyalty

☐ Make them feel like they are part of your company.
☐ Develop identification with your company and its products by:
  • Providing free product samples and advertising items bearing your company name and logo. High quality pens are well received as are items of clothing, particularly hats.
  • Holding regional marketeer conferences, either in their territory, a popular vacation spot, or at the headquarters.
  • Holding performance contests.
  • Assisting in training on an ongoing basis.

Good Communications

☐ Develop a Distributor (Agent) Relations function that is responsible for day-to-day contact.
☐ Assign a headquarter's employee to each distributor or agent and make that employee the spokesperson for the "cause" of the distributor or agent.

Improve Market Share

☐ Organize training programs.
☐ Create joint advertising programs.
☐ Teach marketeer how to improve sales and profits by understanding the opportunities available in after-sale services.
☐ Develop programs that encourage distributors to inventory your products—e.g., additional discounts in exchange for holding larger inventory.

Pricing, Finance, and Credit

☐ Understand credit issues in the territory.
☐ Consider better credit terms in exchange for slightly higher prices.
☐ Consider volume discounts.
☐ Allow distributors to order before raising prices.

210. Improving Distributor Performance

Once you have done your homework and picked the right market, the distributor for your product in that market, and ways to improve results, you should treat your foreign distributor like a partner. Invest time in personal relationships. Be patient. In many regions of the world, personal friendship and mutual respect are prerequisites to the profitable business relationship.

Make sure your distributor knows you are committed to their market and to them as your distributor. If your distributor perceives that you are opportunistic, and are not organized to follow through with the support they need over the long-term, they will usually give less attention to your product.

Make an effort to understand their goals, their business environment and where your product fits into their plans. Show respect for their superior knowledge of how to get things done in their home market. Help them understand how their success contributes to your success and thereby "legitimize" the business reasons for your interest in their success.

Engage in planning and adjust your planning cycle to their time horizon. In many regions of the world, it is not considered realistic to plan a year in advance and commitments to annual goals may not be taken seriously.

Establish mutually acceptable goals, in the same way you would with a partner, rather than an employee. Goals that are unilaterally assigned or imposed may not be taken seriously.

Specific tips that work:

☐ Make sure the economic and financial risks, as well as the benefits of success, are shared fairly between your company and the distributor.

☐ Communicate frequently and offer training to support their success. Also acknowledge the expertise they bring to the "partnership."

☐ Keep them in the "inside" loop regarding new company developments, new products, and competitor intelligence. Especially if they are operating in a newly emerging market, they will appreciate your efforts to share world-wide industry information with them.

☐ Make sure there is someone within your organization who "advocates" for them and takes charge of solving problems they may encounter in export/import logistics, international customer service, engineering, manufacturing, finance, etc.

☐ Hold them accountable, just as you would a business partner. Build the kind of trust that will permit you to compare notes on how well the partnership is working for each of you. Avoid pointing fingers and be prepared to engage them in analyzing problems concerning you.

☐ Always do what you say you will do.

If this approach does not yield results, you may have to reassess your choice of distributors . . . or the suitability of the market itself.

211. Evaluating Performances of Distributors and Agents

At some point, ideally on a regular basis, you will wish to evaluate the performance of your international marketeers. Clearly the best and easiest way to do this is by setting targets and evaluating performance based on these targets. At the beginning of the relationship, this is not easy. The exporter, upon entering new markets, will have only a rough idea of what the market for its products and services will be. The distributor or agent is likely to exaggerate its future performance to obtain the appointment. Therefore, in setting the initial targets, the parties should look to a combination of establishing a target that meets the business needs of the parties but is realistic in terms of market size and conditions.

Another evaluation technique is to compare competitors' sales with those made by your marketeers. If your distributor or agent carries competitive products, you can ask them how they are doing with these products. If there is a problem, and they are good marketeers, they should tell you before you ask. If they do not carry competitive products, consider asking your marketeer to obtain the market intelligence in their home market.

Another good method of evaluation is by setting and monitoring inventory turnover rates. Suppose you agree that a distributor should have a target of U.S.$500,000 for a year, and the distributor places an initial inventory order of U.S.$125,000, with the idea that the inventory should turn over every three months. In that circumstance, the exporter should review its order patterns on a quarterly basis to assure that the distributor orders range in the U.S.$100,000 to $150,000. If they do not, the distributor either is not meeting its sales goals, or is allowing its inventory to be depleted, which may negatively impact its ability to make future sales.

Evaluation techniques also include monitoring requests for direct sales coming from the territory. If the customers are coming to the exporter directly rather than purchasing from your distributor, or ordering through your agent, something is wrong. Either your marketeer is not advertising correctly so that customers are unaware of its presence, or customers are dissatisfied with its prices and/or service. As a rule, requests for direct purchases should be referred to your marketeers in the territory, but the right to make direct sales should be preserved to enable the exporter to sell if the marketeers are not performing properly.

212. Reasons to Terminate Distributors and Agents

Before entering into a marketeer relationship, the exporter should consider what might be the reasons in the future where it would choose to allow its agreements to expire, or to terminate them. Special attention should be paid to termination, because it is often difficult and if the proper measures are not taken, can be very costly to both parties.

The following are all good reasons to terminate:

☐ *To replace them with your own sales office, or with your own manufacturing or assembly operations in the territory.* This is of particular concern in the large markets. You decide to enter the market through marketeers, but it is reasonable to assume that if the marketeer is successful, you will then consider increasing your margins by using your own sales force, and perhaps later, by making the products in country to supply that sales force. If this is within the realm of the possible, you might consider the appointment of a marketeer that can grow with your needs and desires in the marketplace. For example, should you desire your own sales force in the future, would it be possible to acquire the marketeer's company as part of your sales force in the territory?

☐ *To replace an existing marketeer with another marketeer.* Because penalties imposed by some countries for unjust termination are tied to the marketeer performance, it is relatively simple, in almost every country, to terminate the truly poor performers, although occasionally even a poor performer might try to convince a court that it has made considerable effort to build goodwill and therefore is entitled to something, even if it has not sold much of your product.

☐ The more difficult cases would be the *adequate performers*. These fall into two categories:

• Those who miss targets, but still generate sales. For example, a distributor who purchases U.S.$350,000 per year against a target of U.S.$500,000.

• Those who may be making their targets but, in the view of the exporter, whose opinion should be supported by significant data, are not performing up to the potential that exists in the marketplace. That is, they may be making the U.S.$500,000 target, but the exporter is convinced that another distributor could generate U.S.$1,000,000 in revenues.

In the first category, the marketeer may still be able to argue, and perhaps prove, unjust termination if they can show that the targets established were unrealistic, or that business conditions in the country resulted in their inability to reach a target. This will depend on general economic and specific industry conditions, but, as a general rule, 50 percent of the target is probably somewhere near the line that distinguishes the "poor" from the "adequate" performer.

The second category is the most difficult. In these cases, if the law requires, it will almost always be necessary to pay termination indemnities. This will finally come down to a business decision for the exporter: is it willing to pay those indemnities to appoint a stronger organization?

You may need to terminate a relationship with a marketeer if you no longer wish to be present in the market. This may be because the market generates insufficient volume to justify the expense, because of a change in government, or because the existing government has imposed conditions (e.g., exchange controls or local content requirements), which make it difficult, or impossible, to operate in that market.

In some countries that protect marketeers, the simple decision of leaving the country may not be sufficient to meet the standards of just termination, and indemnification may still be sought by the marketeer. In this case, an exporter may decide to ignore court-awarded indemnities (if they have no assets in that country), because it will be difficult to have a court decision in the marketeer's country recognized by a country where the exporter has assets. This approach works often, but presents a risk if the exporter should ever try to reenter the market.

213. Understanding Your Commitments

Just to be clear, it is possible, almost everywhere, to terminate marketeers. The issue is not the ability to terminate, but the monetary costs associated with it.

A substantial number of countries have developed laws and regulations to protect marketeers from unjust termination. These laws and regulations are designed to protect local marketing companies against foreign exporters who use local companies for a period of time to develop the market and create goodwill for the products and services of the foreign company, only to replace them at the end of the period with their own local sales offices.

In principle, these laws and regulations may serve as a mechanism to protect local companies against foreign intrusion. Unfortunately, and in reality, these laws have been greatly abused, and in some cases have resulted in foreign companies having to pay outrageous sums of money to replace marketeers with other marketeers, or to replace marketeers with their own sales force.

These laws and regulations are generally found in some Western European countries (including Germany and France), Central America, parts of South America, and parts of the Middle East. Although the U.S.A. has no federal laws on the subject, about half of the states have some regulations covering agents, distributors, or both. In general, Asia is free from such laws and regulations, although countries like Korea do have some restrictions on the use of agents. Check with your attorney in each case.

Dealer's Acts

Many countries have a specific piece of legislation or a regulation that covers the subject. Other countries (Argentina and Venezuela, for example) bring together specific parts of their civil, commercial and labor codes to reach the same results. A common name given to these laws and regulations are *Dealer's Acts*.

In describing Dealer's Acts, we will discuss what areas they cover, how *just cause* is defined, and what liabilities to the exporter might result from terminating a marketeer without just cause.

Generally, Dealer's Acts cover agents, distributors, and all variants of those two market channels, including dealers, jobbers, manufacturer's representatives, original equipment manufacturers, and value-added marketeers. There are some exceptions. For example, Brazil protects agents but not distributors (directly), while Belgium protects distributors, but subscribes generally to the EEC rules regarding agents, which are not as onerous.

Because most of these countries apply the civil law system, it is possible to prove the existence of marketing agreements through actions and oral statements, even in the absence of a contract. The Dealer's Acts generally cover both goods and services.

Because almost all Dealer's Acts are designed to protect against foreign companies, it is interesting to note that a local subsidiary of a foreign company usually is considered a foreign company. Therefore, a foreign company cannot avoid the Dealer's Act in Belgium by establishing a wholly, or majority-owned, subsidiary in that company, which then appoints the Belgian distributor.

Dealer's Acts allow for termination without indemnities if the marketeer can be terminated for just cause. However, just cause is difficult to prove, and must be based on one or more of the following reasons:

☐ Non-performance of essential acts or omissions of acts that substantially and adversely affect the customers of the exporter
☐ Material breach of contract

☐ Fraud and abuse
☐ Gross ineptitude or negligence
☐ Disclosure of confidential information
☐ Misuse of intellectual property
☐ Significant diminution of business

If it is determined that the marketeer has been terminated without just cause, the exporter will be required to compensate the marketeer for this termination. In some countries, this may also apply on expiration.

Basic indemnification formulas. Depending on the country in which the termination took place, two general types of indemnification formulas are used. In some countries, an *expert* will be appointed by the court to determine the indemnity. The expert will examine the marketeer's efforts to accredit the exporter's products and services in the territory, examine the volume of sales, and try to place a value on the goodwill created by the marketeer in the territory. It is in the area of goodwill where the court will have considerable discretion to increase the amount of the liability to be paid to the marketeer.

In the other countries, a *monetary formula* tied to sales or profits and the duration of the relationship will be applied. A typical formula, for example, will look at the average profit generated by the marketeer from its business with the exporter in the past five years and then apply a one-year average of profit over those past five years, as follows:

Duration of Relationship	Years Profit Awarded
1–5 years	1 year
6–10 years	2 years
11–15 years	3 years
16–20 years	4 years
20+ years	5 years

If the arrangement is less than five years, the court will award one year's profit based on the average profit during the duration of the relationship.

Purchase of unsalable merchandise. In most cases, the court will also determine a value for inventory remaining with the marketeer, and require the exporter to pay that value. The exporter will have the right to the recovery of unsalable merchandise.

Labor obligations. If the marketeer was forced to terminate personnel as the result of the unjust termination, the exporter may be responsible for the costs of termination of those personnel. In countries with strong labor codes, this can be a significant cost.

Failure of exporter to pay. If the exporter decides not to pay the awarded indemnities, the marketeer and/or the court has four basic alternatives:

☐ Seize exporter's in-country assets.
☐ Try to enforce the judgment in a country where the exporter has assets.
☐ Prohibit exporter from appointing other marketeers.
☐ Close the border to future importation of exporter's products and services.

214. Planning Ahead for Termination

Termination problems can be lessened by planning ahead. This can be done by pricing your products or controlling commissions to create a termination reserve. This is a particularly good strategy in countries where time percentage formulas are used. For example, in Brazil, agents are entitled to one-twelfth of their entire commissions for the entire length of service (8.33 percent). In this case, the exporter can reserve one-twelfth of the commission paid as a possible termination payment.

In addition to creating reserves, the exporter may be able to reduce its potential liabilities by considering the use of some or all of the following clauses in its marketeer agreements:

Arbitration—Take the issue out of the courts and put it in the hands of arbitrators who are more likely to make unbiased awards. The International Chamber of Commerce and the United Nations Commission for International Trade Law (UNCITRAL) Rules are good choices.

Governing Law—Try to specify the law of the country of the manufacturer, or a third country that does not have a Dealer's Act.

Future Legislation or Regulations—Have the agreement automatically terminate one day before any negative future legislation comes into effect.

Bankruptcy—Have the agreement automatically terminate if the marketeer files for bankruptcy or any other form of court protection concerning creditors.

Material Default—Define material default to include such things as continuing failure to meet quotas, late payments or non-payment, or misuse of intellectual property. Make a material default an automatic grounds for termination.

Non-Exclusivity, and the Right to Sell Direct—In this case, you may not need to terminate, but merely appoint another, and let your existing marketeer continue its operations, or keep your marketeer, but begin to sell direct. Be careful here, because some countries may determine those actions, under certain circumstances, to be an effective unjust termination.

Assignment—Automatic termination applies if marketeer assigns its rights to others without the exporter's written permission.

Material Change of Ownership and/or Management—Automatic termination, if either occurs. This can avoid a situation where the success of the distributor is dependent on a few key people.

Reserve the Right to Terminate Without Cause—Upon written notice; this normally would not work in Dealer's Act countries, but when coupled with an arbitration clause, and if the notice period is reasonable (three to six months), it may be effective.

Fix the Term, and Require New Agreement for Each Term—This would be of considerable assistance in certain European countries, where nonexclusive marketeers become exclusive if, in certain circumstances, time has passed and no other marketeers are appointed.

Non-Employee Statement—This is essential for agents, and may be of some assistance with distributors, in countries where termination costs of the distributor may become the responsibility of the exporter.

Repurchase Requirements—This is helpful in defining the method and price by which the exporter repurchases the products upon expiration or termination. It may also make good business sense if you no longer wish the former marketeer to have access to your products.

While these clauses are helpful in limiting liabilities, they are far from perfect. Exporters must simply be aware that appointing marketeers may have the additional cost of termination, and should plan for it as a cost of doing business. You should plan ahead, but don't be rest assured.

INTERNATIONAL FRANCHISING

Franchising is one of the fastest growing forms of international business and should remain so for some time to come. Long a standard way of doing business in the U.S.A., where one-third of all sales are made by franchisers, franchising is now an important business component in nearly every country of the world.

In this section we will attempt to understand the tradeoffs of international franchising and explore how to establish and maintain good franchisees.

215. Franchising and its Tradeoffs

Effective franchises have been created for such markets as hotels and motels, soft drinks, car rentals, fast foods, automotive services, recreational services, and business services such as print and sign shops, home maintenance, and numerous other areas.

While franchising is basically a form of technology transfer and licensing, it has some of the characteristics of distributors (e.g., sale of goods and services, after-sale responsibilities, training and stocking requirements). The essential part of a franchise, however, is the transfer of certain industrial or intellectual property rights related to trademarks, servicemarks, trade names, shop signs, utility models, designs, copyrights, know-how, or patents that are to be exploited for the resale of goods or the provision of services to end-user customers.

Overall, franchising has four common elements:

☐ Independent business parties. The franchisor and franchisee are distinct and independent from each other except for the franchise relationship, the major exception being company-owned stores.
☐ The goods and services are sold or offered in a regularized fashion as part of a network established by the franchisor.
☐ The use of the franchisor's trademark, tradename, servicemark, or other intellectual property.
☐ Compensation is received by the franchisor from the franchisee in various forms, including up-front fees, royalties linked to sales, and special fees for assistance provided by the franchisor.

Franchising requires an intense relationship between the franchisor and the franchisee and therein lies the tradeoff in the franchising relationship. Franchisors (those granting the franchise) have the right to require significant fees and substantial compliance to their store design, product mix and ways of doing business. The franchisee (who is receiving the franchise) has the right to expect a high level of services from the franchisor and to be able to depend on its advice to achieve its goals. These rights have been protected by laws so that, for instance, a fast food franchisor can demand its stores be cleaner than the local code requires and the franchisee can demand reasonable financial success if they put their store where the franchisor tells them to.

216. Franchise Methods

There are five major methods used by franchisors in establishing franchise relationships:

Direct Investment—The Company-Owned Store. In this case, the franchisor establishes a direct investment in each country where it will commence operations, normally by establishing a subsidiary company that sets up its own store(s). This will be accomplished when the franchisor:

☐ Desires to approach the market directly
☐ Is unable to locate good franchisee candidates
☐ Wishes to establish itself in the marketplace first and then sell its already-established stores to local companies at a profit

While clearly the most expensive manner to establish franchise operations, this method allows for complete control, and also for the greater potential profit.

Master Franchise. In this method, the franchisor establishes a relationship with one company and grants it the right to establish franchises in the selected country or territory, either on its own, or by giving it the right to sub-franchise. The master franchisee will be responsible for all of the duties of the franchisor in the territory, including collections of royalties and fees from the sub-franchisees, if any.

Joint Venture. In this method, the franchisor creates a subsidiary in the territory, which is partially owned by other entities—at least one of which is a local party. The subsidiary then creates company-owned stores, licenses others, or undertakes a combination of the two.

Appointing of the Franchisee(s) by the Parent Company. In this case, the parent company, or a regional first-line subsidiary, makes a direct appointment of franchisees on a case-by-case basis in one or several territories. No local subsidiary of the franchisor is created. This is probably the most common form of international franchising.

Direct Licensing. This form of franchising is closer to a more traditional technology transfer. In this case, the franchise arrangement may cover only the use of trademarks, trade names, and servicemarks, and the sale of a key component of the product. This form is very common in the soft drink industry, where the franchisor grants use of the intellectual property, along with the sale of syrup, which is then used by the franchisee, normally a bottler, who manufactures the final product.

217. Franchising as an International Strategy

The franchising method is normally used when a company has some valuable intellectual property and methods it believes can be used across international boundaries. Additionally, it will be used when the company feels it is stronger in the development of the product than in the international skills necessary to market the product in other economic and/or cultural environments.

For a company to consider using the franchise method, it should consider the following *internal company characteristics:*

☐ The company (except for the direct investment strategy) does not have the resources or desire to invest heavily in overseas markets.
☐ The company has explored, and rejected, the distributor method.
☐ The company has determined that traditional licensing will not work.
☐ The company normally works through franchisees in its home country, and has developed the appropriate methods and techniques.

Franchising is also dependent upon *product characteristics* of the company. The use of franchises does not make sense if the company manufactures or sells components or products that alone do not lend themselves to franchising. For example, a manufacturer of computer peripherals will not normally establish a computer store, but could become a supplier to franchised computer stores. The same would be true of manufacturers of printing presses or food condiments. Most franchises are established in their home market as distinct operations that are primarily market-driven rather than product-driven. This would not, however, stop a potato grower or marketeer from establishing a separate company that creates a fast food concept based on potatoes as its primary offering.

Market characteristics also help determine whether to franchise. Franchisers of self-service laundries or cleaners may not be able to successfully compete in countries where labor-saving devices and time saving are unnecessary, due to the availability and low cost of labor.

Finally, *legal and financial considerations* must be examined. The U.S.A. and the European Economic Community have very strict laws that favor the franchisee. Canada has no national franchise legislation, but the provinces of Alberta and Quebec do. In Japan, franchises are regulated by very tough laws. These laws sometimes make it difficult to establish controls over franchises and also protect the franchisee against such things as franchisor marketing studies that may exaggerate market potential.

Financial considerations include the problems of obtaining royalties and other payments from soft currency countries, and a greater financial exposure (than, say, straight distributors), if the franchise is inadequately funded or does not work. While distributors may be costly to terminate, it is even more difficult to close franchises that do not work because of the exposure to the value of intellectual property if the company is forced out of the market. A poor franchise might have to be taken over by the franchisor, which would then be pushed into a territory where it had no desire to make direct investments.

218. The Advantages of Using the Franchise Method

Assuming that the company has already developed its franchise system in the home country, this strategy will then offer it the opportunity to enter into the international marketplace with a low capital investment. Many times the up-front fees paid by the franchisee will more than cover the initial costs of locating and appointing them. Thereafter, if all works smoothly, the company will then enjoy a steady stream of revenues that it can take to profit or use to build its markets in other territories.

Franchising allows a company to be present in markets where it is necessary for a local party to be very close to the customers. It allows for international skill centralization with local operational decentralization.

Because the franchisee is more likely to make a larger investment than a distributor, he or she will tend to be more dedicated than a distributor, which may have multiple lines and less at stake. Franchising is also a very effective method to ascribe the company's trademarks and servicemarks in the territory.

Franchising is often the first type of retail business to enter into the emerging market economies. Because of lack of marketing knowledge and practice, the former republics of the old Soviet Union, China, Vietnam, and Eastern Europe are excellent candidates for franchises.

219. The Disadvantages of Franchising

If the company has not developed its franchise system, or if this system must be fine-tuned for the international marketplace (e.g., laundromats in countries where there are few washing machines or dryers), the cost to develop franchises may be very high in the preparation of control procedures and marketing strategies. Franchising requires substantial involvement of the franchisor (or headquarters in a company store) to encourage and enforce product quality, service and standardization.

Franchisers may be subject to possible financial and/or legal exposure if franchisees are provided with improper information or are forced to close because of underfunding, poor products and services, or other reasons. Franchising is also closely tied to an understanding of cultural considerations. Donut franchises have had difficulties in England because that country's citizens were unwilling to replace their traditional pastries with American-style donuts.

Because franchisees do not export, and are much more likely to import, there may be problems in getting paid in soft-currency countries or any country that applies exchange controls.

Finally, as implied above, franchises are much more difficult to abandon once they are established, because more than just money is at stake. The franchisor must also consider the commitments made to the franchisee and the value of its intellectual property, which may be impaired by an unsuccessful attempt to reach a new market.

220. Selecting Franchisees

Before selecting franchisees, a company must do more advanced planning than it would for agents, distributors, or traditional licensing. Because franchisees deal directly with the end-user customer, and because the products associated with franchising are more culturally sensitive, the franchisor must have developed its own understanding of the local market and not rely solely on information provided by its potential franchisees.

Additionally, a franchisor needs to more carefully examine its potential franchisees than it might its potential distributors. Having adequate unencumbered capital and a good status in the community are important elements in franchisee selection.

221. An International Franchisee's Profile

If you have decided to use franchisees as a means to enter international markets, it is probably wise to develop a profile of characteristics you might seek in a good franchisee. This profile might consist of the following characteristics:

Franchisee's Profile

1. Sufficient unencumbered capital for up-front costs and operations
2. Positive reputation in the local community
3. Intense consumer market knowledge and particular knowledge of store location
4. Industry and product knowledge
5. Ability to conform to operations and procedures of the franchisor
6. Ability to work with the franchisor in resolving market and product-unique problems
7. Ability to expand its operations, if successful—if this does not appear likely, exclusivity in a market should not be awarded
8. Knowledge of local personnel practices and issues
9. Ability to make optimistic, yet reasonable, market projections
10. Understanding of the value of and ability to protect the franchisor's intellectual property
11. Willing to accept products and services from the franchisor
12. Willing to participate in advertising programs

222. Maintaining the Franchise Relationship

In no area of international business transactions is the question of maintenance so important as in franchising. There is no question that the franchisor must have a high level of commitment and significant level of control over the franchisee. The franchisee is likely to be the weaker party of the two, not only financially, but also in knowledge level. Additionally, there is far less possibility of the replication of the product or system for a franchisee than a licensee. Overall, a good part of what the franchisee pays the franchisor is for continued commitment and support.

Ideally, the franchisor wants the franchisee to learn its techniques, provide sufficient royalties and other payments, and carry the franchisor's message to the customers. This can only be accomplished if the franchisor has developed the proper techniques and "culturalized" them, to the extent necessary to the local market. There are no substitutes for clear, understandable procedures and organization guides, viable training and advertising programs, and consulting services. The franchisor must make sure the franchisee has learned all of its techniques and will continue to apply them throughout the relationship.

Franchising is a new industry, and global franchising is still in its infancy. The legal system has not yet caught up with the process except initially to provide protection for franchisees against unscrupulous franchisors. However, the law seems to be moving to provide assistance in supporting "reasonable" franchisor requirements. Recently, a French court upheld the termination by McDonald's of a French franchisee who failed to meet McDonald's cleanliness standards, even though it met the less stringent standards of the local health codes.

Franchising is one of the most rapidly growing areas of international business transactions. The next few years will not only bring new laws, but also the development of international standards and codes of ethics. As the most information-intensive of all the transactions, it will be the most likely to continue its development in both form and content in the years to come.

The most important element to be considered in franchising is that both parties to the arrangement make deep and long-term commitments to each other. This makes international franchising a particularly challenging method of global business, but one in which the greatest opportunity is likely to exist.

TECHNOLOGY LICENSING

International licensing of technology is a viable alternative to the exportation of finished products through intermediaries and/or to direct equity investments. Licensing may stand on its own as an international strategy or be part of a larger strategy (e.g., licensing technology to an equity joint venture).

This section examines the various forms of licensing and discusses the pros and cons of technology transfer as a global strategy. It also explores how to profit from licensing and how to protect your valuable intellectual property.

223. Transferring Intangible Property Across Borders

International licensing is normally a contractual arrangement in which the *licensor* (granting company) grants access to its technology, patents, trademarks, copyrights, trade secrets, know how, and other intellectual property to a foreign *licensee* (receiving company) to be used by the licensee in exchange for a fee and/or other considerations. This grant may be in the form of a direct sale of the rights or be limited to a certain period of time.

Technology licensing is a viable alternative to the exportation of finished products through intermediaries (export trading companies, agents, and distributors) or to the various types of equity involvement (joint venture and direct investment), which could be chosen as an international strategy. This strategy can be selected on its own as a global strategy or as part of a broader international strategy, which might include licensing in only selected markets while applying other methods to other markets.

Additionally, licensing may also be a component of another international strategy. For example, licenses may be needed to allow agents or distributors to use certain trademarks, servicemarks, or copyrights. It is also often an integral part of an equity joint venture and sometimes the agreed-to value of the technology is used as part of the equity investment. Finally, many companies use intercompany licenses to protect the intellectual property of the parent company that is held by the subsidiary, and to allow for payments by the subsidiary to the parent of certain license fees.

224. Methods of Licensing

There are five common methods in which technology is transferred through licenses. These fall into two general categories—licensing alone and licensing as part of another transaction.

Licensing Alone

Sourcing

In this case, the licensor might provide technology and other resources (e.g., raw material and/or components) to a manufacturer abroad, that will manufacture either a completed product or more advanced components and send them back to the company for final assembly or sale in its home market or abroad. The foreign manufacturer is normally not charged a fee for the technology, and is not permitted to use it for other than sourcing purposes. It either receives a fee for its work or is allowed to resell the components or finished products back to the licensor for a profit.

Licensing to an Independent Party

In this case, the licensor will license the technology to a foreign licensee to use the intellectual property and/or know-how to make its own products for sale in its home and/or other agreed-to markets. In exchange for those rights, the licensee will pay to the licensor a fee (normally called a royalty), which is usually based on the sale, by the licensee, of the products resulting from the technology. The licensor may also receive other payments, which could result from management, training, and consulting fees.

Licensing as Part of Another Transaction

Joint Venture

Licensing may be used with equity joint venture in two general ways:

☐ As part of the transaction in much the same way as you would license to an independent party (that is, the licensor charges fees to the joint venture which is the licensee).

☐ As part of the licensor's equity contribution to the joint venture. Here the parties will agree to the value of the technology as part of the total worth of the joint venture. For example, two parties agree to create a 50/50 percent equity joint venture with a value of U.S.$2,000,000. The licensee may contribute its share (U.S.$1,000,000) in cash, real property and equipment. The licensor could value its contribution in cash, capital goods, components and technology licenses. In this case, for the sake of discussion, the parties agree to place a value on the technology of U.S.$200,000. This would mean that the licensor would receive its 50 percent for the license rights plus U.S.$800,000 in other contributions. Normally, if done in this manner, the licensor may not be entitled to additional royalties.

Distributor/Agent License

The licensor may need to grant certain rights to distributors and/or agents for the purpose of allowing those entities to use its trademarks, servicemarks and copyrights in the use of business cards, stationery, brochures and catalogs. This license can be included as part of the distributor or agent agreement (it normally is), or by a separate document if the rights granted need to be distinguished from the general marketing rights. Companies using distributors and agents should be aware that the granting of those license rights might require the agreement to be registered and/or approved by a government agency in the home country of the distributor or agent.

Intercompany Agreements

Here the licensor will grant to its subsidiaries or affiliates abroad the rights to certain intellectual property. This is done for a number of reasons:

☐ To identify only those rights which the parent wants the subsidiary to obtain. For example, a marketing subsidiary will not normally obtain the rights to manufacture and may obtain only rights similar to those normally granted to a distributor.

☐ In some jurisdictions, the parent company may be able to charge a royalty or other payments to its subsidiaries and affiliates.

☐ In the case above, these royalties or other fees may allow the parent company to reduce its global tax exposure by charging fees in lower tax jurisdictions. This assumes that the subsidiary will be able to deduct the technology fees paid to the parent as a business expense (e.g., reducing corporate taxes owed in Germany [50 percent], and paying taxes on the additional income in the U.S.A. [36 percent]).

☐ In the case of the subsidiary being sold, only those rights expressed in the intercompany agreement can be sold with the business.

A global company would use intercompany agreements to shift the flow of technology to where it is needed and the flow of royalties to the lowest tax jurisdictions.

225. Licensing as an International Strategy

The international licensing strategy is normally used when a company has valuable intellectual property it believes is suitable in other countries, but the company is not ready to make a direct foreign investment and/or is precluded from importing into the country either because the government limits importation or because market size does not justify direct importation through the use of trading companies, agents, or distributors.

For a company to consider the licensing method, it should consider the following *internal company characteristics*:

☐ The company lacks capital, management resources and knowledge of foreign markets, but is willing to commit some of its technical resources to assist licensees.

☐ The company has, or is willing to spend the time and money to legally protect the technology in the countries in which it will license.

☐ The technologies involved are normally not central to the licensor's core business.

☐ The company has developed a licensing system in the home country that it feels it can take abroad.

☐ The company hopes to be able to take advantage of improvements made by its licensees and to obtain those improvements through cross-licensing.

226. Product and Market Characteristics

Licensing is also dependent upon *product characteristics*. Large and cumbersome products are often good candidates for licensing as are those products that are very basic but have been technologically enhanced by the licensor. For example, a company that has developed a superior building product (such as a brick with a built-in coupling device) is unlikely to be able to export the finished product because of its cost and size, and, because bricks are locally produced in about every country, they may be subject to tariff and non-tariff import restrictions. To take its business abroad, this company is likely to be more successful in licensing the technology for manufacturing the bricks to foreign licensees.

Products subject to rapid technological change are also good licensing candidates, especially if the licensor is continuing to undertake significant R&D. This allows the licensor to keep technologically ahead of any licensee who might become a competitor, and to prevent the spread of the technology by the licensee.

Market characteristics must also be examined in the discussion to license internationally. For many large companies, licensing is designed as a means to enter secondary markets. By secondary markets, we mean:

☐ Those in which the company has decided not to enter through foreign investment or marketing through intermediaries.

☐ Those in which local companies or foreign competitors have a strong presence, so that import of finished products would be difficult.

☐ Regions of the world that are not of primary interest on a country-by-country basis, but where a licensee could produce sufficient products to justify the relationship. For example, a licensee in stable Costa Rica could be selected to manufacture and market to its less stable neighbors in Central America and the Caribbean.

☐ Those in which the company would like to develop a market and establish its goodwill, which then could later be exploited through direct investment.

227. Legal and Financial Considerations

The potential international licensor must look at legal and financial considerations. Often the decision to license has been made since the company has no other alternative because the government restricts direct investment through controls on foreign ownership or because it restricts the development of a marketing network by a number of tariff barriers. Brazil and Japan have used this strategy. In both cases, the countries have large internal markets and public policies in favor of building local industry. While this policy generally worked in Japan, it has failed in Brazil because that country has also greatly restricted the ability of licensors to obtain reasonable royalties and subjected all payments abroad to strict exchange controls.

However prohibitive this proverbial carrot stick may be, some countries that restrict imports do offer a potential "carrot." For licensors who are willing to accept limited royalties and allow for significant assembly or manufacture in their country (value-added), some governments will allow meaningful reductions on the tariffs and other import requirements (e.g., import licenses), on the component parts or finished products. This tends to give the combination licensor/licensee a competitive edge in the market, which could ultimately maximize royalties and the sale of components by the licensor.

228. The Pros and Cons of International Licensing

Pros

☐ Licensing allows the licensor to enter into foreign markets with a relatively low financial risk. In most cases, the licensor will have already made the investment in developing the technology to be licensed. In fact, the income received from foreign licensing may assist the licensor in further developing licensed technology or new technologies.

☐ Licensing allows the licensor to team with a foreign company with adequate capital and a local marketing network to build products or provide services that otherwise would not be sold or provided in that foreign market.

☐ Licensing may enable the licensor to achieve an equity participation in a country that would not permit the establishment of a wholly owned subsidiary. This is a good approach where the value of the license is used as part of the equity contribution.

☐ Licensing can be used to test markets that the licensor may desire, at a later time, to enter with a direct foreign investment.

☐ The potential licensee has the opportunity to acquire technology more rapidly and/or less expensively than it would by developing its own technologies.

☐ Licensing can assist both licensee and licensor when both have significant development capabilities and are willing to cross-license their new developments.

Cons

☐ The biggest drawback to licensing from the licensor's point of view is the possibility of creating a future competitor. Once an understanding of the technology is acquired by the licensee, it may seek to exploit that technology in the licensor's home market or in other countries where the licensor enjoys a competitive position. To a certain extent, this problem can be lessened by three considerations:
  • Restrictions in the legal agreements.
  • Licensing assembly or manufacture of only some of the components—requiring licensee to purchase certain components from licensor. The licensee, therefore, will only be able to *assemble* a completed product.
  • Licensing products that are not state-of-the-art, or products in which the industry or technology is rapidly changing.

☐ If the licensee fails to meet quality standards, it may cause serious harm to the image of the licensor. This tends to be a serious problem where the licensee is not adequately financed or does not have enough trained personnel.

☐ While the licensor may be able to enter markets with low financial risks, it does run the risk of running into a number of licensee demands which could make the relationship very costly. This is especially true for small companies that may find their critical

R&D people constantly on planes to fix the problems encountered by the licensees.

☐ The licensing parties may run into a number of problems in dealing with the government of the licensee's country, and occasionally with the government in the country of the licensor.

☐ Licensing may bring short-term gains but may not be a good long-term strategy if the licensee later is able to block the importation of finished products into the country by the licensor.

☐ Fees received from the licensee may be the easiest to tax and may be subjected to high rates of taxation. Check with your tax experts on the issue of tax withholding on technology transfer.

229. Selecting Licensees

The decision to license is a complex and difficult one. Many licensing relationships do not succeed because the parties fail to understand each other's real agenda. This is sometimes complicated by the fact that the reasons for licensing are not strictly commercial but are determined by government policies and actions.

In the late 1980s, for example, an American company wished to take advantage of the booming market for entry-level mainframe computers in Brazil. Because Brazilian government policies at the time precluded foreign ownership, and because import duties were high, the U.S. company decided to license a prominent local company to assemble their mainframes. The hope was to establish themselves in the market, obtain royalties, and sell components to the Brazilian licensee.

After a considerable search, the company decided to license a Brazilian computer peripheral manufacturer. This company had had considerable success in using foreign licenses to produce high-quality products. Although it had little experience in mainframes, it appeared as if the company was well-funded and was willing to acquire the technical expertise necessary to be successful with this new endeavor.

But the U.S. company misjudged the real intentions of the licensee. The licensee's owner, on the strength of a possible license from a prominent U.S. company, created a new company and took it public. By the time the parties came to the negotiating table, the licensee's owner had already made millions of dollars and was less concerned with the success of the project. Once the relationship got under way, and problems arose, the licensee's owner lost interest and allowed the project to fail. The U.S. company then lost a window of opportunity from which it took many years to recover.

230. A Licensee Profile

If you have decided to use licensing as a means to enter international markets, it is probably wise to develop a profile of characteristics you might seek in a good licensee. This profile might consist of the following characteristics:

Licensee's Profile

1. Understanding of the licensor's products and technologies
2. Experience as a licensee, and perhaps as a licensor
3. Good local reputation in the community
4. Sufficient funds to license technologies, acquire capital equipment, and for working capital
5. Access to raw materials and components
6. Sufficient in-country infrastructure
7. Existence of, or willingness to employ, qualified workers
8. Willing to keep licensor information confidential
9. Willing to pay appropriate license fees and acquire services and components from the licensor
10. Access to local markets
11. Ability to keep up with the technical developments of the licensor and of the industry
12. Ability to develop a network of suppliers
13. Quality orientation
14. Willing to consider nonexclusivity or to earn exclusivity
15. Offers the possibility of improving the licensed product and cross-licensing those improvements to the licensor
16. Potential to be a future equity joint venture partner of the licensor

231. Government's Role in Technology Transfer

As international business transactions become more complex, so does the government's interest in regulating them. This section briefly explores some of the government (state) objectives in technology transfer. You should seriously consider the role the government will play before entering into technology and transfer discussions.

A few nations (primarily the U.S.A.) still have some fairly tough regulations on the *outflow* of technology. The U.S. may have military interests (sale of weapons technology, or of machine tools, which would be used to make weapons), economic interests (to prevent competition), scarce resources, and significant foreign policy considerations, (e.g., to embargo Iraq and promote nuclear nonproliferation), which it applies to the licensing of technologies abroad. Japan is another country with great concerns on the outflow of technology.

Most regulations applied by governments, however, are in the area of *incoming* technology. Here, the state's interests are varied and sometimes complex. Of first concern is to assure that the incoming technology will truly assist in the modernization of national industry. Throughout the 1960s and 1970s, many governments in the developing world adopted the strategy of import substitution. Technologies that did not create replacement of imports were heavily regulated to assure that they were subject to lower royalties and higher taxes.

Some governments tried to regulate incoming technologies so that they were in line with what the government perceived was necessary to defend, or create, a certain lifestyle. The emphasis was to deny technologies that created needs and desires for products and services which were beyond the needs of most consumers (e.g., infant formula or gas-guzzling automobiles). Emphasis was placed on the "appropriateness" of the technology to the level of development and ideology of the state.

Governments also restrict incoming technologies for balance of payments and hard currency considerations. Restrictions on the amounts of royalties and the availability of hard currency to remit abroad are placed on technologies that already exist in the country, or for products deemed unnecessary. Additionally, some countries place currency limitations on needed technologies to allow those technologies to be developed locally. The goal is to create a protected local market before foreign technologies are allowed to enter.

Finally, restrictions are placed on incoming technologies to assist in the improvement of the local intellectual infrastructure. These restrictions are not in the form of monetary limitations, but rather in the form of additional requirements on the licensor. These restrictions are in the area of quality guarantees, contributions to R&D of the licensee, required training of licensee employees, and requirement that the technologies transferred would result in products and services that could be marketed globally.

Determining What to License

Identifying the technologies to be transferred is only part of the licensing decision. Both licensor and licensee must also consider what rights to those technologies are to be granted. Rights granted can range from simple *use of a finished product* to the complete *sale of the rights to the entire technology.*

232. The Right to Use the Product

In this case, the licensor may only be granting the licensee *the right to use the product* for its own recreational or commercial use. The best example of this type of right is in the area of computer software. The software company normally grants only the right to use the software provided on a certain computer (sometimes spelled out by the serial number on the machine). This right might include the right to make a backup copy of the software, but definitely does not include the right to make additional copies for other sale or use. The right to use (only) may also be important in licenses granted in sourcing situations.

233. The Right to Market and Sell

The sourcing relationship is one in which the licensee may have the right to assemble and/or manufacture, but *does not* have the right to market and sell (except to the licensor or customers designated by the licensor). Whatever assembly/manufacturing rights agreed to between the parties, they will need to determine where the licensee is able to market the products that result from the technology. Antitrust laws in some countries (mainly in the U.S.A. and the EEC) prohibit absolute restrictions on the sale of products. However, the licensor can make reasonable restrictions on the licensee's marketing rights. These include:

☐ No marketing where the licensor has other licensees.
☐ Limited restrictions on marketing and sales to the home country of the licensor.

☐ Limitation on sale of the products where the licensee does not have sales offices and/or cannot provide installation and after-sales service.

234. Assembling versus Manufacturing

Is the licensee being granted merely the rights to assemble provided or acquired components or will it receive the technology and rights to undertake "significant transformation" of raw materials into components and/or the finished product?

To illustrate the point, consider assembly versus manufacture of a twist-action writing instrument (pen or pencil). An assembly situation might be one in which the licensee is provided with the right to acquire or purchase from the licensor the finished components, and is given the right to assemble the components into a finished product, which it then places into a container suitable for marketing. A manufacturing situation is one in which the licensor provides the licensee with the technology sufficient to manufacture the components (say the instrument and its ink or lead source) from raw materials, and to design and complete the finished product from the manufactured components.

Licensors looking to protect their technologies will try to limit the licensee's right to either the straight assembly of all components or to the manufacture of certain local components that it will assemble in combinations with other components supplied by the licensor or acquired through third parties. In this circumstance, the licensee never acquires the right to replicate the product in its entirety, and is therefore less likely to become a future competitor of the licensor.

A variant of this approach is the *staged technology transfer* that may begin with assembly rights and allow the licensee, upon reaching certain milestones (which normally include a certain level of payment to the licensor), to acquire more and more manufacturing rights.

235. Limiting Rights to Licensees

If the licensee is incapable (particularly at the beginning of the relationship) to complete all of the assembly or manufacturing processes, the licensor may consider whether to add *"have made"* or *sublicense* language to the assembly and/or manufacturing rights granted. The language would allow the licensee to source some, or all, of its production from third parties. While "have made" and sublicense rights may increase the speed in which products enter the market and reduce the licensee's capital costs, the licensor should be careful not to grant those rights if the licensee plans to use them only to become a contractor rather than a true licensee. Licensees that contract almost everything out may never develop the technological expertise needed to properly service the market and, unless they can carefully control costs, they may never be competitive in the marketplace.

One of the key licensing issues is that of whether the licensor grants to the licensee the rights to the technology at a particular time *(static license)* or the right to the continuous updates and enhancements *(dynamic license)*. A static license has the advantage to the licensor that the licensee is less likely to become a future competitor. It may also make sense to use a static license, at least at the beginning of the relationship, if the licensee has not yet developed sufficient technical capabilities, or the products or services resulting from the technology are, and are likely to remain, appropriate to the licensee's marketplace.

The licensee, however, may demand a more dynamic license, or its government may require it. In some cases, this demand may be reasonable in light of the up-front expenditures that must be made by the licensee, or because the level of royalties and other payments are sufficient to require a longer-term payoff to the licensee. In other cases, the demand may be in line because the market size complexity and/or competitive nature may require the licensee to be on top of all developments. Two compromise strategies commonly used are:

☐ Begin with a static license but allow, in the initial agreement, for updates and enhancements if certain goals are met or conditions occur. Examples of goals might be the payment of a certain level of fees or the assembly/manufacture of a certain number of units. For conditions, the examples might be proof of the availability in the country of more modern versions by their competitors or the licensee's availability to manufacture, sell, and service the more advanced product.

☐ Begin with a dynamic license, but tie the license only to certain versions of products or to certain products in the line. When new products are developed by the licensor, then a new agreement will be necessary.

236. Revenue from Royalties

A royalty is normally a fee associated with the production and/or sale of products and services that result from the use of the technology. It may be a fixed payment per unit (unit charge royalty), or it may be a percentage of the sales price of the products or services (percentage royalty). In designing royalty fee schedules, the parties should consider the following:

☐ When will the fee be paid? Should it be paid upon production or upon sale? If the licensee is able to keep its inventory to a minimum, this would not be a critical issue. If the licensee develops significant inventory, however, it is clearly better for the licensor to be paid on the basis of production.

☐ Make sure you understand *on what* the royalty percentage, or per unit fee, will be paid. In the case of a percentage payment, will the royalty be based on the net sales price of the product to the customer (less taxes and shipping costs), or will it be paid in proportion to the value added to the product or service by the licensee? For example, assume we have a five percent royalty that would be applied to U.S.$2,000,000 in net sales. These net sales were generated by the licensee with a 50 percent value added by it to the product. In the case of a straight royalty based on net sales, the royalty due would be U.S.$100,000. In the case of value added, the royalty would be U.S.$50,000 ($2,000,000 × .05 × .50 = U.S.$50,000).

☐ Determine what is meant by *value added*. This term normally includes not only the value added by the licensee itself, but also any value added for components and services sourced in the licensee's country.

☐ Who will be responsible for the payment of withholding taxes on royalties paid to the licensor? In order to tax the revenues of foreign licensors, many countries place a withholding tax on royalties. These generally range from five percent to 40 percent, with 10 percent to 25 percent being most common. If local law allows, the licensor may require the licensee to withhold and pay those taxes. If local law does not allow for licensee payments of licensor's withholding taxes, the parties may consider increasing the royalty amount to provide the licensor with the after-tax royalty level it requires.

☐ Be sure to establish in the agreement between the parties the appropriate accounting procedures and audit rights to be able to assist the licensor in obtaining its full royalties, and the licensee to assure it obtains its full local tax benefits.

237. Revenue from Other Fees

In addition to the royalties, the parties may consider other fees for the use of the technology. Most important would be an initial or up-front fee. An up-front fee for technology transfer is often demanded by the licensor. This fee could be structured as a nonrefundable fee or it could be an advance on future royalties, or it might be used to reduce future royalties. In any case, the up-front fee is normally designed with the following factors in mind:

☐ It will be used to cover some, or all, of the up-front costs of the licensor in transferring the technology.
☐ It will be used to show the seriousness of the licensee.
☐ It will be used as a hedge in case the licensee is unable to commence production, or is unable to reach adequate production levels. Therefore, from the licensor's point of view, the fee should be due at the latest when the technology is delivered and never be tied to the commencement of production.

What to charge as an up-front fee is clearly subject to the bargaining power of the parties, but in situations where there are strict government controls on technology fees, a large up-front fee should be seriously considered. For example, for years Brazil limited technology transfer royalties to five percent on the Brazilian value added to the net sales price. However, the law did allow the licensing parties to agree to up-front payments as long as they did not exceed reasonable calculations of technology payments over five years, and were present-valued.

Assume the licensing parties were about to sign a five-year agreement at a royalty of five percent on the Brazilian value-added. Assume the value added was reasonably estimated to be U.S.$30 million (e.g., $2 million in the first year, $4 million in the second, $6 million in the third, $8 million in the fourth, and $10 million in the fifth), then the royalties over the period are estimated to be U.S.$1.5 million (five percent of U.S.$30 million). If a five percent interest per year figure was used, the present value of U.S.$1.5 million over five years is .7835 resulting in an up-front royalty of U.S.$1,175,250.

This amount would be subject to withholding tax and the agreement would have to be royalty-free thereafter. The ability to collect this amount in advance, however, might make the transaction quite palatable to any prospective licensor.

238. Sale of Components and Products

The limitation on the amount of royalties that could be charged, plus the heavy taxes associated with such royalties, have caused licensors to look at other means of obtaining revenues through licensing. This has pushed licensors toward arranging transactions in which they will sell components and some finished products to the licensee (e.g., the license is for products A and B in which components are sold by the licensor, and the licensee also purchases from the licensor completed products C, D, and E to have the complete product line). This results in a double benefit for the licensor in that it is able to sell more products while reducing the possibility of the licensee becoming a competitor. It also serves the licensee's interest in keeping its royalties and production costs down.

Another way for a licensor to maneuver around the royalty restrictions and tax problems is to reduce, or eliminate, royalties and raise the price of capital equipment, components, and finished products sold to the licensee. This approach, however, may not work in countries that have high import duties because the additional cost of the duties may exceed the royalties desired. This will depend on many factors such as the ultimate destination of the goods, but it should be considered as one approach to the licensing relationship.

239. Sale of Services

In addition to straight royalty fees and sale of products, the licensor may also consider what revenues can be obtained from the sale of services to the licensee. Said services normally fall into three categories:

☐ *Management services.* The licensor agrees to provide personnel to assist the licensee in managing either the technology transfer or perhaps the plant itself.

☐ *Training services.* The licensor may provide the licensee a certain amount of free training to assist in the original technology transfer. After that point, the licensee must pay for any additional training. While this may be a viable source of revenue, the licensor should consider not to price this so high that the licensee will not take advantage of the training offered, thereby perhaps placing the quality of the products in jeopardy.

☐ *Consulting services.* The licensee may require a certain degree of consulting from the licensor to respond to production problems or to improve production or marketing capabilities. Consulting services can also be used for marketing and sales of the products and services.

MANAGING LICENSEES

Finding and appointing license partners is just the beginning of your relationship. Because licensing is more complex than working with straight marketeers, both licensors and licensees should not enter into relationships with each other unless they feel relatively comfortable that there is a good chance to build a long-term relationship. How to maintain that relationship is the subject of this section.

240. Maintaining the License Relationship

Potential licensors should give considerable thought to whether licensing is to be an occasional or full-blown strategy. If licensing is viewed by the licensor to be an occasional strategy that presents the opportunity to acquire some marginal revenues and/or to address less critical markets, the licensor should focus the bulk of its activities in the selection and appointment process, and try to key in on opportunities that exist from only the more sophisticated licensees. The basic reason for this is that licensors of this type are unlikely to have, or acquire, the resources necessary to properly manage less sophisticated licensees. Under these circumstances, the licensor may be willing to appoint an individual or small team of persons who have licensing as their responsibility, and perhaps make available members of their technical team for occasional consultation and training. The licensee, however, will have to be pretty much self-sufficient.

241. Internal Management Issues

The management of licensee activities can be done from three possible groups: the international division; a distinct licensing function, which may also manage licensees in the home market; or from the operational division, which has responsibility for the technology and the products. All have their advantages and disadvantages and the company may eventually decide to create a matrixed solution.

The international division should be staffed with people who are savvy in cultural and other variables of selecting and appointing inter-

national licensees, but would probably not have the technical expertise to deal with the licensees on a day-to-day basis. A licensing function could be developed with the purpose of optimizing licensing as a
corporate strategy, and it should develop considerable expertise on
how to deal with licensees. However, it would be difficult for such a
function to fully manage the licensor function when it comes to providing technical assistance to the licensees. The operations division
may be able to resolve technical issues and problems, but it may lack
the expertise in cultural and political aspects, and may take a more
parochial view as to how the licensing process fits into the overall
strategic plan of the company.

To solve this potential management problem, the company should
consider the following points and suggestions:

☐ Have members of all groups involved in the selection and
appointment process. Avoid international "deals" teams that find
and appoint the prospects and then turn them over to operations
without that group being sufficiently involved at the outset, or
"bought into" the deal.
☐ Appoint one individual or office that is to serve as liaison with the
licensee. This point of contact should then work with all the
appropriate groups in the company to evaluate and serve the needs
of the licensee.
☐ Develop a system that rewards all involved groups as to revenue
and/or profit credit.
☐ Have top corporate management communicate its feelings
regarding each license relationship to the involved parties, and
identify one individual in top management to resolve any problems
between the functions or departments.

242. Licensor Involvement

Ideally, a licensor would like to limit its relationship to collecting
royalties and selling products and components. Realistically, the licensor is likely to be more heavily involved in the licensee's activities,

especially if the technology is complex, the licensee needs continuing technical assistance, and/or the licensee is having marketing problems.

The licensor needs to decide whether it will take a proactive or reactive response in dealing with its licensees. The proactive response may include management assistance, periodic visits, progress reports and, in extreme cases, actual involvement in the activities of the licensee through board membership, or through the provision of personnel on the licensee's site. The licensor needs to determine which, if any, of the proactive alternatives it is willing to offer. This will obviously depend on the trade-offs involved, but even in situations where the licensee is willing to pay for these services, the licensor needs to think hard before committing human resources that can be used in other ways.

243. The Fairness Principle

Despite the best legal agreements, the balance of benefits between the parties may have to be reassessed and adjusted as the relationship continues. Although licensing may not be part of an equity joint venture in which profits are formally shared, it is a collaboration between the parties in which both parties must benefit. High royalties and/or component prices may have to be readjusted downward if the licensee perceives, and can show the licensor, that it is not receiving its fair share. In this case, it may be determined if lower royalties and prices could result in larger volumes that ultimately would generate more revenues and profits for both parties.

Licensors will soon lose interest in licensees that are not providing them with sufficient revenues and profits to justify the relationship. If the bulk of the benefits are going to the licensee, royalties and products and component price may need to be revised upward, or if that is not legally possible, some other methods must be developed to equalize the relationship (e.g., consulting and/or training agreements).

If neither party is benefiting from the relationship, the parties will need to meet to reassess how to put it back on line or to discuss the best manner to establish a friendly separation. In any case, what we are saying is that a licensing relationship cannot simply be managed from the legal agreement, but that the parties should develop methods to keep the relationship in balance.

244. Misunderstandings and Disputes

Despite many methods of dispute resolution, most misunderstandings and disputes will have to be handled between the licensor and the licensee. To accomplish this in the most efficient manner, consider the following suggestions:

☐ Each party should identify at least one individual who will remain with the project through completion. This individual should attempt to learn and understand the other's side, language, company policies, and cultural variables.

☐ The companies should make a special effort to understand the internal workings of their counterparts. They should share organization charts, company brochures, and other like information.

☐ The parties should communicate regularly by telephone or memos. If possible, a communication schedule should be established and adhered to.

☐ Misunderstandings and problems should be communicated immediately and not allowed to fester.

☐ All parties must continually keep in mind the fairness principle.

Protecting Intellectual Property

All intellectual property is a matter of national law, and property protected in one country is not protected in other countries without registering in each country where protection is sought. A company therefore must decide *where* it will protect its intellectual property rights.

245. Patents

Patent rights and registrations are critical because once a patent is issued it becomes public. A patent provides protection from competition for a limited time (normally 20 years) in order to encourage investment in new technology where secrecy is difficult.

Most countries are signatories to the Convention of the Union of Paris of 1883 and the Patent Cooperative Treaty of 1970. The Paris Convention is administered by the World Intellectual Property Organization (WIPO) and it provides the following benefits to its members.

☐ While patents must be registered in each country, the convention allows the holder of the patent up to 12 months from first registration to file in the other countries. After the 12 months, the first to the patent office obtains the rights.

☐ The Convention assures the right of national treatment. This means, for example, that a U.S. original patent registered in Canada would receive the same treatment as any Canadian patent.

While registration in most key industrial countries is recommended, there are two effective ways to protect patents (at least for a time) in countries where they are not registered.

☐ *Patent pending*—From the time the application is filed with the patent agency to the time it is actually issued, the patent will be in the status of "patent pending." The registration process could take from one to three years during which the patent is not made public. If a company can keep a patent pending for three years plus the one year allowed by the Convention, then it can have up to

four years protection without the cost of registrations. In some industries, such as information technology, four years is an eternity.
☐ *Constantly update product*—Technology is continually updated and enhanced which makes any products that are copied out of date.

246. Trademarks

Trademarks convey the legal right to use a name or a symbol that identifies a company and/or its products. Service marks are also sometimes referred to as tradenames.

Trademarks can and should be registered, but rights to continue them are acquired through use. Trademarks can lose their status if they become too generic (for example, the zipper), so the best tradenames are suggestive (as in Hercules) or arbitrary (such as Kodak cameras or Xerox photocopies).

International protection is provided by the Paris Convention which creates similar treatment as it does for patents except that the period to register is six months for first registration. The Nice Convention breaks trademark registrations down into classes so that except for "famous" trademarks (e.g., Coca Cola), it is likely that you will be protected in one or more classes without being protected in all classes.

The basic legal principle regarding trademarks is to use them or lose them. Trademarks not used for more than three years may be deemed abandoned. Therefore, businesses should be sure they keep their trademarks and servicemarks before the public in countries where they do limited business or are considering doing business in the future.

247. Copyrights

A copyright is a legal right to an artistic or written work including books, films, music and software (which can also be patented). While copyrights are also nationally protected, copyrights come into being when a work is written down or otherwise fixed or recorded. The copyright symbol © in the U.S.A., for example, gives protection although some authors also prefer to register their works.

The Berne and Universal Copyright Conventions provide the general guidelines for copyrights in over 80 nations. Essentially, a copyright is good for 50 years from first use. However, the conventions allow

"Fair Use." Covered in Fair Use is criticism, comment, news reporting, teaching, scholarship, and research. For example, most jurisdictions allow one-time photocopying for educational purposes.

248. Trade Secrets

Trade secrets are any formula, pattern, device, process, tool, mechanism, or compound of particular value to its owner (and, in some cases, his or her employer) that is not protected by patent and is not known or accessible to others.

Because they are not patented, the holder of the trade secret may keep it secret as long as possible (e.g., the formula for Coca Cola). On the other hand, anyone who can figure out the trade secret in a legal manner can share in it.

Trade secrets tend to be protected by state laws (in the U.S.) and national laws in most other countries. The protection may also be found in laws covering the transfer of technology. In general, all laws make it impossible to disseminate or use trade secrets without permission unless they were discovered independently. This is the hardest type of intellectual property to protect.

International Alliances: Non-Equity

While many international alliances take the form of equity joint ventures where a company is owned by two or more parties, there are numerous examples where companies pool their resources for common causes. The three most common non-equity alliances are:

☐ Research and development partnerships—where technology is developed and shared jointly
☐ Joint marketing alliances
☐ Consortium—where parties create a business organization (but not a stock company) to conduct business together

All three types are treated in this section.

249. Using International Alliances

An international alliance could be said to exist when:

☐ Two or more parties contribute tangible and/or intangible assets toward the mutual conduct of business activities
☐ An organization of some type is created between the parties (equity or non-equity)
☐ At least one of the parties is foreign to the targeted market(s)

International alliances can be established between competitors, companies with complementary products and/or services, customers and/or suppliers. They can also be established for an individual project, or as a long-term vehicle to address a particular industry or market.

In today's world, international alliances make more sense than at any time in the history of international trade. The reasons for this include:

☐ The expansion of international competition, which makes it more and more difficult for a company to approach the global market with only its own resources.

☐ The reduction of product cycles, which make it necessary to move faster to establish markets, make sales, and pursue international strategies.

☐ The growing cost of research, product development, and marketing, which force companies to find ways in which to increase efficiencies for both domestic and international markets.

250. Research and Development Partnerships

One common form of a non-equity international alliance is the Research & Development (R&D) partnership. When referring to a non-equity, we are describing relationships in which a new equity company is *not* established, but is instead a relationship between existing businesses.

In an R&D partnership, two or more companies will, by contract, agree to pool their research and development resources to create or enhance technologies and/or products. This can be either companies of different nationalities, or companies of the same nationality, who enter the partnership to develop global products and/or to reach international markets. The products that result from this technology pooling will then normally be distributed by each partner individually within their own international marketing networks, although the R&D partnership could also cover joint marketing.

Another version of technology-sharing is the cross-licensing of existing technologies. In this case, the companies find ways in which to combine their technologies to more rapidly be able to develop products and solutions to sell in the global marketplace.

251. Joint Marketing Alliances

Another non-equity strategic alliance is the joint marketing alliance. This can be of two types. The first is co-marketing ("piggy-backing"). In this case, one business sells the products and/or services of another business along with its own. This type of arrangement is common in the computer, industrial machinery, and electrical products industries, although it is found to some extent in nearly every industry. In the second case, both companies agree to handle the products of the other within their respective international marketing networks. This strategy can work very well where the companies market in different territories, or even within the same territory, but to different customers. Again, this can be structured in a distributor or agency-type of relationship.

252. Consortia

Still another non-equity strategic alliance is the consortium. In a consortium relationship, several participant companies come together to pool their resources to bid on a significant project or group of projects. Normally, each company would have a different specialty which, if bid on or offered alone, could not win the project, but together with other companies with different specialties, could result in offering a viable and complete solution to the customer. Consortia are also sometimes created for the production of specific products.

In creating a consortium, each company retains its individual identity, but together create a *business organization* that does not fit into the standard partnership or corporate form. In fact, no specific "legal entity" is created.

Since the consortium is not considered a legal entity in the manner of a partnership or corporation, it is not treated as such for tax purposes. Each party to the consortium will be responsible for their own taxes. Additionally, the consortium avoids the problems of partnerships in that, if one party pulls out or is adjudged bankrupt, the consortium may continue to exist between the remaining participants. A partnership would have to dissolve.

Consortia are normally created for the purpose of bidding on a series of projects over a given time period and are common in the infrastructure industries. Consortia have also been created for the purpose of jointly producing products, either to meet the specific needs of an individual customer or on a longer-term basis, to provide a source of products to all participants. Our experience indicates that the production of products over the longer-term is best served through the creation of an equity joint venture. However, filling short-term needs may work very well through consortia.

INTERNATIONAL ALLIANCES: EQUITY

An international equity joint venture (IEJV) is similar in many ways to an international alliance, except that an actual company is formed and registered with the appropriate government agencies. In this section, we will explore the advantages and disadvantages of this transactional type and some of the key issues in IEJV formation. We will also review the terms that need to be included in the IEJV agreement.

253. International Equity Joint Ventures

The definition of an international equity joint venture is similar to the definition for an international alliance, except that an actual company is formed and registered with the appropriate government agencies. To reiterate, an international equity joint venture could be defined as two or more parties that contribute tangible, and perhaps intangible, assets toward the conduct of business activities. These assets are used to form a legal entity (partnership, limited partnership, limited liability company or a corporation). The legal entity formed is a distinct company with its own shares, board of directors, officers and employees. It has its own budget and conducts business as a distinct entity. At least one of the parties is foreign to the targeted market(s).

International equity joint ventures (IEJVs) come in many types and styles. The five examples below are illustrative of the types of IEJVs that have been created:

☐ Two or more foreign companies of the same nationality creating an IEJV in a third country. For example, two U.S. corporations, Honeywell and Control Data, created a company in Portugal (called MPI) to manufacture products needed by both foreign companies in their global markets.
☐ A foreign and domestic company creating a joint venture in the domestic country. This is a very typical form of IEJV.
☐ Two or more companies of different nationalities creating an IEJV in a third country. For example, a U.S. and Japanese company creating a joint venture in India.

☐ A foreign company and a domestic government company (or parastatal company—partially government-owned). This type of relationship has become common as the result of the privatization of many companies that has occurred in Great Britain and various Latin American countries.

☐ A foreign company that creates an entity abroad, and then makes a private placement or takes the company public in the country where the company is located, or in global financial markets. This results in the creation of an IEJV.

254. Characteristics of the IEJV

IEVJs may be said to have the following unique characteristics:

Separate legal identity. As stated before, the company formed has a separate identity. Its shares are normally held by its participants, but the company will have its own officers, directors, and employees. Normally it will have its own facilities and will be operated as a distinct company.

Ownership and control is divided among the parties. While ownership is usually divided in the form of shares or quotas, with the company holding the largest or majority shares in theoretical control, it is also necessary to look at other forms of control. A minority party may have considerable influence or control by virtue of being the major technology supplier, the provider of key management, the major customer of the IEJV, or simply because one of the minority participants is a larger player in the international marketplace.

IEJVs are formed through a combination of resources. They are normally formed where no single party possesses all of the assets needed to exploit the available opportunities. To best explore how these resources are combined, we will examine the creation of a sample joint venture between a global company located in the U.S.A. and a local partner located in a developing nation. The IEJV will be located in the developing nation and its purpose will be to finally assemble and sell the products in the developing nation, and those nations in the same geographical area.

The expatriate partner would normally contribute:

☐ Capital—which might include cash, lines of credit, and capital equipment

☐ Technology—various forms of intellectual property, which could include assembly, technology, and marketing know-how
☐ Management expertise
☐ Training and consulting
☐ Finished product and/or parts and components

The host-country partner may also contribute any of the items mentioned above, but may also contribute:

☐ An existing physical presence in the country, including use of real estate and other property
☐ Knowledge of language, culture, and local business conditions
☐ Rights from the host country government to undertake the proposed activity
☐ Access to special government benefits
☐ Lower cost sources of labor and/or raw materials
☐ Marketing and sales contracts or expertise

255. Advantages of IEJVs

IEJVs make it possible to share and reduce risks. Companies will enter into IEJVs when they believe that the project is too large or risky to be handled alone. This would be especially true in markets that do not justify full-blown subsidiaries, or in markets where the costs of doing business are high.

IEJVs create economies of scale. Economies of scale can be produced when less efficient local production techniques, coupled with low labor costs, can be combined with foreign technology to achieve efficient production techniques at low cost. This is particularly valuable in the IEJVs between parties from developed and developing nations.

IEJVs also allow smaller or medium-sized companies to combine resources to permit these companies to compete more favorably with their larger competitors.

IEJVs allow access to market and better penetration of the market. Some countries may require a local presence, which normally includes at least some local assembly or manufacture, before products are allowed to enter the market. Even if this is not the case, a local presence, and the existence of local stocks, might be advantageous in reaching government customers and in bidding government projects in countries where local companies are given preference. A foreign company might also achieve better market penetration if it uses the same resources to establish two 50 percent/50 percent IEJVs in two separate countries rather than establishing one wholly-owned subsidiary in a single country.

IEJVs establish more effective relationships with host governments—reducing foreign identity. It is worth mentioning a few areas where establishing a more effective government relationship can assist the foreign party. They include:

☐ Reduced risk of expropriation/nationalization
☐ Prompt political acceptance and local identity
☐ The satisfaction of local legal requirements for ownership and/or local content

IEJVs allow for the exchange or pooling of technology. When IEJVs are created between technologically sophisticated parties, the result could be the creation of new and/or better technologies. General Motors and Toyota created a joint venture to manufacture lower-cost small cars in the U.S.A. The joint venture allowed General Motors to learn Toyota's production techniques for the manufacture of high quality, but lower-cost, motor vehicles. Toyota received technology associated with design and style which has assisted it in developing automobiles which are suitable to American tastes. Additionally, it had some access to GM's marketing network and was able to improve its marketing techniques.

With an IEJV, companies can tap into local capital markets and use concessionary financing. The more countries where a company has a presence, the more likely it will have access to local financing. This allows companies to achieve a more global financing strategy, borrowing in currencies at rates that are most favorable to its global position. Additionally, companies willing to invest abroad might find, in some countries, attractive government-supported financial packages and incentives.

IEJVs may offer access to natural resources. Countries with critical natural resources may give preference for their exploitation to local companies. This is true even for a few products (such as red cedar shingles) in the U.S. Additionally, even abundant natural resources may be cheaper for local companies. Mexico, for example, as part of its National Industrial Development Plans, during the 1980s, provided electric energy, residual fuel oil, natural gas, and basic petrochemicals at a discount to companies, Mexican or foreign, that produced products in areas designated for development, and especially to companies that were willing to locate in designated geographical areas.

Better labor relationships are possible with IEJVs. Having a local partner in the host country is sometimes instrumental to creating and preserving better labor relationships. The local partner will understand the workplace environment and how to deal with difficult labor problems. It will also know how to motivate the local workforce on all levels.

IEJVs provide immediate market strength when local partners have established distribution and contacts. As stated previously, Japanese automobile manufacturers have used their IEJVs with American auto manufacturers to establish a larger presence through the use of the dealer network. Ford and Mazda have also used their IEJV to establish a market for Ford's light pickup trucks in Japan. Similar marketing arrangements exist in the liquor industry and among various producers of food products.

256. Disadvantages of IEJVs

Profit sharing comes with the sharing of risks. This issue, however, becomes even more problematic when one partner desires the IEJV to be profitable while another partner would prefer to make its profits from selling to, or buying from, the IEJV. This problem is most likely to occur when a larger foreign company links with a smaller domestic company. Still another issue over profits comes when one partner desires to distribute profits to the shareholders while the other wishes to put the profits back into the business.

If one party to the IEJV is the major contributor of technology, it will often seek to maintain **control over that technology** while the other partner may wish the technology to be controlled by the IEJV itself. Even if this problem can be resolved, there are likely to be disputes over how the technology is exploited. For example, the foreign partner may desire that the IEJV produce a more sophisticated product for export while the local partner may desire to produce a less sophisticated, or "appropriate," product for the local market.

It is appropriate to compare an IEJV to a marriage. At the beginning of the marriage, both partners may seek the same goals. As the marriage progresses, **one partner's goals may evolve in a different direction** or both partners may wish to pursue different courses.

One IEJV, for instance, started with an agreement that a substantial amount of the production would be exported. This suited the foreign partner, who needed "export credits" from the host country to sell its other products in that country. At first, the domestic partner went along with this approach because the IEJV was weak in marketing and desired that the foreign partner be responsible for the largest portion of the offtake. However, once the IEJV established a viable marketing function, the domestic partner realized that considerable demand existed in the host country for the IEJV's products (and at good prices), and continued to push for a shift toward domestic sales. As happens in many IEJVs, one company eventually bought out the interests of the other. In this case, the domestic company bought out the foreign company.

Differing management styles, controls and responsibilities may arise out of dissimilar size and cultural differences. Partners to IEJVs must decide how the entity will be controlled. Here, there are three reasonable choices: The foreign partner controls the IEJV, the domestic partner does, or the partners agree to have the IEJV create its own controls. If anything else exists, the partners are normally asking for trouble. One IEJV, for example, was created between a large global company and a small family-owned company. Both companies were very good at what they did but had entirely different goals and management styles. The small local company had 80 employees, 21 of which were family members, including an uncle who had never been at the company's facilities (he lived in another city), and a 10-year-old nephew of the local company's president. The purpose of this company was to meet the needs of the extended family and, given the high local income taxation, it was determined to be better to have all family members on the payroll at lower individual salaries.

This situation was absolutely intolerable for the global company, which initially agreed to allow the smaller company to control the IEJV, but could not resist repeated visits by employees of its human resources department with their strong anti-nepotism bent. The result of this was first a serious decline of morale followed by a decline in production quality and quantity. Eventually the partners dissolved the IEJV and went their separate ways.

Changing government policies may create problems for IEJVs. The marriage analogy also applies here, but in this case, the marriage may be of the "shotgun" variety, arranged by the government of the host country, or at least by its policies. During the 1970s and 1980s, many governments, particularly in the developing world, pursued policies that made it necessary for foreign companies to establish a local assembly or manufacturing presence. To reduce costs, many foreign companies responded to these policies by entering into joint ventures with local companies. When these countries moved toward market economies in the late 1980s and 1990s, the purpose for the IEJV for the foreign partner's point of view lessened or dissolved.

With lower tariffs and direct access to markets with finished products, the original purposes of the IEJV no longer existed. As this occurred, the IEJVs became more difficult to manage and many of the foreign partners pulled out. While there are still many valid reasons for the IEJVs, potential partners "foreign" to the entity should carefully consider entering into IEJVs if a major purpose is to satisfy government requirements.

Major Issues in Forming an IEJV

Before an IEJV is formed, the prospective partners should examine a number of critical issues, which, if understood and handled adequately, could result in limiting problems at a later date. Topics that should be discussed include how the partners will be compensated, the control issues, calls for additional capital, staffing of the IEJV, and termination issues.

257. Partner's Compensation

Eventually, all partners will desire to be compensated for their efforts in the IEJV. The forms and manner of compensation, however, can raise considerable concern as the joint venture progresses. In some cases, the IEJV itself will be designed to maximize profits. In this situation, the parties need to consider how, and when, such profits will be distributed.

Normally, profits will be distributed in relationship to each party's percentage of ownership. However, the shareholders should also recognize the respective roles of each party in the operation of the IEJV. For example, if one party contributes a larger share of the management, marketing efforts and/or technology after the IEJV commences, that party may be entitled to, or demand, a higher proportion of the profits. To the extent that this can be recognized during the formation of the IEJV, it should be provided for and the IEJV documents should, in any case, be flexible enough to allow for changes in IEJV compensation as the operation changes through time.

When IEJV profits are distributed is another potential problem area. This is especially true when one party may be looking for longer-term gain, while another one is oriented toward shorter-term gain. The first company may desire to defer profit distribution in order to use those funds to expand the business while the other company may desire more immediate distribution of funds to meet the current needs of the investing company and its shareholders. This is of particular concern when one contributor is an individual or a smaller family-owned company while the other is a larger, more global organization. This problem can be partially solved through the creation of a dividend policy at the outset that can be adjusted after a number of years.

In other cases, the IEJV will not be established to maximize its own profits, but rather to maximize the profits or goals of its owners. In this case, to the extent allowed by the local taxing authorities, the IEJV would be established as a break-even proposition, and may even be designed to lose money in its early years.

Illustrative of this point is a joint venture that was designed to break even. The foreign investing party desired to make its profits directly through the sale of components, management contracts, and license royalties and fees. The local investing party desired to make its profits from the IEJV through management services, and by the purchase of the bulk of the output of the IEJV which the local company was to sell at a considerable profit in the home country.

258. Controlling an IEJV

The most common manner of controlling an IEJV is through equity control. However, equity control does not always indicate effective control. The following are some methods in which a minority equity party can establish and maintain effective control of an IEJV. For the sake of discussion, let us assume the minority equity party holds 40 percent of the shares while the majority party(ies) holds 60 percent of the shares. In this case:

☐ The minority party provides the key technology to the IEJV.
☐ The minority party provides the key manufacturing parts and components to the IEJV.
☐ The minority party manages the IEJV.
☐ The equity of the majority parties is split among many partners or is traded on a local or global stock market.

Typically, relatively equal parties to an IEJV will attempt to balance control either by the creation of a set of checks and balances or by a 50 percent/50 percent split in equity. This works part of the time, but also fails frequently.

The most famous example of a "balanced" IEJV that failed is Union Carbide India Ltd. (UCIL). UCIL was created with Union Carbide owning 50.9 percent of the equity while local Indian investors owned 49.1 percent. The Indian shareholders were given control of the board of directors and appointed the majority of the management. While the critical technology was provided by Union Carbide, the Indian partners suggested that it be adapted to Indian safety standards, and modified to provide for more Indian content in the construction of the plant. Both, Union Carbide claimed, were also requirements of Indian law.

Toxic gas leaked from the plant in Bhopal on December 3, 1984, resulting in numerous deaths and injuries. Charges and countercharges continued throughout the entire litigation process. The case was settled for U.S.$470 million in 1989, and the Bhopal IEJV stands as one of the greatest failures of the IEJV process.

The conventional wisdom that 50/50 IEJVs do not work was seriously questioned when two specialists with McKinsey & Company[6] examined 49 alliances of the top companies in the U.S., Europe and Japan, and found that:

☐ 51 percent were successful for both parties; 16 percent for one party, and 33 percent resulted in failure for both. Success was defined as both parties having recovered their financial costs of capital, and making some progress toward their strategic objectives.
☐ Alliances were more effective for related businesses or new geographic areas.
☐ Alliances between strong and weak companies are least likely to succeed.
☐ Alliances with evenly split financial ownership are more likely to succeed (50/50 percent), than those in which one owner holds majority interest. Percentages of ownership are less important than establishing clear management control.
☐ More than three-fourths of alliances have terminated with the acquisition of the IEJV by one of the owners.

Therefore, the issue of who controls the IEJV may be more important than ownership percentages. In dealing with the issue of control, it is probably best when initiating the IEJV, to determine which party should logically control it in the early years. If the project is one where technology is critical to success (e.g., Bhopal and Union Carbide), it may make practical sense to have the technology supplier control the IEJV until the technology is fully absorbed by it. If the project is one where finished, or near-finished, products are being introduced into a new geography, and the local party is well placed to market in that geography, then the local partner should control the IEJV. The parties might also consider including in the IEJV agreements a provision that calls for control of one party for a certain period of time, but with a gradual shift of control to another party as the entity becomes firmly established.

259. Capital Needs and Guarantees

Determining the financial needs of the IEJV is not always easy. There is always hope that the IEJV will generate enough capital for its own needs and that additional equity and/or debt will not be required. However, in the real world, this is not often the case. To prepare for the eventuality of the need for additional capital or debt financing, the parties should determine at the outset what their policies will be. In regard to additional capital, the following should be considered:

☐ Is the capital needed for growth or survival?
☐ If needed for survival, at what point do the parties agree to "pull the plug"? What would this entail?
☐ If needed for growth, how do the parties assess growth opportunities?
☐ If one party wants to grow and the other does not, can the party seeking growth provide the bulk or all of the growth equity in exchange for reorienting the ownership percentages in favor of the investing party?
☐ To what extent will the parties provide for third-party investors to cover growth needs? If this is acceptable, in what form would the equity be achieved (e.g., take public and/or sell to one or a few private investors)?

In the area of debt financing, a similar set of questions might be posed, but the parties may also consider to what extent, if any, they would be willing to guarantee the debt acquired by the IEJV. This is commonly required of IEJVs, particularly in their early years.

260. Management and Staffing

To succeed, an IEJV must be properly staffed and managed. Staffing of non-management employees is normally accomplished in the local market. Top management, however, is a different matter. If the foreign party uses its management in key IEJV positions, it will obtain near effective control of the venture, but the IEJV will begin with expatriate management that may not be as effective in the initial years of the venture.

If top management comes from the local partner, it will give that partner near effective control of the venture, and a strong local presence, but may put in place individuals who are not as familiar with the technologies and products. Generally, a compromise is established where the various parties contribute the management with, perhaps, some management being recruited from outside the companies. The problem with this approach is that it often results in creating a management team that is pulled in different directions to the satisfaction of none of the parties. Therefore, it is important, at the outset, to determine clear management control. This may mean that one party concedes management to the other, but this might be preferable to mixed management. The decision of who manages must be made on the basis of the real needs of the IEJV. If technology is critical, the party providing technology should provide management in the early years. If local production or market conditions prevail, management should come from the local partner.

261. Terminating an IEJV

As we have stated previously, with regard to agents and distributors, the time to plan for termination is when the relationship is being established. Because many IEJVs wind up being acquired by one of the partners, the parties should consider the possibility of building into the agreement buy-sell provisions that allow the selling party to recoup all of its financial investment, plus a reasonable amount of growth and its technology, if the seller is a party that contributed technology.

If the IEJV is to be terminated and/or liquidated, the parties should contemplate what happens to the contributed, or otherwise acquired, technology and critical equipment. Provisions should be built into the agreement allowing the parties who contributed the technology at least the right of first refusal to reobtain the technology and equipment as part of the liquidation procedure. If, for no other reason, this will prevent the technology and equipment from being acquired by a third party competitor in the liquidation proceedings.

ESTABLISHING DIRECT
OPERATIONS ABROAD

Most large global companies have moved from working with others to establishing their own operations in most, if not all, jurisdictions. Ownership of your overseas entities gives you the most effective control over your destiny and the ability to move from being an international company to being a global company.

This section looks at the issues associated with direct ownership and explores the types of organizations that are most often formed to meet the interest of companies—both large and small. It also looks at important issues of subsidiary-parent relationships.

262. The Importance of Direct Operations

The establishment of your company's own operations abroad is perhaps the most complicated and expensive of all of the international business transactions. For definitional purposes, we are describing the acquisition of, or the formation of, a wholly-owned direct operation outside the territorial boundaries of the home country.

The direct operation is more complicated for a number of reasons. First, everything associated with the direct operations will have to be performed by the company. Using agents, distributors, licensees, or joint venture partners gives you a local presence that now must be acquired through your own efforts. Second, you now must deal directly with the local government agencies including those associated with granting licenses and, with the exception of the creation of a representative office, the local tax authorities.

Third, you need to consider the staffing problems associated with your own operations. These are particularly difficult in the initial years where you may wish to use a number of expatriates to get the business going and to train their local replacements. Finally, there is the issue of conforming your local operations to the overall goals and strategic objectives of the parent company. This becomes particularly complicated when the parent company begins to develop global tax strategies that may require the foreign direct operations to "minimize" their profits. This may require companies to develop incentive packages based on "company contributions" rather than "company profits," and this becomes very difficult in countries where profit sharing is required among the local employees.

Yet most major companies prefer, where the market dictates, to create their own direct operations abroad. For this, there are many reasons; the three most important are *control, profit maximization,* and *global image* (see tip #264).

While some companies prefer to start their foreign operations with the direct approach, most companies "graduate" to direct operations after experimenting with other forms of international business transactions. An agent or distributor's business may have grown in the market to the point where the economies of scale dictate the establishment of your own marketing subsidiary. Your company may desire, after an effective licensing arrangement, to manufacture and sell the product on a direct basis. Direct operations are also created by the purchase of the entire equity in an existing equity joint venture. Finally, the foreign company may establish direct operations through the merger or with the acquisition of a local company.

263. Forms of Direct Operations

As with other international strategies, establishing a network of direct operations may stand alone or it could be combined as part of a global strategy that uses a combination of direct operations in key countries, distributors and agents in others, and licensing in still other countries. Often, regional wholly-owned subsidiaries are established to service the needs of agents, distributors, and licensees.

Direct operations can take many forms. These include:

☐ A *representative office,* where a small staff is located in a jurisdiction to explore possibilities and to fly the global corporate flag.
☐ A *financial subsidiary,* which is established primarily to take advantage of the availability of financing and/or for tax reasons, including the use of tax treaties.
☐ A *regional headquarters,* which is established to service marketing and manufacturing entities in a particular country or region (e.g., Europe, Latin America, or Asia).
☐ A *marketing subsidiary,* which is normally established to provide a direct sales force in a particular country or region.

☐ *A manufacturing subsidiary,* which is established to take advantage of the benefits of local manufacturing.
☐ *A full subsidiary,* which could perform finance, marketing, and manufacturing functions.

264. Advantages of Direct Operations

The major reasons why companies establish direct operations abroad are control, profit maximization, and global image. These and other advantages of direct operations are explored below.

Control. The major reason why a company will establish direct operations is to achieve the control it cannot achieve with other forms of international business transactions. The more global a company is, the more it will attempt to rationalize manufacturing, sales, services and R&D to achieve its various global strategies of revenues, market share, and profit maximization. This can best be achieved by obtaining, and maintaining, direct control over all of its operations. For example, in the area of marketing and sales, the company knows its customers, and their needs. It receives direct feedback from its direct sales force and can adjust to customer needs and market forces.

Direct control also allows a global-oriented company to be more flexible, which allows it to respond more rapidly and effectively to global changes in such areas as taxation, accounting standards, and currency fluctuations. Production and sales can be moved to areas of more favorable tax regimes or weaker currencies, allowing for the rational policies previously mentioned.

Finally, direct control provides the greatest amount of protection of a company's intellectual property. Agents and distributors could negatively impact a company's trade names and trademarks. Licensees can do the same, but also may bring into question a company's patents, trade secrets, and know-how. The same problems could result from consortium and/or equity joint ventures.

Profit maximization. The truly global company will have, as one of its highest priorities, the maximization of its profits on a global basis. This can best be accomplished with direct control over all foreign operations. This is normally achieved through a combination of creative sourcing, tax incentives, transfer pricing, intercompany royalties, global management, and control of currency fluctuations. Central management can direct captive operations to achieve maximum results for the benefit of the entire company.

Global image. It is more difficult to create a positive global image if the company's international strategy is subject to the whims of "partners" who may see things differently than headquarters. Larger companies may be expected by their customers to have direct operations in the key countries, particularly if they are providers of goods and services to other global companies. Corporate image, goals, and objectives can best be accomplished when the company directly controls the forces which assist in establishing those images, goals, and objectives.

Barriers to entry. A company may wish to establish direct operations in order to overcome barriers to entry which are imposed by various countries or regions. Many companies have established direct operations in the EEC in order to qualify as a European company, and thereby enhance their access into the EEC. Asian and European companies have established operations in North America to take advantage of NAFTA.

Government incentives. Most governments now have some forms of financial and market incentives to companies willing to locate in their countries. Some of these incentives are on the state or provincial level. Various Canadian provinces offer incentives, as do countries like Belgium, Ireland, Luxembourg, and Spain within the EEC. These incentives may include free manufacturing space, worker reimbursement, training, and various tax incentives.

Availability of local financing. The ability to develop a global financial strategy may be enhanced by having direct operations in numerous jurisdictions. The establishment of local operations normally enhances the ability to borrow in the local market. Sometimes the funds acquired in one country can be used in others. Therefore, a global company may be able to borrow in countries with lower interest rates and expand operations in countries with higher interest rates.

Attraction of the best human resources. It is almost conventional wisdom to suggest that the best and the brightest people are more likely to be attracted by the global corporation than by their domestic counterparts. Global corporations may offer better financial packages and benefits, more global opportunities and more prestige.

Legal insulation. If a company has a direct local presence and contracts locally, it may have created a certain level of legal insulation for the parent company. This tends to lessen the number of lawsuits and decrease the amounts paid in settlements.

265. Disadvantages of Direct Operations

The complexity and expense of direct operations are their greatest disadvantages. Those, and other disadvantages, are explored below:

Complexity. The commitment to establish direct local operations is a complex one. The best way to characterize this is to describe the events of a small U.S. company that decided to establish its first overseas direct marketing operations in England. The company felt that England was the logical place to establish its first direct operations because of the size of the market—plus what it felt were language and cultural similarities.

In reality, however, it learned quickly that England was indeed a true foreign operation. In acquiring its property lease, the company was placed up against a property system that was totally different from anything it had experienced in the U.S.A. It had considerable difficulties in obtaining permission to send one of its employees to manage the operation. Recruiting local employees was a nightmare, as was obtaining local licenses. It had little idea of the costs of doing business in the London area, including such basics as telephones and office supplies.

Finally, the company had considerable difficulty in importing its first product shipment. Nevertheless, all problems were eventually solved in England and the local operation has been a success. The moral of the story is that setting up direct operations in any country will require infinite commitment and patience.

Direct operations involve more capital and risks than IEJVs. Clearly the advantages of licensing and equity joint ventures are the ability to share the costs with your technology or equity partners. Additionally, the start-up costs associated with a direct operation are normally much more than twice the value of a 50-percent ownership in an equity joint venture. This is because the costs of outside advice, initial travel, and deposits are considerable. If establishing a direct operation requires the use of expatriates, the cost soars. The cost of an employee, spouse, and two children, living abroad normally can be 2½ to 3 times that of New York if placed in London or Frankfurt, and four times the cost if placed in Tokyo.

With the increased costs come increased risks. The company establishing the direct operations now must bear all risks associated with the local operations. Risks may also be increased during the learning curve when the company is becoming more familiar with local customs, procedures and laws.

Higher tax liabilities. The foreign tax liabilities associated with agents and distributors, if handled correctly, should be negligible. With licensing, there may be some royalty withholding taxes but the foreign party is usually spared other taxes including corporate tax. With a consortium, tax liabilities are considerably lessened and in the equity joint venture, tax may be limited to the participant's percentage of ownership plus, perhaps, taxes on royalty withholding and some taxes on profit repatriation. With a direct operation, all taxes could apply, and it will be easier for the tax authorities to locate and collect taxes.

Disfavor of local governments. Although this has changed for the better in the past decade, some countries still look with disfavor on foreign wholly-owned direct operations. They may be restricted in bidding government projects and, in some cases, wholly-owned operations have been under considerable pressure to bring in local partners.

The experience of the Control Data Corporation in Mexico is illustrative. Because it was created prior to 1973, Control Data de Mexico (CDM) was "grandfathered"—that is, it was able to remain 100 percent foreign-owned. In 1985, CDM desired to expand its space in Mexico City. It was told that it could not do so unless it sold some of its equity to Mexican nationals or companies. CDM was allowed to go ahead with its plans without "nationalizing" after a major earthquake in Mexico City lessened the amount of available commercial property. CDM agreed to lease some of its space to a Mexican government agency in exchange for being allowed to retain its total foreign ownership.

266. When to Use a Representative Office

Sometimes also known as a liaison office, this type of direct operation is established when a company wishes to explore a market but is not yet willing to establish an operation that will subject the parent company to taxation. It is also used in cases where a company is unable to sell in the local market, because of boycott and other restrictions, but wants to plant its flag so that it is able to operate quickly when the boycott is lifted. Representative offices were popular for U.S. companies in Vietnam during the 1990s, for instance, and are used frequently in Algeria because it is illegal to appoint agents and distributors in that country.

Once established, a representative office allows you to establish a few people in the country and to rent space for the purpose of conducting business on a limited basis. Marketing (not sales) personnel are free to call on prospective clients for the purpose of distributing sales brochures and, in some cases, product samples. The office can also rent, or lease, a hotel room or apartment for the purpose of serving company personnel and others who visit the territory. However, the office itself is not allowed to book orders or to receive payments from customers of any kind or it will lose its tax-free status. Orders can be passed back to the foreign parent for "acceptance" at home.

The cost of representative offices are often shared by a number of companies who wish to leverage the opportunity to serve markets in the future. This was common in the People's Republic of China in the 1970s and in the Soviet Union in the 1980s. Today, in Vietnam, many consulting and law firms have opened representative offices in Hanoi or Ho Chi Minh City (Saigon), which can be used for marketing purposes and product promotion.

267. Establishing a Branch Office

Normally, a company would consider a branch office if it desires total home office control, secrecy, and simplicity of management. A branch office is exactly how it sounds. Rather than establishing a legally distinct subsidiary in another country, the branch is registered with the local authorities as another office (branch) of the parent company, or in some cases, a branch of a subsidiary of the parent company. The major disadvantage of the branch office is that it subjects the parent company itself to local taxation. Additionally, the assets of the parent or subsidiary company are also exposed in the country(ies) of registration.

Most international lawyers would generally advise against using branch offices because of the exposure of the parent company to local taxation, but in some cases they may be necessary or the favored form of direct operations. A branch may be necessary for American companies who make a Subchapter S election for tax purposes. Subchapter S corporations are precluded by law from having foreign subsidiaries. While this election generally applies to smaller companies (although some have been known to reach more than U.S.$100 million in revenues), some Subchapter S corporations do establish foreign operations.

If the operation to be started abroad is likely to have substantial losses in its initial years, the branch office may be a viable alternative. Just as all profits will be ascribed to the parent company, so will the losses of its foreign branches. Taking these losses against the profits of the parent company may then result in a significant tax savings to the parent company. Therefore, a company may desire to begin as a branch operation and shift to a subsidiary form when the branch office becomes profitable.

As mentioned previously, one of the major advantages of a branch office over a subsidiary is the simplicity of management and secrecy. In most countries, branch offices are easier to set up and dismantle. Because the office is completely controlled by the parent company, the parent company can maintain full control and secrecy over company records and intellectual property. Although there are a few exceptions, the U.K. included, most countries do not require financial disclosures of the branch office, while such are required for subsidiary entities.

268. Establishing a Foreign Subsidiary

When a company creates a subsidiary, it creates a distinct company (in this case, foreign), which, although it might be entirely owned and "controlled" by the parent company, or a second-tier subsidiary, it is distinct in terms of having its own stock and management team, as well as physical and intangible assets and liabilities. Figure 4 illustrates the forms a subsidiary might take.

In the case of *direct parent ownership,* the company creates a subsidiary in another country that is directly owned by the parent. This is used most commonly when a company will have only one or a few foreign subsidiaries, or if the subsidiary is primarily for manufacturing. Often companies will attempt to create a buffer between the parent corporation and the subsidiary. This is normally done for two reasons: to provide a legal buffer between the parent and the subsidiary, or to divide the company into specific geographies for management purposes. If the buffer is set up in the home country, the subsidiary would be considered *local second-tier.* If the buffer is set up in another country, the subsidiary would be called *foreign second-tier.* In the example cited in Figure 4, a first-tier subsidiary was set up in the U.K. to service all European operations.

Once you have decided to use a subsidiary, it is important to select the type of subsidiary company that is appropriate to the company's business. A "stock" company is the appropriate type of subsidiary if you are creating a large company, bidding on large projects, or planning to take the company public. A "limited liability" company is preferable for ease of administration, along with fewer reporting

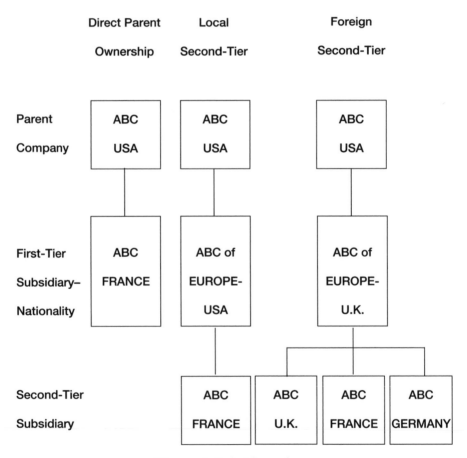

Figure 4. Subsidiary forms.

requirements and expenditures. This type of company is most similar to the privately-held U.S. corporation. Almost every legal system provides for both stock and limited liability companies. The table below indicates some of the types of companies available.

Stock Corporations and Limited Liability Companies

	Stock Corporations	Limited Liability Companies
Brazil	Sociedade Anónima (SA)	Sociedade Limitada (Ltda.)
U.K.	Public or Private Company, Limited	Private Company, Ltd. (Pte. Co. Ltd.)
France	Société Anonyme (SA)	Société a Responsibilité Limitée (SARL)
Germany	Aktiengesellschaft (AG)	Gesellschaft mit beschränkter Haftung (GmbH)
Italy	Societa Per Azioni (SPA)	Societa a Responsibilita Limitata (SRL)
Japan	Kabushiki Kaisha (KK)	Yugen kaisha (YK)
Republic of Korea	Chusik Hoesa (CH)	Yuhan hoesa (YH)
Spain	Sociedad Anónima (SA)	Sociedad Limitada (SL)
Turkey	Anonim Sirket (AS)	Turk Limited Sirket (TLS)

269. Converting from a Distributor to a Sales Subsidiary

Often a business will decide to establish a sales subsidiary after they have successfully tested the market with a distributor. This decision is usually made after a cost-benefit analysis of whether market potential exceeds the additional costs of setting up the sales subsidiary. In making this analysis, consider the following factors:

☐ *Costs, financial and otherwise, of replacing the distributor.* In Tips #211 and 212, we discussed the financial issues associated with distributor termination. Additional to those costs might be a degree of bad faith among local customers which results from a local company (the distributor) being deserted, not because it failed but because it was successful. Often, businesses will decide to buy the distributor out rather than to terminate them to avoid the bad faith problem.

☐ *Analysis of the local market for your products.* One of the disadvantages of a distributor is that the principal will not be able to become familiar with the local market because that is normally the distributor's responsibility. While your company will know the amount of product sold to the market, it will still need to do an economic analysis of the market and consider such issues as:
• How much of those sales were dependent on the distributor's contacts and know-how?
• How quickly can you learn local marketing and sales techniques?
• To what degree can you replicate and improve upon the distributor's service capabilities?

☐ *Analysis of costs and financial factors.* Besides the actual costs of establishing the subsidiary, you need to consider the issues of local taxation, collections, and repatriation of capital. These were the problems of the distributor which are now passed to the subsidiary.

☐ *Local subsidiaries' impact on global strategy.* What will the impact of the establishment of the subsidiary have on other stakeholders in the company? For example, will replacing a distributor with a subsidiary in France negatively impact distributor relations in Germany and Italy? If the new subsidiary fails, will this alter global strategy (e.g., is this the right market at the right time)? On the positive side, will selling your own products help to encourage a market for other products of the business which the distributor did not handle?

270. Choosing a Foreign Manufacturing Site

The decision of where to establish a manufacturing plant abroad is a complex one. Below are 100 points to consider. In reviewing these points, it is clear that not all will be of equal importance to every company. It is therefore suggested that this list be scrutinized to see which points apply and what values should be assigned to each point in making your site determination.

Overall Country Considerations

1. Size of internal market
2. Degree of government regulations
3. Nature of the economy—stable growth or roller coaster growth and decline
4. Dependence on the global economy in relation to the internal economy
5. Currency stability/convertibility
6. Balance of payment position
7. Economic balance—industry/agriculture/service
8. Population/population growth
9. Per capita income
10. Income distribution
11. Inflation as an issue
12. Customs duties/non-tariff barriers

Regional Considerations

13. Size of regional market
14. Physical access to the regional market
15. Free trade agreements or common markets with access from the target country
16. Regional problems and issues

Political Considerations

17. Form of government
18. Stability of government
19. Degree of unification of the political entity— cultural/economic/political
20. Acceptability to other trading partners
21. National/regional restrictions on trade (e.g., political embargoes)
22. Attitude toward foreign investment
23. Restrictions on foreign investment—formal and informal
24. Privatization of state industries—complete or in process
25. Threats of expropriation/nationalization

26. Attitude toward technology transfer
27. Favoritism toward locals
28. Concentration of political/economic power
29. Relationship with your government

Government Considerations

30. Relative day-to-day freedoms—freedom to travel
31. Government policies related to business
32. Degree of bureaucracy and red tape
33. Degree of honesty of government employees—levels of corruption
34. Will the current government stand behind commitments made by the previous governments
35. Favoritism toward locals
36. Reasonable and modern laws/legal codes
37. Protectability of intellectual property
38. Fairness of court system
39. Availability of alternative dispute resolution mechanisms
40. Immigration policies

Geographic Considerations

41. Recreational opportunities for expatriates and visitors
42. Costs of land and/or building
43. Leasing opportunities
44. Availability of local plants
45. Efficiency of internal transportation
46. Port facilities
47. Airport facilities
48. Availability of free zones and bonded warehouses
49. Proximity to export markets
50. Availability of raw materials
51. Availability and reliability of utilities
52. Waste disposal availability and issues
53. Environmental protection considerations

Human Resource Considerations

54. Availability of people who speak the major language(s) of your company
55. Availability of skilled labor
56. Availability of professional labor (such as engineers, accountants)
57. Level of employee productivity
58. Role of unions and other labor organizations
59. Non-labor/sheltered labor possibilities—use of consultants and advisors
60. Public training facilities
61. Quality of public educational institutions
62. Required employee role in management
63. Freedom to hire and fire
64. Legal requirements upon termination
65. Salary issues
66. Required fringe benefits
67. Required or customary profit sharing

Profit Retention Considerations

68. Tax rates
69. Types of taxes
70. Rates upon repatriation of capital or dividends
71. Attitude toward intercompany pricing strategies
72. Fairness and honesty of the tax system
73. Complexity of the tax system
74. Ability to put profits back into the business
75. Taxation and inflation issues
76. Tax incentives and disincentives
77. Depreciation rates
78. Tax rates on importation of capital equipment
79. Duty drawbacks
80. Number and quality of tax treaties
81. Tax treatment of expatriates

Financial Considerations

82. Degree and quality of government regulation
83. Local availability of financial resources
84. Cost of local borrowing
85. Ability to convert currencies
86. Currency stability
87. Reasonable lending terms
88. Government assistance in export financing
89. Availability and use of credit cards
90. Stable banking system
91. Availability of non-bank financing
92. Local stock market

Miscellaneous Considerations

93. Availability of home country investment/political risk insurance
94. Local business morality and ethics
95. Local systems of distribution
96. Availability of good service providers (accountants, lawyers)
97. Consumer protection
98. Antitrust and restrictive practices
99. Competitive nature of the population; competition in your industry
100. Amenities available to expatriates and their families

271. Choosing the Subsidiary Form

The structures of German companies provide good examples of the types of subsidiaries that may be formed, along with examples of the pros and cons of the stock and limited liability companies.

Aktiengesellschaft (AG)—The Stock Company

This company is normally used for large operations, or for those companies that require a substantial registered capital in order to bid on large projects, particularly government projects. An AG can also be traded on local, and perhaps foreign, stock markets. To start an AG, a minimum of 100,000 deutsche Marks (DM) are required as registered capital, of which 25 percent must be paid in. The AG requires a minimum of five shareholders (which can be natural or legal persons). This prevents, at least in a formal sense, 100 percent ownership by the parent, or first-tier, subsidiary. If 1,000 shares are issued, 996 might be held by the parent and one share each by four trusted individuals, normally company employees. This nominal ownership does increase paperwork and sometimes creates problems when one of the employees leaves the company, retires, or dies.

An AG must have both a supervisory board and a management board. The supervisory board must be composed of at least three natural persons elected by stockholders or in some large companies, by stockholders and employees. The supervisory board controls and supervises the management board. The management board may be composed of one or more natural persons. They are appointed by the supervisory board and are responsible for day-to-day management of the company. Additionally, the AG has a greater responsibility of reporting its activities to government agencies.

Gesellschaft mit beschränkter Haftung (GmbH)— The Limited Liability Company

The GmbH is the most frequently chosen by foreign investors because of its lower costs and simplicity of operation. It cannot be publicly traded and may place the company at a disadvantage if it plans to bid large public projects. The GmbH requires a start-up capital of DM 50,000 (with at least DM 25,000 contributed when application for registration is made). It requires only one shareholder who can be a natural or legal person.

Management of a GmbH is much less complex. No supervisory board is required unless the GmbH regularly employs more than 2,000 people. A management board is also not required, but the company must have a managing director who is responsible for managing and representing the company. This must be a natural person, but there are no citizen, domicile, or residence requirements for the managing director. The company, however, must have a corporate office within Germany. In summary, with a GmbH, a foreign investor can hold all of the shares and appoint someone to manage the company who does not have to be present in Germany.

Acquiring a Local Company

Some companies will choose to establish direct operations abroad through the acquisition of an existing local company. This is often accomplished through the acquisition of an existing distributor, licensee, or joint venture partner. In other cases, a company will try to acquire a totally unrelated party. In either case, acquiring a local operation is normally undertaken to capture or establish market share, to create a local presence and acquire local facilities, to acquire products and services that are unavailable to the foreign investor in order to complement existing product lines, and/or to enter into new or related markets.

The rules and techniques for acquiring companies are fairly standard throughout the world, but the acquiring companies must also look for certain country-unique variables which are imposed by local governments. Examples of these local requirements are limitations on foreign ownership, (Mexico, India), reservation of certain industries for local ownership and other requirements for employee retention, reporting, and additional investment considerations.

The two general ways to acquire a foreign company are to acquire either part or all of its assets, or to acquire all or part of its stock. Because asset and stock purchases are very different, each will be discussed individually.

272. Asset Purchases

An asset purchase is where one party purchases all, or part, of the assets of a company. That is, Company F, the foreign company, purchases assets from Company L, the local company. Because the stock of Company L is not purchased, that company continues to exist—at least on paper. Company F will then need to place the assets within an existing local company, or establish a new company in the local jurisdiction, in which to place the acquired assets.

Foreign companies undertake asset purchases for a number of reasons. Asset purchases allow the company to acquire only those assets needed. This is particularly useful if the foreign company only wishes to acquire part of the business. This would also allow the remaining part of the acquired company to continue its operations. It is common for one company to purchase only a division or product line of another company. For example, this approach is useful if Company L has three divisions and/or product lines and desires to sell only one division and/or product line to acquire cash or other assets needed to invest in the other two divisions and/or product lines.

Another advantage of the asset purchase approach is that the acquiring company should not be responsible for any liability not assumed, although some contractual and labor obligations may have to be assumed. In a stock purchase, all liabilities associated with the shares will normally be assumed by the purchaser. Finally, it is sometimes a better approach for the seller to separate the assets from shares and sell each as separate transactions to different parties.

For example, in a transaction that happened in Brazil, all of the operating assets except the real estate of a foreign-held corporation were sold to a local Brazilian party. This party did not assume any liabilities, except those associated with the particular assets. The foreign-held corporation sold the real estate in the local market and used the proceeds, in part, to pay off remaining liabilities.

The foreign-held corporation then sold the shares to another foreign party. The additional foreign party desired the shares of the paper company because it had some tax losses and registered capital. The tax losses can be carried forward for up to five years and the purchaser desired to apply such losses to their current profits. The registered capital could be used to remit profits at a lower tax rate since the allowable amount of remittances at the lower tax level was dependent upon the total amount of registered capital. Registered capital is that amount registered with the Central Bank of Brazil, and the parties were allowed at that time only to repatriate up to 12.5 percent of that amount at a lower tax level.

273. Stock Purchases

A stock purchase is one in which the foreign company (F) acquires some, or all, of the stock of the local company (L). In this case, Company F will be acquiring not only the assets but also the liabilities of the company through its acquisition of the company stock.

On the surface, this appears to be a much simpler transaction than the asset purchase. For starters, it is possible to avoid dealing with company management by going directly to the shareholders. Additionally, the purchaser should be able to avoid having to establish a new company by transferring all documents as part of the transaction. Corporate identity is also preserved as it should be easier to reserve the corporate name and logos. Finally, if the commercial contracts and intellectual property agreements have a "successor in interest" clause, it may not be necessary to assign them.

However, the stock purchase is not without its disadvantages. Some of these include:

☐ Disagreements among shareholders which could hold up or prevent the transaction.
☐ More due diligence may be required, because you are assuming all liabilities.
☐ If the stock is publicly traded, the purchaser may be required to obtain the approval of a local securities and exchange agency.
☐ The purchaser is more likely to have to assume employee contracts and liabilities. In some countries—such as Germany, Austria, and Benelux—workers councils or union approval may be required.
☐ The purchaser will also need to acquire all outstanding stock options and warrants.

274. Due Diligence

In both an asset and stock purchase, the buying company should perform very careful due diligence on the assets to be acquired. This due diligence would cover the following assets (and the liabilities, if any, tied to the assets):

Cash on hand and in financial institutions.
Real and personal property. In the case of real property, the buying company should make sure that a foreign company has the right to acquire it. Mexico, Switzerland, and certain parts of Australia, along with the U.S., are examples where restrictions against foreign ownership of real estate may apply. It is also advisable to check states and provinces. In the state of Minnesota, for example, foreign individuals and companies cannot acquire certain agricultural properties. Additionally, in Eastern Europe and the

former Soviet Union, land titles may not be clear and it may take years to establish ownership.

Accounts receivable. These should be reviewed carefully and aged. In the case of government debt, be sure it is assignable.

Inventory. This should be checked carefully. Boxes should be opened. One company found empty boxes after acquiring the inventory. The purchaser may wish to hold back on some of the payment until the usability of the inventory can be determined.

Contracts. If acquiring contracts (e.g., purchase and sales, distributor, etc.), make sure they are assignable or have been assigned before closing.

Intellectual property. Check registration, ownership and assignability of the intellectual property. One transaction was stopped when it was determined that so-called license rights were really only unassignable distribution rights.

Employment agreements. These can be a benefit or a detriment depending on who is covered, and under what circumstances. In countries with tough labor laws (Western Europe and Latin America are regions which come to mind), the purchaser may wish to decide which employees it wants the seller to terminate before assuming ownership. In places like Germany, be very careful to determine all labor rights before acquiring any assets or stock.

Miscellaneous. Insurance, telephone lines, and so on. Be very careful to understand your acquired liabilities and the cost of insurance. In certain countries, such items as telephone lines and equipment may be very valuable. Up to a few years ago in Mexico you needed to purchase stock in the telephone company before you could acquire telephone lines. In Brazil, a company acquired a whole business in order to acquire access to telephone lines. Be particularly cautious in Eastern Europe and the former Soviet Union.

275. Government Requirements

Besides the considerations applied to asset and stock purchases, a company may need to consider additional requirements that might be imposed by governments (national and local). These may apply even if a new foreign investment is made, but governments are particularly concerned when local companies are acquired. In addition to the real estate ownership prohibitions, there may be other basic requirements, including balancing imports with exports, training of local personnel, restricted geographical access, and the requirement to use state-of-the art technology.

In recent years, the trend has been to lessen these government-imposed requirements. Mexico, for example, in its Foreign Investment Law of 1993, considerably weakened, or ended, all of the above requirements that had existed for 20 years.

RELATIONSHIPS WITH SUBSIDIARIES

Now that you have created your direct operations, you need to examine how they will be managed and controlled. In this section, we will examine the general approach you can take to operations management and how to evaluate performance. We will also discuss motivation techniques used by successful companies for their foreign operations. This discussion centers around the foreign subsidiary, but it also can apply to representative offices and branch companies.

276. Strategies for Success with Subsidiaries

Historically, how companies managed and controlled their overseas operations was, in part, a result of home country culture and relative positions of their countries in world trade. After World War II, the U.S.A. was predominant in world trade, and the internationalization of U.S.-based companies tended to reflect this predominance. Beginning in the 1970s, and strengthening throughout the 1980s and early 1990s, Western Europe and Japan arose as significant challengers to the U.S.A. for a major portion of trade between, and among, nations. This was further complicated in the 1980s and 1990s by the creation of globally-oriented companies.

American companies expanded abroad in the 1950s and 1960s as the result of post-war reconstruction, and the pent-up demand for products and services which the U.S.A. was best able to provide. Significant U.S. companies developed an *"international" strategy.* That is, one in which development of overseas subsidiaries was centered around products developed in the U.S.A. which were then "internationalized" for global use. Research and development tended to take place primarily, or totally, in the U.S.A. with overseas subsidiaries producing products and services to U.S. specifications and with only marketing and sales left to local control. This was a logical outgrowth of economic conditions, and the American "can do" attitude.

European companies took a very different approach. For starters, more significant European companies were still family-owned, which allowed for more independence of action. Additionally, Europe was more oriented to smaller, more independent markets. As a result, the

Europeans tended to take more of a *"portfolio" approach* to international management, where each foreign subsidiary was allowed to operate independently in meeting the needs of its local market, subject primarily to overall financial bottom-lines.

The approach of Japanese companies was different than either that of the U.S. or European companies. The Japanese developed an *"export-based" strategy* in which the world was treated as a single market but tied to tight control from the home office in product creation, production, marketing, and sales. This was the logical outgrowth of the lowered trade barriers brought about by GATT, and the policies of the Japanese government which imposed limitations on overseas investment.

While all three strategies were somewhat effective in the 1980s, the world of today and of the 21st century calls for some creative approaches to subsidiary management which need to keep the following factors in mind:

☐ The need to create international opportunities for all key employees. Suffice it to say that a German engineer has more in common with an American engineer than a German farmer.
☐ The need to take advantage of the creative skills found in all countries, rather than reliance on home-country talent only. This has required a shift in thinking among some American and Japanese companies in particular.
☐ Creation of global competitiveness to capture economies of scale. Knowing what products and services can be globalized, and which products and services might respond to local considerations.
☐ The need to understand and react to the contradictory world forces on one hand, with the increasing globalization of communications, transportation, banking and finance, and data management; while on the other hand, the increasing desire of humans to establish their own national and ethnic identities has resulted in the explosion of nation-states and inter-ethnic conflict.

277. Evaluating Subsidiary Profitability

Evaluating the performance of domestic operations is difficult enough, but once you cross international borders, the process becomes considerably more difficult. This is especially true if the company has developed a global approach to its operations, products, and profits.

As a company develops a global, profit-maximization strategy, each subsidiary may be asked to sacrifice some, or all, of its individual profits for the sake of the entire company. In those cases, the company may wish to develop a performance criteria which is based more on "country contribution" than country, or subsidiary, profit.

Normally, the parent company, or one of its first- or second-tier subsidiaries, can attempt to reduce the taxable profits of the subsidiary through *transfer pricing*. Transfer pricing is the intercompany pricing practice which applies to goods, services, technical assistance, trademarks, or other assets that are transferred between related parties. This policy would also apply if the subsidiary was transferring the above items *to* the parent company, or the subsidiaries of the parent company.

Companies wishing to maximize their global profits will attempt, to the extent possible, to take their profits in lower tax jurisdictions. As an example, if American corporate income is taxed at 36 percent, while German corporate income is taxed at 50 percent, then a global company with American operations may wish to charge the German subsidiary at a higher rate so that it maximizes its profits in the lower tax jurisdiction.

Transfer pricing is scrutinized very heavily by the respective governments. The standard applied by most countries is that sales between related parties must be priced on an *arm's length basis*. An arm's length price is the price that would exist if the related parties to the transaction were dealing with each other as independent parties. The U.S.A. has recently toughened its transfer pricing regulations, making transfer pricing one of the most difficult financial issues facing companies in that country. In addition to transfer pricing, governments also have developed other methods to assure that the local operations retain their profits. One such scheme is limiting the percentage of royalties which can be charged to related companies.

Nevertheless, companies with sophisticated tax and treasury departments have been successful in making global profits through transfer pricing. This creates a dilemma in subsidiary management, especially if a subsidiary's performance is to be judged on a financial basis.

For example, a marginally profitable U.S. parent company desires to increase the intercompany royalty amounts and transfer prices from goods and services provided to its very profitable Mexican subsidiary.

While the effective corporate tax rates in the two countries are similar, the U.S. company has sufficient losses in previous years for which it has substantial tax loss to carry forward. The company was able to obtain approval from the Mexican tax authorities to increase the inter-company royalty and transfer prices to the local subsidiary.

This created an additional problem for the Mexican subsidiary because local law requires that 10 percent of adjusted taxable income must be given to the subsidiary employees as part of a nationally mandated profit-sharing plan. Therefore, the parent company's policy of profit maximization impacted, in a very real sense, almost every employee of the Mexican subsidiary.

The problem was solved in two ways. First, the company developed a policy of country contribution, which valued the financial contribution of the subsidiary based on many factors including what its arm's length profits would have been, and, in this particular year, ascribing a "contribution" to the subsidiary for its assistance in obtaining the Mexican government's approval to increase transfer pricing. Second, the parent company allowed the Mexican subsidiary to pay bonuses to employees that were similar to what was lost through profit reduction.

278. Other Subsidiary Performance Issues

In addition to financial considerations, a subsidiary's performance can be evaluated on the basis of *market penetration*. The parent and subsidiary can agree on each year's marketing plan to a percentage of the market that the subsidiary will achieve in the coming year. This performance evaluation criteria is particularly important in the early years while the subsidiary is trying to achieve the economy of scale which would justify its costs. Additionally, even if the subsidiary is not profitable, if its market penetration is able to increase the economies of scale and reduce production costs in other countries, that factor should be given consideration.

Productivity is another measure of performance evaluation. If the subsidiary is assembling and/or manufacturing products, various techniques in the areas of quality, quantity, production time, and amount of scrap can be applied. If the subsidiary is marketing finished products and services, techniques such as sales per employee and customer retention can be applied.

Subsidiary performance evaluation should take into consideration product performance. Since the subsidiary will often serve as the "local" home office for customers in its territory, the evaluation process should consider whether the subsidiary is installing and maintaining the products up to global standards. This, along with other measures of customer satisfaction, should be considered.

A subsidiary should also be evaluated on its ability and willingness to develop a highly-motivated and efficient local workforce. Because locally-developed and trained employees will almost always be less expensive than expatriates, sufficient career opportunities must be created, and an understanding of the company's global vision should be instilled in the employees of the subsidiary. Additionally, local management should be able to respond to, and limit, any potential labor problems.

Success or failure is often dependent upon the subsidiary's *ability to create a positive image of the company and its products and services in the local market.* This is especially true in creating *good relationships with the local government agencies.*

279. Subsidiaries and Global Planning

Many companies have, historically, developed their global plans without sufficient input from their foreign subsidiaries. A truly global company will solicit ideas from subsidiary management on how the plan will impact that country or region, as well as solicit ideas on the entire global plan. This is not only a useful way to acquire information, but it also allows the company to select individuals in the subsidiaries who could be promoted to positions in global management and operations.

Motivating Subsidiaries

Establish a global plan and let each subsidiary know its role or mandate within that plan. Once you cross international boundaries, the levels of perceived, and real, misunderstandings are bound to increase. It is very important that the subsidiary not be allowed to operate in a vacuum. Subsidiary leadership must be told and, if necessary, be made to understand the global vision and plans. The given role of the subsidiary within that plan must also be understood, and

advice and counsel should be sought from subsidiary management
before the plans are finalized and put in place.

If subsidiary management understands and feels that they have
been made part of the global vision and plans, they will logically
work harder to see that it is implemented. Be prepared, however, to
make changes on the advice of local management. Encourage con-
structive criticism, and act on it when the criticism is valid.

Establish a fair assessment of subsidiary performance. Consider the
use of a "country," or "subsidiary," contribution to replace a bottom-
line financial assessment. Develop criteria based on market penetration, productivity, product and personnel development and performance, public and government relations, and contribution to global
planning.

**Consider the creation of a career-oriented international division and
company foreign service.** Many international companies consider foreign assignments for home office personnel only—to be given either to
people on the "fast track" to season them for greater opportunities, or
to technical types for the purpose of addressing individual assignments
or problems. Foreign employees are seen as staying in their own subsidiaries with only occasional placement in other operations.

With the growth of international business and the increasing need
for people with international orientation, companies should consider
offering long-term opportunities within an international division.
International work requires a somewhat different skill set. Interna-
tionalists will tend to be generalists with an entrepreneurial bent, who
function well in diverse and ever-changing environments.

Graduate schools of business are beginning to understand this, and
many have developed international concentrations in their MBA programs and/or individual Master of International Management programs which reflect the above-mentioned characteristics. Graduates
of these schools, and others, are looking for international careers
which normally include a mixture of expatriate assignments and
home office positions with international responsibility. People interested in doing international business are required to learn a second
(or third) language. The language itself is not as important as the
learning process, which requires the individual to learn and absorb
cultural differences.

With this in mind, consider rotating country managers and other
key individuals. Knowledge of the company and its products, and
experience in international assignments, are the key variables to con-

sider even over nationality. If people in the subsidiaries know there are true opportunities in the international (global) division, they are then more likely to advocate company goals over local considerations.

Allow all significant employees to visit the corporate headquarters on a regular basis. The clearest way to increase understanding is to have all key individuals know the persons on the other side of the international phone call, e-mail, or fax. Consider providing this opportunity to all loyal and effective employees, no matter what their level. For some lower-level employees, the company-sponsored international trip may be the opportunity of a lifetime and would ensure their loyalty for some time to come.

FAMILY BUSINESS CONSIDERATIONS

In most countries, the family business is the most typical form of business organization. In the past, families, tribes and co-religionists have formed global alliances to pursue the interests of all parties. Today, more than ever, the advantages achieved by the family business are particularly useful in globalization. The ability to move fast without the constraints brought about by shareholder bottom-lines, gives the family business a somewhat unique advantage in the years to come.

280. The Globalization of Family Businesses

The leveling of the economic playing field has opened up many new opportunities for family businesses. Beginning in the 1980s and accelerating through the early 1990s, both developed and developing countries have weakened or ended onerous foreign investment laws that have kept all but the largest global companies out of the market.

As part of the general movement toward market economies, governments have decentralized services and simplified processes for gaining approval of everything from creating companies to winning import licenses. Many have streamlined their tax codes and relaxed laws limiting payments for transfers of technology. Today foreign companies are given relatively free access to the economies of almost all nations and now receive fairer royalties for products and technologies licensed in these countries.

The days of the old craft-based manufacturing methods are returning. The 20th century may be remembered as beginning with the rise of mass production and ending with its decline. Whether it's making hand-tooled Chrysler street roadsters or specialized tortillas for the "breakfast burrito," the movement back to craft-based methods favor family owned and privately held businesses, and will be a factor in their global expansion. Such businesses tend to be more responsive to the niche markets and are able to move at a more rapid pace in spotting opportunities and converting them to successful businesses.

The movement to market economies abroad has led to exponential growth of family businesses. With the exception of North Korea, it is very difficult to find a true command economy left in the world today. The first step normally taken by governments that want to liberalize their economies is to allow the formation of small family businesses. Thus, family businesses formed in the late 1970s and early 1980s in Hungary and the Czech Republic now compete with the newly-privatized state industries in many key areas of the economy. In fact, many privatized state firms were acquired by family firms.

Significant growth in family enterprises is occurring in the developing world as well. Starting with Margaret Thatcher's United Kingdom in the early 1980s, most countries in Europe are moving to privatize major state-owned companies. The same trend is apparent in Latin America. Even in countries where large public businesses have been sold to global companies or publicly traded local companies (ports, airlines, and utilities), these new companies need to be more responsive to local businesses and are far more likely to source from the hundreds of thousands of family owned companies that have arisen to supply or service them.

The development and strengthening of global "tribes" will provide unique advantages for family firms. This will be discussed in more detail in tip #281.

As laws are simplified and regulations relaxed, it is becoming easier to operate within the legal "white market." Until very recently, many family firms from Brussels to Buenos Aires operated in a legal twilight zone; they sold legal goods while not conforming with many government regulations. The so-called "gray market" constituted upwards of 30 or 40 percent of businesses in some countries, often employing more people than the legal "white market." Many family businesses simply found it impossible to do business with full legal status because of high incorporation and notary fees, difficult documentation, burdensome employee-withholding requirements, and high corporate taxes. Governments tolerated the existence of the gray market because it was important to their economies and, in many cases, because they simply lacked the ability to enforce the laws.

Today, companies are operating in a similar manner to family businesses in the U.S.A.—the result of major changes in law and policy. Decentralization of government, reductions in taxes, simplification of bureaucratic rules and procedures have now brought the gray market into the white market. As a result, these companies are more likely to trade and partner with foreign companies.

281. Finding Your "Tribe"

Recently, two Jewish school friends who owned an American business that had grown from a garage-based operation to almost $100 million in sales, sought to take their business abroad. The owners had selected a smaller but substantial Jewish-owned business in Mexico City to assist them in their expansion into other Latin American countries.

Given the diversity of Latin America, it is suspicious when a local firm in one country wants exclusive rights to distribution in other countries of the region. The Mexican company did not have offices outside Mexico. What it did have, however, was relationships with a number of Jewish-owned companies throughout Latin America. Some of these relationships were with relatives, some were with similar types of distributors, while others were merely personal contacts in their network. The owners of the American company found this series of relationships to be perfectly acceptable and agreed to give the Mexico City company rights to distribute through them in all of Latin America.

Joel Kotkin described these new cross-border business networks in his controversial book, *Tribes: How Race, Religion and Identity Determine Success in the New Global Economy* (Random House, 1993). Kotkin argued that two factors are critical for success in today's global marketplace—geographic dispersion and belief in scientific process. He identified five "tribes"—Jews, the British, the Japanese, the Chinese, and Indians—that are highly successful at doing business abroad because of a strong ethnic identity and a sense of mutual dependence. All five have a global network based on mutual trust as well as a passion for technical and other knowledge.

Kotkin suggested that six other groups are developing similar networks and may in the future qualify as global tribes under his definition—the Armenians, Lebanese, Koreans, Vietnamese, Iranians, and the Mormons.

Finally, the importance of relationships in building a global business may also lead to the creation of networks based on other ties besides ethnic group, religious affiliation, or nationality. Business contacts often result from cultural and/or student exchanges, for example. People with common educational backgrounds or professional credentials retain close ties which open doors across borders that may otherwise be closed. Other groups sharing the same interests—collectors, sports enthusiasts, hobbyists of all kinds—may form strong enough networks in the future for doing business abroad.

282. Establishing a Global Family Vision

Since your business should project your family's vision, the globalization of your business should force you to think about a global family vision. In developing this vision, you should consider the following points:

☐ *Is your family international?* Are there branches of your family in more than one country? If so, would you look to that family to be part of your global business network?
☐ *How do you define family?* Must it be blood or direct descendants? Does it include children, godparents, and "political cousins"? Does it include trusted employees? Can friends be considered family?
☐ *Does your family believe itself to be part of a tribe?* Are you willing to give special preference to members of your same ethnic and cultural group when doing business abroad?
☐ *Do you seek business relationships with other family businesses?* Is dealing with family businesses a preference or a requirement?
☐ *Does your family have a vision that it believes should be shared across borders?* Is there a unique or special way that you do business? Do you treat your employees and suppliers as extended members of the family? Are you open to sharing that vision and perhaps combining it with those of related companies?

283. International Expansion Issues

Incumbent with international expansion are its impact on the issue of succession and on its ability to attract and retain better employees. In both cases, it can be said that the impact is positive.

Succession: For some families, the expansion into international markets can be used to test and season members of the younger generations. This is based on the probably valid assumption that if you can find a way to make profits abroad, you should be able to do so in the home market. Sending the younger generation on international assignments may even be an alternative to having a family member go work elsewhere before returning to the family business.

In other family cultures, global expansion may be an excellent "wind-down" strategy for the older generation. This allows the younger generation to take over domestic operations while their elders travel abroad not only to see the world but in connection with expansion. Either approach is an excellent way to build the business and revitalize cultures suffering from a status quo mentality.

Employee attraction and retention: Companies with substantial international business can attract and retain better people because they offer greater opportunities and perceived stability. This is especially true for retaining employees in the home market. The chance to broaden your cultural, intellectual, and business horizons is an attraction that cannot be matched even by the best domestically-oriented companies. Just look at the lists of the best places to work and you will find that an overwhelming majority are companies with significant international operations.

Capitalizing on International Trends

As global business enters the millennium, it has become more important for astute businesspersons to understand the way in which the world is evolving around them and what to expect for the future. This section explores six important world trends and concludes how these trends may impact your future business. Although, overall, the trends look quite favorable to global expansion, it is still necessary to have a clear understanding of these trends so as to avoid any potential negative impacts.

284. Understanding the Major Trends

The world around us is changing more rapidly now than at any time in the history of humankind. While the last years of the 20th Century seemed to be more peaceful and prosperous than other periods in recent times, it is clear that we are undergoing a significant transition in the political and military arenas with the end of the Cold War and the breakup of the Soviet Union and certain Eastern European nations. This, coupled with the continuing knowledge explosion and the exponential growth in international trade, makes it more and more difficult to determine what the world will look like in the near future.

To view international business in the years to come, it is necessary to have at least some understanding of six major trends taking place today. These are:

☐ The end of the Cold War.
☐ The explosive growth of global finance, trade and commerce, and the continued strengthening of global companies.
☐ The continued population growth, with its positive and negative implications.
☐ The explosion of knowledge.
☐ The development of a global culture.
☐ The growth of the number of national units, coupled with the increasing inability of nations to control their own destinies.

285. The End of the Cold War

Anwar Sadat and Mikhail Gorbachev will be remembered as two of the most important people of the last quarter of the 20th century. Anwar Sadat promoted the creation of diplomatic and trade relationships between Egypt and Israel, thereby ending an over thirty-year period of extreme hostilities, which included four significant wars that had bankrupted Egypt. This set off a process that ultimately resulted in the creation of a Palestinian nation and the development of commercial ties between Israel and its neighbors, thereby likely defusing one of the key powder kegs of international violence.

When late 20th century history is written, Mikhail Gorbachev will be remembered as the primary reason behind the end of the Cold War between the so-called "capitalist" and "communist" worlds. The Cold War did not end because of U.S. geopolitical containment or the Reagan military buildup of the 1980s; it ended instead because a new generation of Soviet politicians realized the need for a political awakening.

Throughout the late 1970s and 1980s, the Soviet Union's economy was growing at a respectable rate. While income and product distribution remained key issues, that alone would not have brought down the Soviet Union in 1991, if it were not for the political chaos brought about by Gorbachev's policies of *perestroika* and *glasnost*. These policies started a political force that could not be stopped.

This emphasis on political change may be the short-term legacy of the end of the Cold War. What we have seen since the late 1980s is the increasing growth of political and ethnic nationalism brought about by the fall of the "Soviet Empire." This is not only true in the former Soviet Union and its socialist siblings like Czechoslovakia and Yugoslavia, but it has also exacerbated the sense of national identity in North America (Quebec), Africa (South Africa, Burundi, and Rwanda), and Asia (India and Pakistan).

The end of the Cold War may also result in the changing nature of warfare. Major military conflicts will be all but unthinkable, because the concern over nuclear destruction has been replaced with the mutual interest of nations that are interdependent on the global economy.

286. The Continued Strengthening of Global Companies

There have been substantial international trade and global corporations (such as the Hudson Bay Company) for hundreds of years, but it has only been for the past 50 years that we have seen the explosive growth of international finance and trade, and the massive expansion in numbers and powers of businesses engaged in global business. This explosion has been the result of many causes, a few of which are presented here:

☐ Exponential growth of communications and production technologies.

☐ Rapid increases in the methods and speed of international transportation.

☐ Development of international monetary and trade mechanisms, including the GATT and the World Trade Organization (WTO).

☐ The relative freedom and power of the United States of America which, in the 1950s and 1960s, controlled over 40 percent of the world's trade, and in the 1980s and 1990s, developed the marketing and cultural tools to dominate significant aspects of popular global culture.

☐ The rise of Western Europe, Japan, and the Asian "Tigers" (Hong Kong, Singapore, Malaysia, Thailand, South Korea, and Taiwan) as significant global economic actors, which have challenged the U.S.A.'s economic position with the ability to compete with U.S.-headquartered companies on a global basis.

☐ The privatization of public companies which began in Britain in the 1970s and has continued to the present in most parts of the world.

The growth of global finance has been occasioned by a combination of government actions and the adaptation of technology. Throughout the 1970s and 1980s, government after government went through periods of deregulation followed by regulation and then again by deregulation. In response, a number of internationally-coordinated efforts were launched by the major banks and financial institutions that set global rules of engagement. This movement toward globalization was encouraged by the widespread use of computers and artificial intelligence to create new products and services.

One major result of this movement was the process of disinterme-diation—or the removal of banks as intermediaries in the accessing of capital markets, usually accomplished by the issuance of commercial paper. This process, which began in North America, is now pretty well complete among the major Western European states, except Germany, where a close relationship still exists between local banks and companies.

While the volume of global financial transactions increased dramatically, the number of banks will continue to decrease, and the remaining banks involved in international transactions will have to become more and more specialized to meet the needs of their increasingly sophisticated customers. The decline of the traditional bank is further exacerbated by the increasing abundance of money coupled with the decline of the banknote as a vehicle of business. Being more plastic, or electronic as the case may be, money will be less subject to definition and control, by banks or by governments.

These trends will continue into the 21st century as financial services reach the home computer. Investors of all sizes will have global portfolios designed to match their demographics. Corporate and commercial borrowers will use the services of the financial industry to place their securities with these "global" investors. As information becomes cheaper and artificial intelligence is used to analyze the information and suggest investment alternatives, the power once employed only by big investors will become available even to small investors.

The expansion and strength of global corporations is another phenomenon of the second half of the 20th century. Global corporations can be defined as a cluster of business entities with different nationalities that are joined by a common parent through bonds of ownership and/or control, that respond to a common global strategy and share a common pool of human, financial and physical assets. Some global corporations have become so large that their annual revenues could compare favorably with the gross domestic product of many middle-sized nations (e.g., General Motors, AT&T, and Mitsubishi, as compared with Norway or Chile).

While global trends continue to show that most jobs and a substantial part of new technologies are being created by smaller non-global companies, there is no question that large global corporations are now significant factors on the world scene and likely to remain so for some time to come.

287. The Population Growth

Barring any major catastrophe, it seems clear that the world's population will continue to grow well into the 21st century. While this probably will not be at the rate of the last 50 years, global population will be about 6 billion in the year 2000, and somewhere around 8.5 billion by 2025. This growth will have a number of positive and negative implications, although it will, overall, be favorable to the growth of international business.

From a business perspective there seem to be three important demographic trends:

☐ If one looks at demographics from a regional perspective, North America, with its slow growth rate, will be better off (e.g., with more stable economies) than Europe and Japan with their no-growth rate, and Asia, Latin America, and Africa with their higher growth rates.

☐ The majority of population growth in the "third world" will be felt in the urban areas, creating considerable infrastructure problems and substantial business opportunities. In general, the expanding countries of Latin America and Asia will create massive markets for consumer goods.

☐ The rapid growth of the Islamic population is the most significant wildcard in demographic projections. Pessimists suggest that the growth rate may be a continuing cause of wars and civil strife, and point to the current chaotic conditions in parts of the Middle East, India subcontinent and Indonesia. Optimists suggest that resources in the Middle East coupled with pent up demand will bring one billion new Muslim consumers into the world markets in the next 25 years.

288. The Knowledge Explosion

In the past 35 years, the amount of knowledge available to humankind has multiplied 10 times—yet all the technical knowledge we work with today will, according to experts, represents only one percent of the knowledge that will be available in 2050.

While the accumulated knowledge has to be considered positive, too much knowledge, too soon, may lead to individual and/or societal overload. The knowledge explosion is upon us, so the question is if our institutions can evolve and survive to deal with the paradoxes that are sure to result.

Medical knowledge is now growing at an exponential rate. The science of genetics has now unlocked 8–10 percent of the human genetic code versus less than one percent known 20 years ago. While this can end suffering and extend life, it can also lead to ethical considerations that did not exist in the past. We can only imagine what further knowledge and ethical concerns will arise as the frontiers of space and the sea are explored.

Also needed to be addressed is the tremendous impact the field of robotics may have on our conception of, and ability to, work. While the Industrial Revolution of two centuries past replaced hand work with machines, the post-Industrial Revolution of today is replacing factory workers with robots, thereby lessening the necessity of bringing human beings together at a place of work. Facsimile machines, modems, and other communication devices are doing the same to the white collar office environment.

The world of the future may best be described by Charles Handy,[7] who offers nine paradoxes that result from the knowledge explosion. Three such paradoxes are mentioned here:

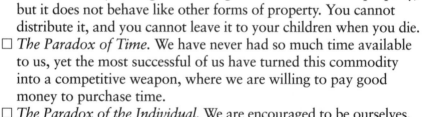

☐ *The Paradox of Intelligence.* Intelligence is a new form of property, but it does not behave like other forms of property. You cannot distribute it, and you cannot leave it to your children when you die.

☐ *The Paradox of Time.* We have never had so much time available to us, yet the most successful of us have turned this commodity into a competitive weapon, where we are willing to pay good money to purchase time.

☐ *The Paradox of the Individual.* We are encouraged to be ourselves, to be entrepreneurial. The knowledge explosion allows us the freedom to pursue our own course as long as we respect the rights of others. Yet, it is difficult to make a phone call without being asked, "Whom do you represent?" or "What organization are you from?"

Therein may be the business advice for the early 21st century: Gear products for individuals, for leisure time activities, and for planned obsolescence. Remember that the bulk of technological innovations, however, will continue to spring from corporate laboratories, or be acquired from individuals or smaller companies, by the corporate giants. These giants will have a great interest in keeping these developments proprietary. Coupled with the growth of global corporate structure, the bulk of technology will be passed between the segments of related corporations, and while knowledge will expand, much will be kept in private hands.

289. A Global Popular Culture

As communications, finance, and business techniques become more global, it seems logical to address whether this will result in the development of a global culture. The answer, depending on how you ultimately define the question, is probably, "Yes." In our view, we are entering an era in which there will be three types of global cultures. The intellectual culture, which will be, as it has always been, a mixture of the perceived "best" from all cultures; the professional culture, which will be most heavily influenced by the culture, or cultures, that most impact each profession; and the mass, or popular culture, in which the American culture will predominate.

The world anticipated by Marshall McLuhan, who coined the term "Global Village," is already here.[8] A billion telephones are in place, all interconnected and capable of reaching each other, and the phones are used across borders. In the U.S.A. alone, the number of international calls originating from that country increased from 23 million in 1970 to 580 million in 1987, and then tripled in the next 10 years.

The growth in telecommunications is being accompanied by growth in the various forms of video communications, especially through the use of television. Today, nearly 80 percent of U.S. homes are cable-connected, and specialized cable information services are an increasingly cost-effective way for business to communicate with niche markets. A recent conference of U.S. cable companies and suppliers estimated the global market for cable services between 1994 and 2004 to be more than U.S.$3 trillion.

While the manner of "delivering" culture may change from the printed word to the visual image, and perhaps from more live performances to more videotape and cable television, intellectual-oriented culture will remain much the same. Intellectuals throughout the world will continue to opt for the perceived "best" of what is being offered in the arts, literature, and the stage. Availability will increase, and a greater number of cultures will be represented, but people considering themselves to be intellectuals will still orient themselves to the global great masters.

Popular, or mass culture, is, and continues to be, overwhelmingly dominated by American culture. In fact, it is probably safe to say that as global communications accelerate, and American marketing techniques and institutions grow, popular global culture will be an extension of American popular culture.

While it seems clear that American films, music, and fast food will dominate popular culture, and indeed create a global culture, we should not leave this discussion without mentioning the manner in which the U.S.A. has begun to dominate university education. While the U.S.A. is soundly criticized for its pre-university education, few question the quality of its top universities and the solid quantity available through its thousands of institutions of higher learning.

Today, while less than 100,000 Americans may be studying abroad at any time, six times their numbers are currently foreigners studying at American universities. While American schools have become of particular interest to Asians in recent years, it is fair to say that the U.S.A. enjoys large numbers of foreign students from all regions. This has become big business, and has played a major role in keeping some economically marginal colleges and universities afloat.

The *Wall Street Journal* published a front-page story that illustrated the influence of America's top universities on the world.[9] The story tells of the meeting of three Latin Americans at universities in Cambridge, Massachusetts (Harvard and MIT) in the 1970s, who developed life-long friendships and ultimately became, at the same time, the finance ministers of Argentina, Chile, and Mexico. Whether referring to Pedro Aspe (of Mexico), Domingo Cavallo (of Argentina), or Alejandro Foxley (of Chile), all have developed and applied similar free-market techniques to open up the economies of their respective countries. This has, in part, resulted from their exposure to the "cutting-edge" economic theory taught at the universities at that time, and the advice and counsel shared with their student colleagues and professors over the years.

290. The Growth of Nation-States

For the past four centuries, the nation-state has served as the chief organizing unit for human activity. In fact, the number of nation-states has grown throughout that period; now, over 200 exist. (More than 3,500 groups exist that call themselves nations.) If one considers the number of nationalities that would like to achieve nation-state status, that number could easily be doubled.

A nation-state can best be defined as a national unit, or units, which has achieved sovereignty (the ability to make and enforce independent decisions). Few nation-states consist primarily of one nationality (such as Japan and Iceland). Most consist of a multitude of nations and nationalities. Some nation-states have done a relatively good job of integrating nationalities (Brazil, the U.S.A. and France), while others have had considerable problems (Canada with Quebec, Nigeria with Biafra). The recent trend has been for the expansion of the number of nation-states. The United Nations was founded in 1945, with 51 members. There were, at that time, another 20 nation-states. By the end of the colonial period in the 1970s, the numbers had doubled, and continued to grow throughout the 1970s and 1980s.

With the end of the Cold War came another proliferation of nation-states, with the breakup of the Soviet Union and Yugoslavia, and the separation of the Czech Republic and Slovakia.

Nation-states, as organizing units, reached the height of their economic power in the middle 20th century, and have been in economic decline since that point. The nation-state is now in the middle of a profound transformation. Economic forces seem to be moving in a direction that implies that in the future there will be no national products, no national technology, and probably no national industry in the sense that we use these concepts today.

The concept of national economy is becoming obsolete as capital, technologies, and products become more global. The process of privatization of state-run industries in places as disparate as Great Britain and Bolivia further exacerbate the process. The nation-state, while desired and admired for its nationalism, common history and symbols, is a probable casualty of the first five trends discussed in this chapter.

Yet, the nation-state has not gone away, nor is it likely to do so for some time to come. The nation-state is likely to remain as the political organizing unit and primary source of people's identity well into the 21st century. Nothing as yet has been developed to replace it. While the United Nations and other global organizations have strengthened, and while economic regionalization is certainly the trend, humankind has not developed a viable option for the nation-state.

The degree to which international business will continue to grow will be dependent upon whether nation-states will attempt to reassert their control over the economy or whether nation-states will move away from economic nationalism to an approach that Robert R. Reich (the former secretary of labor under U.S. President Clinton) calls "Positive Nationalism."[10] Economic nationalism (which is another name for protectionism), is the recognition of the rights of nation-states to control their economic destinies within the framework of the international economic system, but, if necessary, to move within their own borders to change the rules of the game by which global business is transacted.

Economic nationalism was popular during the 1960s and 1970s, but began to decline in the 1980s as more nation-states moved toward free-market economies. Aspects of economic nationalism are:

☐ Nationalization, expropriation, and confiscation
☐ Restrictive foreign investment laws—which limit foreign ownership and reserve certain industries to locals
☐ Artistic or cultural restrictions
☐ Domestic content requirements
☐ Technology transfer restrictions (as to royalties permitted) and requirements (e.g., quality guarantees)
☐ Restrictions on foreign workers
☐ Foreign exchange requirements
☐ High tariff and non-tariff barriers

These types of restrictions are more likely to succeed in countries with larger markets, or as countries attempt to form economic unions. NAFTA, although presented as opening up a free-market union amongst its members, has elements of nearly all the above-mentioned examples as European and Japanese manufacturers are now virtually "required" to manufacture products in North America to remain competitive with local manufacturers in the region. Additionally, all three countries retain strict restrictions on certain artistic and cultural artifacts.

The other scenario for nation-states in the coming decade is to recognize their loss of control in the economic sector and concentrate instead on developing a "positive nationalism." This approach is based on a number of factors. These are:

☐ A certain sector of the population will benefit from the global economy.
☐ While these people will be influenced by the global economy, they will still be oriented to the nation-state as their source of nationalism and politics.
☐ The future of the nation-state will not be in national control of the economy but will be in preparing their populations to be part of, and compete in, the global economy.
☐ The government will play some role in assisting the nation-state to compete in the new realities by assisting in the preparation of citizens with global awareness and purchasing power. This will require the rich to share with the poor.[11]

We suspect that the next few decades will bring a mixture of these approaches with the poorer nations attempting a return to economic nationalism, while the richer nations will, at least, try to develop some aspects of positive nationalism. Nation-states still possess a number of weapons to be used to reestablish the economic side of their sovereignty and the battle for control of the global economy is far from over. The clash between the rapidly expanding economy and the traditional means of politics should be interesting to watch.

291. Politics and the Nation-State

The following seem likely in the coming years:

☐ The number of nation-states will continue to proliferate.
☐ Developing states will attempt to bring about economic growth and stability before undergoing democratization and other political development.
☐ Nation-states will attempt new techniques to reassert their economic independence.
☐ Urbanization and infrastructure development will be the biggest challenges to the nation-state in the early 21st century. They will also offer the greatest business opportunities.

☐ Tremendous business opportunities will exist in much of the developing world, Eastern Europe, and Russia; they will be especially interesting in China, Indonesia, Palestine/Jordan, Vietnam, South Africa, and a unified Korea.

In the next three to four decades, another 30 to 40 nation-states will join the community of nations. While obvious new players may be Quebec and Palestine, it is also probable that large parts of Africa will be redrawn to reflect traditional ethnic, tribal, and language groups. The former Soviet Union will also continue to splinter with the creation of the possible Armenian and Georgian nation-states. Additional changes are possible in the area stretching from the Middle East to Southeast Asia. This proliferation of nation-states will result from continued ethnic uprising and racial/ethnic conflict. This will be true even in the multi-ethnic states that survive, and will result in the need to maintain armed forces and the continued need for substantial defense budgets.

Defense needs will also be enhanced by the continuance of the acceptance by national leaders of the process of economic development before political development. The success of South Korea, Chile, and Mexico of putting their economic house in order before moving to democratize their political systems will continue to be used as models by other "developing" nations.

Additionally, the selection of this approach is likely to sit well with existing power structures, which can use it as a means to continue in power for some time to come. The economic-before-political strategy, however, will put considerable pressure on nation-states from those groups of persons that do not benefit immediately from the economic progress.

While the actual ownership of the economy is not as likely to be in nation-state hands, governments have not lost the ability to tax and regulate those who do business in their country. As countries have moved away from economic nationalism, governments have shifted the focus of regulating behavior to concern themselves with quality, safety, environment, anti-trust, and consumer protection. The clearest example of this is Mexico, which liberalized its foreign investment and transfer of technology laws, but has increased its scrutiny over brand labeling, qualifying products to certain safety and usage norms, and enforcing its rigorous environmental protection laws. This will provide work for a wide variety of professional consultants.

The process of urbanization is unending (with minor reverse trends in certain developed nations). With urbanization comes the need for infrastructure. Companies providing infrastructure products and services will have ample business opportunities in the years to come. Even developed countries such as the U.S.A. will need to rebuild much of the national highway system built in the 1950s and the infrastructure of its great cities.

Additionally, as privatization continues into the 21st century, global companies will have infrastructure opportunities which never existed in the past. Post, telephone, and telegraphs will be privatized, and private toll roads will be common. Municipal services will go to private providers (e.g., trash and street cleaning), and education institutions will be run by private management firms. There are even some who predict that police, fire, and the military will eventually be privatized.

While we now look to China (whose gross domestic product, or GDP, is expected to exceed that of the U.S. sometime between 2005–2010), as well as Mexico, Brazil, and India as major areas of expansion, there are a number of other countries we should look at as potential growth areas. These are:

- [ ] *Indonesia*—200 million people with substantial physical resources, including a middle class the size of many of the larger European countries.
- [ ] *Palestine/Jordan*—The advantage for Palestine is that it has a number of wealthy Arab neighbors who recognize the value of preserving and enhancing its existence. Look for a number of infrastructure opportunities in the projects financed by Saudi Arabia, Kuwait, and the United Arab Emirates.
- [ ] *Vietnam*—Nearly 80 million people with a long tradition as traders, with one of the lowest standards of living in the world. Excellent natural resources and substantial infrastructure opportunities. An especially good opportunity for U.S.A. products.
- [ ] *South Africa*—A potential economic powerhouse in its own right, South Africa has now begun to attract human talents from the north, and expand its business into such places as Tanzania and Kenya, as racial barriers fall.
- [ ] *Unified Korea*—If and when it happens, bringing the North up to the standards of the South will rival German reunification, and a unified Korea will receive substantial world assistance for having helped to defuse a major global hotspot.

292. The Impact of International Trends on Economics and Business

Due to the current international explosion of knowledge, the world economy is indeed shifting from a command model to a knowledge model. While it is still necessary to be well connected, *who* you know is less important than *what* you know. The amount of knowledge available is, and will be, so large and diverse that the future will be bright for those who know how to organize knowledge into niches and distill it into components which are more easily absorbed.

Knowledge, and the complexity of knowledge, will define hierarchial structure and rewards. A corporate treasurer, with a staff of five, may be more responsible for corporate success than a larger Human Resources or MIS department. Because of the resources available, all employees will be given more responsibility for their actions. Finally, knowledge and knowledge access will be even more critical to performance.

One would think that the existence of facsimiles, electronic mail, and video conferencing would lessen the need for business travel, but it is likely that the opposite will be true. People, despite any amount of electronic gadgets, will still believe in face-to-face contact and interaction. Additional means of communication will only increase the number of people who come in contact and ultimately increase travel among those people. Travel will also be increased as more smaller and mid-sized companies enter into the global marketplace.

293. Structuring Global Relationships

Look for the following changes in the ways global businesses will be structured:

☐ Large global companies will continue to dominate significant parts of world business. Local autonomy and decision-making will increase, however.

☐ Smaller and mid-sized companies will "go global," and U.S., European and Japanese multinationals will begin to see significant competition from companies headquartered in the "developing" nations.

☐ The traditional forms of international business (agents, distributors, franchising, licensing, and equity joint ventures) will remain, but unique types of strategic alliances will develop in response to changing conditions and government deregulation.
☐ The time it takes between making the decision to "go international" to the creation of a true global company will be shortened.

The 21st century will still belong to the large global corporation, but it will evolve in a manner that reflects global trends. Headquarters will still define global strategy, business relationships, global profit maximization, and tax minimization. Global products will still be sought, as will networks of distribution and service. Some level of decentralization, however, will occur on the regional, national, and sub-national levels. Local subsidiaries and offices will be given more authority over marketing and sales, and in dealing with local suppliers. Additionally, local employees will be able to offer suggestions to headquarters, and global careers (where employees move between numerous countries) will become the norm rather than the exception.

One advantage of the exploding technology in communication and transportation is that it will let smaller and middle-sized companies operate as true global companies. In some cases, these middle-sized companies (with their unique technologies, more manageable product lines and limited bureaucracies) will actually have an advantage over the global giants. IBM found this out when EMC, a storage disk driver manufacturer out of Massachusetts, took a good part of its European market. EMC's international sales went from zero in 1989 to over U.S.$400 million in 1994.

As middle-sized companies begin to assume a larger share of international markets, the nationality of these companies will become more diverse. Strong local players in national economies in developing nations, now faced with open borders within a free market economy, will strike out for international markets. Mexico, with its new contingent of billionaires created by privatization, has been particularly aggressive. In the past few years, Mexican companies have acquired U.S.A. competitors in the areas of ceramics/glass, food products, and motorbus manufacturing. This trend will continue and will become a major vehicle for businesses in such countries as Hungary, Poland, and Brazil.

Whether large or small, more and more global players will look for different ways of operating in the international marketplace. While the traditional forms of operation (direct sales, agents, distributors, licensing, and equity joint ventures) will continue, companies will look for different ways of conducting business. The following lists some of the possibilities:

☐ Joint R&D and product development. This has been encouraged by the weakening of some anti-trust laws, which now allow competitors to cooperate.
☐ Outsourcing of all but critical components or technologies. Global products produced in a number of locations by a number of suppliers and/or competitors.
☐ Sharing of distribution networks between companies with complementary products and/or customer bases.
☐ Strategic alliances (consortiums) between suppliers of related products and services to respond to project-type business.

International Negotiations

Whenever there are two or more people in close proximity, and the laws of physics prevail, some kind of negotiating is most certainly taking place. This section will help you identify the basic skills required for negotiating across national and/or cultural boundaries; it will also help you plan for and manage the negotiating process in a number of different cultural settings.

294. Selecting International Negotiators

If you face the prospect of selecting candidates whom you feel will best serve your company's interests in international negotiations, here are some traits, knowledge, skills, and abilities to look for:

- ☐ *Flexibility and adaptability:* International negotiations often require long workdays as well as work on weekends and holidays. This is due to the fact that negotiations often have to be conducted and concluded within a limited timeframe. It is also due to the requirements of travel, changes in time-zones, and different national holiday schedules.
- ☐ *Strong interpersonal skills:* The ability to quickly establish rapport and elicit cooperation are crucial to effective international negotiations.
- ☐ *Excellent communication skills:* Cross-cultural negotiations often require well-developed listening, observing, and speaking skills—preferably in the native language of the counterpart.
- ☐ *Entrepreneurial approach to business:* Negotiations, especially when conducted far from "home base," often require a high level of independence, creativity, and risk-taking.
- ☐ *Technical competence:* Your counterparts will expect the negotiator(s) to possess a firm grasp of any underlying technical information.
- ☐ *Special knowledge and awareness of the counterpart's country:* Its history, economy, and prevailing cultures.

295. Selecting a Winning Team

For larger companies facing a complex international undertaking, one individual negotiator may not have expertise that is broad enough or deep enough to handle all issues that are likely to appear on the agenda. In these circumstances, it is wise to create a team whose members, ideally:

☐ Can add value to the negotiating process, based on their expertise
☐ Provide competencies that match those of the counterpart team members
☐ Have strong international negotiating skills
☐ Have complementary communications skills, e.g., listeners, talkers, observers
☐ Can handle long work days and the rigors of international travel
☐ Can work together as a team

If the entire team is to go on the road, it is important that the team have an opportunity to work together before embarking on the negotiating mission, and to establish "ground rules" for managing the negotiating process and for handling communications with the counterpart team. It is wise to appoint a person with broad management authority as team leader and this leadership arrangement should be made clear to the counterpart team.

For smaller companies, it is often impractical to assemble a complete negotiating team and send it abroad, no matter how complex the undertaking. When the company chooses to send a "solo" key manager as negotiator (often a founder, owner, or chief executive), it is still wise to appoint a team *within* the company. The purpose of this team is to:

☐ Prepare the negotiator to competently handle the range of issues that might arise during the negotiations abroad
☐ Serve as a resource to the negotiator, while he/she is on the road
☐ Begin to prepare the negotiator's own organization for follow-up negotiations around technical issues
☐ Create a receptivity ("buy-in") within the negotiator's own organization, in order to facilitate implementation.

In this case, the selection of the team may have more to do with creating future "buy-in" than with individual technical expertise or international negotiating skill. If there is no such "buy-in" on the part of key managers "back home," the negotiator may face a "disconnect" when he/she returns home and attempts to implement the negotiated agreement.

296. Improving Your Listening and Observation Skills

A successful international negotiator has well-developed listening and observation skills. The negotiator must use these skills in tandem in order to make the most of the negotiating opportunity. Here are some tips for developing and improving these skills for use in international negotiations:

☐ *Preparation—know what to "look and listen" for:* The more you know about the language, culture, education, social standing, and professional or business background of your counterpart, the better able you will be to use your listening and observing skills productively during the negotiations. It is important to learn as much about your counterpart as possible before any negotiations. It is also important to take advantage of every opportunity to engage in "pre-negotiation" social activities with your counterpart.

☐ *Know yourself:* Enlist the help of others to evaluate your own listening and observing skills. Identify your strengths and weaknesses, and plan how you will compensate for any weaknesses you perceive. Consider teaming up with someone who has skills that complement yours.

☐ *Practice concentration:* Before embarking on the negotiations, practice giving someone your undivided attention. Make notes on what the person said, comment on their choice of words, and his or her apparent emotional state. Include notes on their posture, their manner of dress, and a description of what he or she is wearing. Analyze your notes and discuss and compare them with your subject and with other observers. Do this as often as you can. Develop your own system for ensuring concentration.

☐ *Use silent periods or breaks:* During negotiations, some negotiators may use silence as a negotiating tactic. Periods of silence give you an excellent opportunity to analyze your thoughts, notes, and impressions and to identify particular things you may want to listen and look for during the next stage of the negotiations.

☐ *Be aware of your "talk/listen" ratio:* In some cultures, frequent or continuous talkers are not taken seriously. In many more cultures, careful listening is taken as evidence of wisdom and as a sign of respect. Keep track of how much you are talking versus listening.

297. Key Variables in Negotiations

Once your have determined that you need to "make a deal," it is important to sit back and consider the many variables that make up the negotiating process. Here is a checklist of the most common variables:

Negotiating leadership: Do the negotiations require technical expertise, professional competence, or management seniority?

Negotiating goal(s): Do you seek to merely complete a transaction or are you beginning a long-term business relationship?

Negotiating attitude: Do you anticipate a hostile, adversarial response or a friendly, cooperative response from your negotiating counterpart?

Negotiating outcome: Are you committed to a "win-win" outcome; or must you win, no matter what?

Negotiating style: Do you expect the negotiations to be very formal and structured, or informal and loosely organized?

Communication: Do you expect the give-and-take to be very direct or somewhat indirect and diplomatic?

Language/interpreters: In what language will you conduct the negotiations? Do you plan to use an interpreter?

Time sensitivity: Do you anticipate deadline pressures or will you be able to proceed at a relaxed pace? How about your negotiating counterpart?

Emotional level: Do you or the other party have a large personal stake in the negotiations? Are there sensitive issues involved that might provoke strong emotions?

Form of agreement: Do you expect the agreement to contain "all the usual boiler-plate" material or will it contain unique technical/legal provisions?

Use of prepared agreements: Will it be acceptable to work from a generic agreement prepared in advance?

Role of the government: In what ways will the laws or rules of your government or that of your counterpart influence the handling of specific negotiating items or the type of agreement that will come out of the negotiations?

Renegotiations: Is it likely that there will be a need to renegotiate certain agreement provisions in the future?

Team organization: Who will make up the negotiating team on the road and back at headquarters? How will the team divide up the negotiating roles and tasks?

Process for reaching agreement: How will the negotiation outcome be determined—i.e., by the team or by a higher authority back at headquarters?

Risk-taking: Are there large risks inherent in the negotiating process or in the outcome? How much risk will the negotiator be expected to take on?

Procedure for ending negotiations: Have you envisioned how you will end the negotiations, if you find it is in your company's best interests to do so? Will you be able to break off negotiations without "burning bridges"?

298. Planning Negotiations

Regardless of the nature of the business that is to be negotiated, the negotiator should consider the following factors when planning international negotiations:

Location: Where would it be most advantageous to conduct the negotiations?

Communications—language and culture: What are the language and cultural differences, if any, and how will the negotiator accommodate them?

Technical complexity: How does the negotiator intend to handle the complexities?

Team or solo—numbers of people: How many people will likely be involved on the counterpart's team?

Relative rank of negotiators: What rank does the counterpart negotiator hold within his/her organization?

Relative size of counterpart companies: Are the counterparts the same, similar, or different in size?

299. Negotiating Strategies that Do Not Work

The following negotiating strategies and tactics are losing favor in most parts of the world and are not recommended for use in international negotiations:

☐ *"Good Guy" vs. "Bad Guy"*: One person takes a very hard, aggressive negotiating stance with the counterpart, and the other team member takes a more conciliatory and sympathetic stance with the counterpart. This strategy is hard to carry off in a credible and convincing manner, and if it is apparent to the other party, it loses its desired effectiveness.

☐ *Sequential negotiating agenda*: The negotiator reduces the negotiating task into logically ordered, sequential steps, so that he or she can focus on and dispose of one item at a time. Unfortunately, in many business cultures, your counterpart will prefer to approach negotiations in a more "holistic" manner and will feel free to re-open items already negotiated.

☐ *Confuse and distract*: The negotiator deliberately creates an environment in which the counterpart will feel "off balance," confused, or distracted.

☐ *"Slash and Burn"—"Take No Prisoners"*: The negotiator dominates the agenda and uses intimidation to force concessions from the counterpart and creates an agreement that is clearly balanced in favor of his or her interests.

☐ *"Bring in the Closer"*: The negotiator appears to have all the authority required to negotiate an agreement; at the conclusion, however, a higher authority is introduced to seek additional concessions from the counterpart.

300. Using Interpreters

It is always best to be prepared to conduct international negotiations in the language of your counterpart or in a common language that both parties thoroughly understand, but this is not always possible. When one party or the other is not able to (or prefers not to) conduct negotiations in a common language, then it is wise to either agree on a third-party interpreter or to bring your own interpreter to the negotiations. Here are points to consider when it comes to using an interpreter:

☐ If possible, select an interpreter who is familiar with the subject matter to be negotiated. Brief the interpreter about the subject in advance.

☐ Speak clearly and at a moderate pace.

☐ Avoid colloquialisms, regional dialects, metaphors, or analogies that may be difficult to translate.

☐ Explain major ideas in two or three different ways to ensure that they make it through the translation.

☐ Allow the interpreter to interpret in frequent intervals. Do not talk for more than a minute or so without allowing the interpreter to interpret.

☐ Allow the interpreter to make notes while you talk.

☐ Do not lose confidence in your interpreter merely because he or she has to use a dictionary from time to time.

☐ Give the interpreter sufficient time to interpret and to clarify complex matters.

☐ Do not interrupt the interpreter. Interruptions create confusion and miscommunication.

☐ Avoid long sentences and double negatives. Use simple declarative sentences whenever possible.

☐ Avoid using superfluous words, multiple adjectives, and adverbs. These will tax the abilities of the interpreter without adding to the central information that must be communicated.

☐ Try to be expressive. Don't hesitate to use appropriate gestures to reinforce points you wish to communicate.

☐ Provide a written outline of the main points to be covered during the meeting. This way, the interpreter and the other party can more easily follow the course of the communications.

☐ Prepare a written summary of the meeting to confirm understanding of what has been communicated and agreed upon.

☐ Provide periodic "comfort breaks" for the interpreter. Interpreting can be stressful and you want your interpreter to be at his or her best.

☐ Consider having two interpreters available for protracted negotiations, so that a fresh interpreter can step in as the first one begins to tire.

☐ Don't be concerned if your counterpart rambles on for five minutes and your interpreter takes only two minutes to interpret what was

said. Some languages require a relatively large number of words to express certain concepts.
□ Be patient with the interpreter's mistakes.
□ Ask the interpreter for advice if communication problems arise.

301. Negotiating Styles

It is wise to avoid stereotypes and generalizations when preparing to negotiate with counterparts in or from a particular geographic region. It is always preferable to do your homework and base your negotiating strategy on what you have learned to be true about your counterpart. Keep the following factors in mind when approaching international negotiations:

□ *Language:* Depending on the region, English may or may not be used as a common business language among the educated elite; it is likely, however, that the local language will be used at some point in the negotiations. Plan on hiring an interpreter or using a bilingual member of your own organization.
□ *Formality:* Expect a high degree of formality in the initiation of the relationship and at the start of the negotiations. The larger the counterpart organization, the more structured and ritualistic the negotiations, particularly in the early stages. Expect social preliminaries and intermittent social events throughout the negotiations. These should be considered mandatory parts of the negotiation process. Your counterparts will use these occasions to learn more about you; you should do likewise. Expect seating arrangements and other meeting-room logistics to have significant meaning in rank.
□ *Numbers:* Larger numbers of people could be involved or just key participants, both in the social preliminaries and in the actual negotiations. It is important that you observe carefully and identify the ranking individuals.
□ *Pace:* Expect long periods of intensive negotiation. The use of interpreters will require an adjustment and will tend to slow down the pace of negotiations.
□ *Approach to agenda:* Expect your counterparts to revisit or re-open negotiations on issues that might have been resolved earlier in

the process. Expect your counterparts to be quite comfortable tracking a number of issues concurrently.

☐ *Special features:* Expect periods of silence throughout the negotiations. Expect your counterparts to use this silence to concentrate on complex issues and to weigh the relationship between one issue and another.

302. Preparing for Renegotiation

In this rapidly changing world, it is wise to anticipate the possibility that some points in your recently signed agreement will have to be renegotiated as circumstances change. This is particularly true in the case of international agreements because the parties must address a greater number of variables that are often beyond their control, e.g., currency exchange rates, national laws or rules, and import duties. Here are a few points to keep in mind:

☐ *No deal without a relationship:* A written agreement is only as good as the relationships that sustain it. During negotiations, it is important to lay the foundations for a sustainable, long-term relationship based on mutual trust. If a change in circumstances triggers a re-examination of the agreement, the relationship must be strong enough to survive a re-negotiation.

☐ *Conditions will change:* As the saying goes, life is what happens while you are making other plans. Assume that change will occur. Discuss with your counterpart how you will respond to changes that materially affect the negotiated agreement.

☐ *The key players will change:* The fact that people and their personal commitments come and go is perhaps the best argument for entering into formal written agreements. Agreements should be written with these changes in mind and it might be wise to record "statements of intent" for posterity.

☐ *Anticipate that changes might occur:* When certain changes are predictable, consider building flexible, adjustable change parameters into the agreement so change can be accommodated without full-scale re-negotiations.

☐ *Change can bring benefits to both parties:* Change can be a "two-way street." You may be the one facing circumstances that make re-negotiation attractive.

INTERNATIONAL ETHICS

The increasing globalization of commerce has raised the awareness that business practices still vary widely from one country to another. This is certainly true in the area of business ethics, where business practices that have survived for thousands of years are now being challenged and debated within countries, between countries, and within multilateral agencies like the United Nations.

This section describes the emerging standards for international corporate conduct, the sources and venues for the ongoing debate about business ethics, and offers some practical insight into evolving business practices. This information is organized to help you develop appropriate standards of conduct for your own business and to help you prepare to manage your way through the differing practices around the world.

303. Good Corporate Citizenship

The notion that corporations can and should be "good citizens"—and that good citizenship requires more than providing secure employment and paying taxes—has been spreading throughout most countries. The larger and more visible your enterprise, the more likely that government and the general public, along with special interest groups, will expect corporations to "behave" according to certain standards. Here are a few areas of international "corporate citizenship" your company may be asked to address:[12]

☐ Compliance with international law
☐ Compliance with local laws in all countries in which you operate
☐ Non-discrimination in hiring and promoting
☐ Adequate wage levels
☐ Workplace safety and health
☐ Working hours and overtime
☐ Freedom of association and right to organize
☐ Child labor and force labor
☐ Freedom from political coercion
☐ Environmental protection
☐ Protection for whistleblowers

304. Establishing a Worldwide Image

A properly planned and executed "worldwide image" can enhance your company's balance sheet and reputation for goodwill, as well as the value of its associated brand names. Here's how to go about creating a positive worldwide image:

☐ Adopt a "world corporate mission" statement
☐ Get in tune with the expectations of key local stakeholders
☐ Be aware of your company's local impact everywhere
☐ Communicate frequently and through local channels
☐ Strive for mission consistency in advertising and promotion
☐ Strive for mission consistency in business practices
☐ Support local "good causes"

305. Graft and Corruption

It is fair to say that graft and corruption exist to some degree in every country. Corruption is more sophisticated and subtle in some countries than in others. Here are some practical guidelines for the international businessperson:

☐ *Awareness:* It is important to understand what a "corrupt" practice is so that you can recognize it at home or abroad. There are a number of points of reference available, e.g.; the *Foreign Corrupt Practices Act* enacted by the U.S. Congress. At the same time, it is wise to be aware of how other business people regard these practices.
☐ *Adopt policies and/or principles:* These should include a definition of the corrupt behavior that is to be proscribed by the policy.
☐ *Communicate the policies and/or principles:* It is essential that every employee, agent, distributor, customer, supplier, etc., have an opportunity to become familiar with these policies and principles.
☐ *Audit performance:* It is important that your company perform periodic audits to determine the degree of compliance with your company's policies and principles.
☐ *Stay informed:* The definitions of corruption change over time, as do corporate policies and practices that respond to them. It is wise to update your company's policies to reflect these changes.

306. Demands for Information

In some parts of the world, corporations are required to register with the federal government and with other units of government and to supply a substantial amount of financial and/or ownership information. Even exporters without operations abroad may face requests about product components and their costs from third party services hired to ensure compliance with national import regulations. Often the requested information may be considered proprietary and/or confidential. Here's what you can do to minimize undesirable disclosures that may harm your competitive position.

☐ *Create an international subsidiary:* Since it is the subsidiary that conducts business in the country in question, the required disclosures can be limited to those regarding the subsidiary itself.

☐ *Create a foreign sales corporation:* Same as above; expect that the financial disclosures can be further limited and certain attractive tax relief can also be obtained.

☐ *Limit information disclosed:* Follow the *Dun & Bradstreet*® format and disclose only information that is already in the public domain.

307. Corporate Philanthropy

Although tax considerations may vary from country to country, corporate philanthropy can be an important component in a company's approach to the global marketplace. The discipline and market knowledge required in developing an approach to global giving might very likely contribute to the successful implementation of other elements of a company's market strategy. Here are some points to keep in mind:

☐ *Think globally, act locally:* Establish corporate philanthropic priorities at the world headquarters level, but involve local management, employee, and community groups in their application locally.

☐ *Seek coherence:* Select philanthropic priorities that reflect and/or enhance the global corporate image you are seeking to perpetuate.

☐ *Seek focus:* By concentrating on a few well-advertised priorities, a company will acquire expertise and some degree of acclaim for accomplishments in a specialized area of philanthropy.

☐ *Seek leverage:* Take opportunities to collaborate with other local and global entities to carry out the local philanthropic mission.

☐ *Seek recognition:* Seize opportunities to publicize the impact of the chosen philanthropic activity—not only in the local press but also through the media that reaches your company's customers and other stakeholders at headquarters and other subsidiary locations.

308. Standards for Corporate Behavior

A number of international private and public groups have developed and circulated international standards for corporate behavior. Here's a short list of these groups:

☐ The Caux Roundtable's "Caux Principles" (adapted from the "Minnesota Principles")

☐ The United Nations' "Universal Declaration for Human Rights"

☐ The Organization for Economic Cooperation & Development's "Guidelines for Multinational Enterprise"

☐ The International Labor Organization's "Minimum Labor Standards"

☐ The U.S. Government Department of Commerce's "Model Business Principles"

REFERENCES

[1] *INCOTERMS 1990.* International Chamber of Commerce, Paris, France. ICC Publishing S.A., 1990.

[2] Czinkota, Michael R., Ronkainen, Ilkka A., and Moffett, Michael H. *International Business,* 4th ed. Orlando, Florida: Harcourt Brace, 1996.

[3] Muller, Gerhard G., Gernon, Helen, and Meek, Gary K. *Accounting: An International Perspective,* 3rd ed. Burr Ridge, Illinois: Irwin, 1994.

[4] Muller, Gerhard, and Meek.

[5] Window on the World, Inc., Minneapolis, Minnesota.

[6] Bleeke, Joel and Ernst, David. "The Way to Win in Cross-Border Alliances." *Harvard Business Review,* November–December 1991, Vol. 69, No. 6, pp. 127–135.

[7] Handy, Charles. *The Age of Paradox.* Boston: Harvard Business School Press, 1984.

[8] McLuhan, Marshall. *The Global Village.* New York: Oxford University Press, 1989.

[9] Moffett, Matt. "Seeds of Reform: Key Finance Ministers in Latin America are Old Harvard-MIT Pals." *Wall Street Journal,* August 1, 1994, p. A1.

[10] Reich, Robert B. *The Work of Nations.* New York: Vintage Books, 1991.

[11] Reich, Robert B.

[12] Kidder, Rusworth M. Interview for The Institute for Global Ethics, Camden, Maine, 1997.

INDEX

A

Accounting
  assets, 122
  audit examinations, standards, 120
  checklist, 120
  cultural implications, 118
  Current Cost Accounting (CCA), 122
  Current Value Accounting (CVA), 122
  definitions, 122
  differences, 117, 121
  financial information, analyzing, 120
  General Price Level Accounting
    (GPL), 122
  Generally Accepted Accounting
    Principles (GAAP), 117
  historical cost principle, 122
  international, 118
  International Standards on Auditing
    (ISA), 118
  models, 121
  pension accounting, 122
  practices, 117, 118
  principles, 117, 118
  standards, 117, 118, 120
  systems, 118
Accounting authorities, international
  African Accounting Council, 119
  American Institute of Certified Public
    Accountants, 120
  ASEAN Federation of Accountants, 119
  Asociación Interamericana de
    Contabilidad, 119
  Association of Accountancy Bodies of
    West Africa, 119
  Confederation of Asian and Pacific
    Accountants, 119
  European Community (EC), 119
  Fédération des Experts Comptables
    Européens, 120
  Financial Accounting Standards Board
    (FASB), 120
  International Accounting Standards
    Committee (IASC), 118
  International Federation of Accountants
    (IFAC), 118
  Org. for Economic Cooperation &
    Development (OECD), 119

Securities and Exchange Commission
  (SEC), 120
U.N. Intergovernmental Working Group
  of Experts, 118
Acquisitions, 286–288
Agents, 2, 10, 24, 73, 109, 129, 142,
    146, 187–189, 191, 195, 197,
    199–202, 232
  application, 207–211
  evaluating, 205, 215–216
  motivating, 200, 213
  non-performance, 219
  performance, 142, 199–200, 215, 217
  profile, 207
  replacing, 189, 207, 216–218
  selecting, 199, 212
  termination, 199, 216–219
Agreements, legal concerns, 22, 43,
    183–185, 189–190, 232
  alternative dispute resolution, 27,
    182–184, 188
  arbitration, 27, 112, 144, 183, 221
  bankruptcy, 221
  contracts, 174
  disputes, 27, 51, 53–55, 250
Alliances, 2, 10, 76, 139
  chaebol, 76
  consortia, 2, 256
  equity, 257
  keiretsu, 75
  marketing, 255
  Ministry of International Trade and
    Industry (MITI), 71
  non-equity, 254
  sogo sosha, 75–76
  strategic alliances, 2, 76, 139
  trade, 43

B

Banks, financing trade, 75
  branch, 110
  correspondent, 110
  Export-Import Bank of the United
    States, 66, 126
  foreign credit financing, 110–111
  offshore, 111
  representative, 111